# Survivor

# Survivor

Biography of
Master Sergeant Frank Nathaniel Lovato
ARMY/USAF Retired

*Prisoner of the Japanese*
*1941-1945*

Written by
Francisco L. Lovato

To all the brave men and women of the
"Battling Bastards of Bataan" those courageous
defenders of freedom and liberty,
alive and deceased, who gave every ounce of
their being so that we and our children can live in
a free world then and forever.

---



*The Prisoner's Song*
Written by Guy Massey
Used by Permission of Shapiro, Bernstein & Co., Inc.

Francisco L. Lovato lives and writes at his home in the Sierra Nevada foothills of Northern California. He enjoys listening to and promoting original music, as well as performing traditional Latin music with his partner, Teresita Juarez.

www.FranciscoLovato.com

Library of Congress Control Number: 2008902083

# Introduction

Throughout my childhood, Dad rarely spoke of his three and a half years as a POW in Japanese prison camps. When asked by relatives at family gatherings during the holidays what it was like to have survived the infamous Bataan Death March or Prisoner of War camps, he usually just closed his eyes, bowed and shook his head and said, "It was hell, just hell." Dad would often change the subject and talk about a happier time before that fateful day he and over twelve thousand other American soldiers, and sixty thousand-plus Filipino soldiers were surrendered to the Imperial Japanese Army at Bataan on April 13, 1942. He would rather tell short stories of his half-track (armored artillery vehicle) unit's triumphs over the invading Japanese, or humorous anecdotes. It seemed clear that Dad did not want to talk about the details of life and death in the POW camps.

The first time I heard my father say anything about a specific incident in the American POW camps was sometime in the Fall of 1964, as we sat down following the National Anthem at a University of New Mexico football game. The twenty thousand or so Lobo football fans had just sung the National Anthem with particular zeal and enthusiasm. Even though he had not worn his military uniform since he retired from active duty in 1961, Dad always stood as if at attention, and saluted the flag during the playing of the Star-Spangled Banner. With a tear in his eye he cleared his throat and said quietly to me "When I hear thousands of people singing like this, I'll never forget that night in the (POW) camp when we all stood proud and sang "God Bless America." As the UNM football fans cheered the start of the contest, Dad sat as if in a trance, his eyes fixed on the flag, with a distant, somber look on his face. I had intended to ask him later to tell me more about that night that moved him so, but at age fifteen my own life's challenges and experiences occluded that well-meant intention.

I left home a year later to attend Eastern New Mexico University where I graduated, taught psychology courses, and became a psychotherapist in Los Alamos, New Mexico. The remote, mountain plateau city of Los Alamos is the birthplace of the two atomic bombs that were dropped on Hiroshima and Nagasaki, resulting in the end of hostilities between Japan, the United States, and eleven other countries, liberating Dad from the POW camps.

After nine years of working as a psychotherapist and administrator of programs for the developmentally disabled, I retired from my profession and moved to Northern California to pursue a career in the music business. I formed an events production company and promoted local and regional musicians in a variety of concerts, special events and showcases. My children's mother and I divorced after seven years and I soon became the single parent of my two beloved children, Eric and Jordan. I wrote grants to start a comprehensive senior citizens' center, and managed a community radio station while pursuing my love of original music, musicians and live musical performances.

Following his retirement from a distinguished career in the Army and Air Force, Dad continued his working life as a civil servant in the Army Corp of Engineers, and the Internal Revenue Service. He had achieved his goal of obtaining the rank of Master Sergeant earlier than he had expected, had received numerous Good Conduct medals, two Purple Hearts, three Presidential citations including a fourth from the President of the Philippines, and a Bronze Star. He retired as a result of a back injury and continued to live in his home in Albuquerque with his only wife, my mother Evangeline, helping his children and grandchildren with everything from plumbing to auto tune-ups. Never one to give up on anything, regardless of the difficulty or personal time and effort involved, Dad remained a shining example of tenacity and resourcefulness to everyone that he met.

Still no one, including his beloved wife "Vangie," ever knew of the horrible memories he harbored of his three and a half years as an American POW in prisoner of war camps in the Philippines and Japan.

Even though he always moved forward in his life duties as a responsible husband, parent, and proud American, it was inevitable that the repressed, painful memories would eventually emerge from the dark depths of his psyche. In 1978 he began to experience what the Veterans Administration physicians first called "idiopathic seizures." The episodes began with a trance-like stare, hand tremors, and rapid breathing. His unemotional stare quickly turned into, and remained for about a minute, a horrified expression of abject fear. Although his eyes were open and he appeared to remain awake, he clearly was dissociated and unresponsive to anyone around him. When the symptoms of the episode subsided, he became conscious and aware of his surroundings, and recognized that he had "one of those spells," but could not remember anything that happened during the episode. If an episode occurred when he was standing, he could neither sit or lay down; he fell, but still remained awake and detached. My mother also related that he had always had occasional nightmares of someone chasing and wanting to kill him. According to her, from the time of the onset of the seizure-like episodes, the nightmares also increased. Examinations, including electroencephalograms (EEGs) performed at the Veterans Administration Hospital were still inconclusive regarding the source of his "seizures." Anti-convulsive and psychotropic medications reduced the frequency but not the intensity of the almost-daily episodes.

Dad continued working on all his Mr. Fix-it projects during his retirement and accepted as a matter of fact that the episodes were just something he and the family must endure like any other chronic illness or physical disability. Dad's never-give-up-on-anything attitude and approach to life's problems, that he so valiantly displayed since I could remember, allowed him to move forward, unabated except for a short rest after each episode.

I asked Dad to request a copy of his medical record and I recall reading there was virtually no mention, at least in connection to his seizure activity, of his history as a POW. Even in my psychological studies during the late 60's, dissociation symptoms of Post Traumatic Stress were generally related to case studies of the civilian population who were victims of natural disasters such as earthquakes, floods, and tornados. According to my Mother, the episodes sometimes occurred when Dad got "nervous" about something or in response to a loud, unexpected noise like when a kitchen pan fell and hit the floor or a jet aircraft created a sonic boom. The incidents were reported to the VA, medications were adjusted, and the episodes continued with no regularity or pattern. Over time Mom and the family adjusted to the fact that Dad had the "spells" and although they feared that one day they might result in a more permanent injury or even his death, life at home went on as usual except for the occasional episode and a feeling of frustration about their origin and what could be done to prevent them.

Even fifty years after the war, family discussions of Dad's war history and experiences within the Prisoner of War camps were limited to only a couple of humorous stories we heard about buddies he called the Chillicothe Kid, Brewster, and Captain Perrenault, the night the POW's sang "God Bless America," a successful tank ambush incident, and the morning the "Japs" landed. The rest, including the infamous Death March, Dad just said was "pure hell."

Upon telling a friend of some of the incidents that Dad had related, I realized that I needed to know as much as possible about what actually happened before it was too late. I returned in the spring of 1997 to Albuquerque with a video camera and a list of questions, intending to record whatever Dad could recall from that significant time.

What happened during those first eleven hours of continuous interviews changed my life forever. This book is the result of hundreds of hours of in-depth interviews over an eight-year period. As I relived with my Father the individual incidents of war battles, personal triumphs of spirit over extreme adversity, painful losses of buddies, and personal freedom, I vowed that I would write his first-hand account of those almost four years of unbelievable pain, courage, and survival. He told of hair-raising battles between American/Filipino mobile artillery units and invading Imperial Japanese infantry in wooden landing craft as they approached the beaches of Northern Luzon, fighting and destroying advancing Japanese tanks at night and, of course, the almost unbelievable horrors of being a prisoner of the Rising Sun.

I felt compelled to visit the Philippines during the months of March and April 1998, to visit the sites that Dad had told me about with such detail and to experience same seasonal extreme heat and humidity he experienced during the Death March. I traveled to the Philippines with only a backpack, Dad's hand drawn maps, and an intention to walk on the ground made hallowed by the tens of thousands of defenders of the Philippines. I was greeted at the Manila airport by my new friend and guide, Reynaldo Cervania and his wife and family, without whom I would not have been able negotiate the unfamiliar terrain.

With Dad's notes and guidance of a local fisherman, I was able to find remote locations like the crescent-shaped beach where the first land battle took place between American/Filipino troops and the invading Imperial Japanese forces. Later, with the help of another former Philippine Army sergeant and friend, Felix Ledda, we found Cabcaben Field, an old abandoned airfield near the tip of the Bataan peninsula where the Death March began for Dad and many others. There were no historical markers at these desolate sites where history is forgotten except in the minds of those who fought for their lives there fifty-seven years earlier. A few vandalized markers along the Death March route and a Philippine National Museum on Mount Samat were the only reminders on Bataan of the heinous actions by the Imperial Japanese Army that resulted in the destruction of over ten thousand lives after the joint American/Filipino soldiers were forced to surrender by their commanding officers. A small shrine and a partially finished monument had been erected at the infamous prisoner of war Camp O'Donnell, where hundreds of American POWs and Filipinos died daily from disease, starvation and abuse.

With the help of an article published in the nationally-distributed newspaper, the Philippine Star, and the Filipino veterans' organization "The Defenders of Bataan and Corregidor," I attempted to find the other twenty-five Filipino soldiers who were in my Dad's self-propelled artillery battery. The Filipinos lost over thirty-five thousand men in Camp O'Donnell the first six months of captivity; few remain alive today. I did find one Filipino Scout Lieutenant from another half-track battery who remembered my Dad. He and his men destroyed their four half-tracks by pushing them over high mountain cliffs near Bagio when they ran out of ammunition and were about to be surrounded by thousands of infantry men from the Imperial Japanese invasion force. They escaped over a high mountain pass and later joined up with the remaining half-track units in Bataan.

Perhaps the greatest miracle in the process of writing Dad's accounts was finding Dad's only American buddy in their predominantly Filipino mechanized artillery unit. Dad thought, as did Burl A. Brewster, originally from Portales, New Mexico, that each had died in the massive prisoner of war camps. So of course, they never tried to find each other. With the miracle of Internet people-search capabilities and a hunch I might find a relative of Mr. Brewster, I found him alive, but not too well, in Pismo Beach, California. Again, I took my video camera. I wanted to hear his account of the events they endured prior to their sixty-year separation. He graciously, but with a great deal of emotional difficulty, corroborated Dad's accounts of their trials during the many battles for the defense of the Philippines. Like many other POWs, he could only speak in brief phrases about the time beginning with the Death March and concluding with his release from the POW camps. Dad and I are eternally grateful for Mr. Brewster's recollections of theirs, and the other half-track batteries' significant contributions to the defense of the Philippines. Most are lost to history, which is why we devote an entire section to the brave and courageous fight before the fall of the Philippines.

Many of the stories contained within this biography took several years to assemble from the indelibly tortured memory of my Father. Because the memories were so painful to all the survivors, daily POW life is largely unknown to the majority of us for whom they fought and died everyday and night from December 7th, 1941 to even after the war was over on August 15th, 1945.

Without my training as a therapist, I doubt I would have been able to elicit the details of the horror stories and still be able to facilitate any degree of healing at all. To dig into that hell-hole of pain and suffering without responsibility to my dad's wellbeing would have been another cruel and undeserved assault to his psyche. For this reason, please read with care and caution this brave and honorable man's account.

If your father is a veteran of any war, he harbors an unthinkable burden, which he may never share. Courageous heroes rarely disclose the details of their suffering. Rather, they continue to do what they were trained to do: to protect their families.

I am still learning every day how to protect my father from the worst of his fears: how to navigate life without his "Vangie." My mother passed away during the time of writing this book. She was his hope, his light, even before he met her; it was the hope of her, and of the family they would create, which kept him alive those nearly four years as a POW. Now, he looks to his great-grandchildren for that hope. As do I.

# Contents

PART I

# The Fight for Freedom

*December 7, 1941 – April 9, 1942*

CHAPTER 1

# "…just the beginning."

*Sunday, December 8, 1941 (December 7th across the International Dateline in Hawaii.)*

Private Frank Lovato
Fort Bliss, Texas 1941

*What a beautiful peaceful Sunday morning in paradise,* I thought as I looked out at the tropical panorama of green foliage, soft blue sky and thin high clouds over Clark Airfield, Luzon, Philippines. Even though we were on full alert following the startling information earlier in the morning that Pearl Harbor had been attacked by the Japanese, the sound of birds chirping in the acacia trees made it feel like another day in paradise. From my vantage point on the open grass of the parade field, I could see Mt. Arayat, the towering cone-shaped volcano, jutting up majestically behind the broad expanse of runway densely rimmed by flowering acacia and mango trees. All of our B-17s, which had been up all morning on alert, had landed and were parked neatly along the runway while their pilots and crews, had lunch. My fellow soldiers of the New Mexico 200th Coast Artillery Anti-Aircraft had an early breakfast of scrambled eggs and bacon and had been in their emplacements since 0500 and were ready for lunch. The trucks transporting their hot meals arrived and set up a portable mess tent to serve them on the grass field.

We were all shocked to wake up and hear that Pearl Harbor had been sneak-attacked by the Japanese Navy, and I was equally surprised when Captain Grimmer of the 200th gave me orders to report with my truck to a new unit. "Lovato! You are to report to Captain Travis Perrenot at the parade field at 1300. He is an excellent artillery officer. We are forming several new tank and half-track artillery units.

Your chances for promotion will be better in this predominantly Filipino unit because your responsibilities will be greater. Good luck, Lovato, and say 'hi' to Captain Perrenot for me."

*I like Captain Grimmer.* He had seemed genuinely concerned when I described my frustration at not being considered for promotion when I knew I deserved it. Although I didn't realize I was going to be transferred completely out of the 200th, but orders were orders, and a chance for promotion sounded pretty good to me.

Bugler 1st Class
Atanacio Lovato
Post "Great War"1918

I was proud of my father, who fulfilled his patriotic duty in the Great War with his bugle and Springfield rifle so that our country and allies like France and England could remain free of tyranny and oppression. His duty was to communicate messages and orders from the commanding officer to the troops with bugle calls. Dad knew almost three hundred different calls that included reveille,(wake-up) chow-time, charge, retreat, and of course, taps. A bugler was an important and necessary person on the battlefield at a time when walkie-talkies and other electronic communication devices were virtually non-existent.

Now that the Japanese had attacked Pearl Harbor and we are the nearest Americans to Japan, I realized it was now my turn and responsibility to uphold the defense of these same principles that protected my family and country.

I thanked God that I had just finished enjoying a three-day pass to Manila before this state of war had begun.

It was about 1230 hours when I put my canteen down and looked up at a massive tight V formation of white bombers and escort fighter planes against the powder-blue sky. With one hand palm up to block the brilliant rays of the noonday sun, I proudly announced as I pointed upwards toward the approaching warplanes, "Hey, guys, look, the Navy's on the job!"

"Hooray for the Navy!" cheered the other guys, thinking that reinforcements had arrived to bolster our Philippine-based air force of B-17s, B-26s and P-40s.

Suddenly, mirror-bright objects began falling from the bellies of the oncoming planes. Without warning the peaceful morning erupted with the high-pitched sound of bombs screaming through the air. Almost immediately, the air raid sirens signaled that we were under attack.

Dec. 8, 1941 – Japanese attack Clark Field ten hours after Pearl Harbor sneak attack.
*Ex-POW Ben Steele*

"Hell, they're not our navy! They're Japs!" someone shouted. For an instant, we stood frozen like rabbits in car headlights staring incredulously at the bombs plummeting towards the neatly parked B-17s on the runway.

The ground shook and my teeth rattled from the thundering explosions of the first bombs hitting their targets. Overlapping explosions from the striking bombs electrified the stunned onlookers with a jolt of adrenaline, and in a frenzy of yells the men scattered to foxholes and their anti-aircraft emplacements. Clark Field was under aerial attack by nearly a hundred enemy aircraft as our airplanes sat liked sitting ducks on an open pond. Low-flying Japanese Mitsubishi Zeroes, with big cherry-red suns emblazoned on their wings and fuselages, roared in at treetop level, machine guns blazing at anything or anyone in their path. I ran and jumped into my truck, which was my primary responsibility to protect, and headed for cover away from the runway. Gas pedal to the floor, I charged, engine roaring, toward a group of trees on the other side of the railroad tracks. Even through the noise of the Chevy engine pounding full throttle, the fighter engines thundered in my head.

Private Lovato chased by Japanese fighter plane
*Drawing by Francisco Lovato*

*I've got to save the truck!* I repeated to myself as the enemy fighters swooped down less than fifty feet from the ground. Their engines buzzed like angry bees as they shot at our stationary bombers, fighters, and anti-aircraft guns that had already begun to return fire. Over the mechanical whine of my truck's gears, I heard, but couldn't see, the staccato firing of an airplane's machine guns growing louder as I approached the railroad track. For a moment, I had to slow down and was totally vulnerable as I crossed over the multiple rows of train track. Sharp, metallic rings of machine gun bullets ricocheting off the steel track alerted me that one of the Zeroes had a bead on my truck.

*Oh my God! I'm being strafed from behind!* In a blur of dust I careened wildly over the tracks and onto the dry dirt road, as rows of machine gun bullets kicked up columns of dirt on both sides of the truck. The Japanese fighter roared past and arced upward to possibly circle around and try again. "Man, that was too close," I yelled out loud.

Shaking like a leaf, I stomped the pedal to the floor and headed toward a dense row of trees that bordered the airfield. *If I could just make it to those trees, I would at least have overhead cover to hide me and the truck, from the vision of those fast enemy fighters.* Crashing through the thick brush, I wedged the big truck into a canopy of leaves, grabbed my .30-caliber Springfield rifle, jumped out of the truck, and began to shoot at the low-flying planes.

I fired my Springfield bolt-action rifle at the light-gray bottom, olive-green top planes, until I ran out of ammo. The huge cherry-red suns emblazoned on the fuselage and wing tops made good bulls-eye targets to line up a shot at the pilot. They flew so low I could see the pilots' goggled faces in brown leather helmets with a white scarf tied across their foreheads.

As quickly as the enemy planes appeared and wreaked their havoc, they withdrew and disappeared, leaving behind burning rubble of what had once been combat-ready aircraft and fuel trucks. I drove my ton-and-a-half out of the cover and back toward my buddies in what seemed like only a few minutes after the attack. Smoldering remains of P-40s, B-26 medium bombers, and smashed hulks of the once mighty B-17 Flying Fortress of MacArthur's Far East Air Force lay broken in the aftermath. Heavy black smoke rolled in thick clouds from the burning fuel depot on Clark Field. Flames crackled everywhere from the bonfires of burning barracks, storage hangars and overturned vehicles. Gaping pock marked craters perforated the once smooth runway and aircraft staging areas. I cautiously maneuvered my way through the destruction, shocked at the results of the Japanese attack. Fire crews scrambled to put out the raging fires while other soldiers stumbled out of their dugout trenches and walked about aimlessly as if in a trance. Everyone looked coldly grim in the aftermath of our baptism to war.

Even though Pearl Harbor was attacked ten hours earlier, we had absolutely no warning of the Japanese raiders coming in on us from the northeast, and for this ignorance we paid the price of being unprepared. Virtually all of our aircraft were on the ground, with the exception of a few Curtiss P-40 fighter planes that managed to get up.

*By Francisco Lovato*

I drove my truck through the burning, smoking piles of twisted aircraft to follow my orders to report to Captain Perrenot at the flagpole by the baseball field. I thought to myself, *We sure got off on the wrong foot in this war.* In the depressing aftermath I still felt proud I had saved the truck to fight another day, and maybe I even put a few holes in one of the Japanese planes. I wondered what was coming next.

En route to the baseball field, I saw the medic units and ambulances weaving through the smoldering remnants of aircraft, picking up the injured and dead. The Japanese had successfully unleashed this assault abruptly on our unsuspecting forces. The once picture-perfect military base with its snow-white buildings and neatly parked aircraft was now charred and crumbling. *Didn't our military intelligence know hostilities with Japan were imminent? And wasn't our new radar was supposed to spot oncoming aircraft?* Most of our planes had been up earlier in the morning but had returned and parked out in the open like sitting ducks in a shooting gallery. I kept asking myself, *How could this have happened?*

This was a day of new beginnings for me. First I was told I was no longer with the 200th Coast Artillery and had been assigned to a new unit, then came the attack, and now I was to report to an officer I had never met before. *Well, I am alive, and the truck is in good shape. Right now all I have to do now is find Captain Perrenot.* The Japanese caught us with our pants down. *What other surprises do they have for us? When will they attack with their navy and infantry? Will we be prepared with ordinance and troops to battle them on equal ground?*

Captain Travis E. Perrenot *Photo courtesy of Perrenot Family*

Old Glory hung limp in the warm, tropical air over the neatly cropped green grass. It was amazing that the Japanese bombs had missed the playing field. Across that immaculately manicured grass, I spotted someone walking directly toward me with a peculiar gait that made me chuckle. It was as though one of his legs was longer than the other. As he got closer, I noticed the embroidered bars on his khaki uniform, indicating that he was a captain. I stepped off the truck hood and stood at attention as he neared. His piercing blue eyes and curled brow seemed to ask if I was the one he was looking for.

"My name is Private Lovato, Sir. I was sent by HQ Battery, 1st Battalion, 200th Coast Artillery. Reporting for duty, Sir," I said as I saluted him.

Captain Perrenot returned the salute and answered, "Don't bother saluting me anymore Lovato. We're at war. We have no time for formalities. We don't have much time for anything. I'm going to Manila to get Filipino soldiers and four half-tracks. We need to train and prepare them quickly before the Japs arrive. You'll be joined by another GI with a deuce and a half (a two and a half ton truck)." He looked upward into the sky and said, "That was just the beginning."

"What's a half-track, Sir?" I asked.

The captain drew a rough sketch of one on a piece of paper while he described the anti-tank machine. "The rear drive is like a tank's caterpillar treads, but the front end uses large truck wheels and tires. It looks like a cross between a tank and a truck. A French 75-mm cannon is mounted on the mid-section behind the cab and extends forward. Behind the cannon is mounted a .30-caliber machine gun with a 180-degree radius that rides on a track that loops around the rear perimeter of the half-track."

In the past two and a half months in the Philippines, I had never seen a single half-track on the base. *Where will he get them,* I wondered.

"The half-track is considered primarily an anti-tank weapon," the captain continued. "Lovato, since you are the first to report, I must ask you to prepare a bivouac area while I am gone. Here is your authorization and a list of supplies I want you to get. The supplies are for thirty men for thirty days." The list included food, pistols, rifles, ammunition, medical supplies, gasoline and oil, helmets, uniforms and tents. "Get everything you can. It won't be easy," he said.

"Is that all, Sir?" I asked.

He looked at me and grinned. "One more thing. As soon as you secure an area, make directional signs from here (the flagpole) so I can find you when I return. We are G-Battery, 2nd Provisional Group, Self-propelled Artillery." He paused and looked at me as if he was reaching in to my soul. I felt a certain closeness then that I hadn't felt before with any of the other officers. Maybe it was the urgency of the moment or the need to form a bond of trust in this harrowing time. With a genuine smile, he offered his hand to shake mine.

"Good luck, Captain. I'll take care of everything here."

"Thanks. I'm going to need it." chuckled the Captain as he turned around and started walking back to his Jeep. "I'll probably have to round up the men we need off the streets of Manila." He remarked sarcastically with a serious tone of voice.

In five short minutes I had met my new commanding officer and discovered what kind of unit I would be fighting with. I had also been handed a list of new orders and was ready to get to work. My first duty was set up the bivouac area. We needed a secure place for tents, equipment, and supplies. I remembered what they taught us in training at Fort Bliss: when establishing a bivouac area, find a location that is on high ground so that rainwater won't flood the position. Find an area that has good access from more than one direction and a canopy of trees for camouflage and protection from the elements.

As I drove my truck around the rubble looking for the ideal bivouac area, I couldn't believe the degree of destruction that our base had sustained. I wondered how the rest of the guys in my old unit were doing and how they had fared during the attack. From what little information I gathered while searching for the bivouac area, we apparently had not lost very many men in the attack, which was probably due to the fact that we had dug deep trenches around the perimeter of the runway for such an eventuality. While we were digging the trenches we thought it was a colossal waste of time, but they had proved to be lifesavers during the attack. I wasn't going to find a decent bivouac area in the main part of the base, so I drove back across the tracks where I had hidden my truck during the air raid. Fortunately, I soon found the perfect location. It was almost completely sheltered from above by huge native trees that was surrounded by thick vegetation. It was slightly higher for good runoff in case of rain, and only about a quarter of a mile from the parade grounds. I made some signs out of wood slats and cardboard and staked them conspicuously where the captain would see them. G-Battery had a home.

My next objective was to start obtaining the supplies on the list. As I drove back beside the runway, I saw that the medics had laid out the charred remains of one of the burned B-17 crews alongside their plane. Ambulances rushed about everywhere on the flat landscape of burning planes and buildings. Soldiers and aircrews wasted no time making repairs re-stocking their ammo supplies. Every group had to establish their priorities specific to their unit's needs. As Captain Perrenot had said, " This is only the beginning."

A burning oil dump belched copious clouds of black, acrid smoke into the fog-like aftermath of bomb; anti-aircraft and gunfire smoke, made the dismal scene even darker. Upon reaching the depot I parked my truck where I could keep an eye on it for security reasons. I was wary about whom I could trust after I heard a rumor from one of the anti-aircraft guys that a spy had been shot at the communications headquarters for purposely directing our planes to land before the attack. Someone had said he was actually a German spy working for the Japanese now that they were allies.

I handed the quartermaster the list Captain Perrenot had given me. He looked at it and shook his head. "I'll get you what I can, but we're short on most supplies. The Japs got some of what you want with their bombs," he sighed. He made notes on my list, and gave it back to me to fill. "Take these now and come back tomorrow for the rest." I loaded what he gave me into the back of my truck and returned to the bivouac area.

By dark I had unloaded and stacked everything neatly. With my flashlight, I reviewed the list for tomorrow's haul. Debris fires burned everywhere on the base. Buildings that had collapsed and could not be made operational were left to burn. I was startled when a nearby ammunition dump exploded like a 4th of July firework display. The huge initial blast eerily lit up the already smoke-filled night sky. Although it seemed like everything was in total turmoil and confusion following the attack, I forced myself to remain focused on the job to get my orders completed. I don't remember sleeping much, thinking about what was going to happen next. Like Captain Perrrenot had said, "This is just the beginning!"

*December 9, 1941*

I was the first in line at the supply depot the next day to plead our case for the precious supplies. Little did the quartermaster know that I was representing a phantom unit not yet assembled. I had complete faith that Captain Perrenot would deliver the men and half-tracks as planned, so I felt it was my duty to prepare for that, come hell, high water, or more Japanese.

That same morning Private Burl A. Brewster arrived. "Are you Lovato, Sir?"

"Yes, I am and you don't have to call me 'Sir.' I am a private just like you, and I am very happy to see you," I replied. "Where's your deuce and a half, Brewster?"

" Just outside the bivouac area." he replied.

Private Burl A. Brewster
*Courtesy of the Brewster Family*

Brewster stood about six-foot-two, had dark wavy hair and resembled the handsome movie actor Gilbert Roland. He was from eastern New Mexico near the Texas border and spoke softly with an easy manner of speaking. We spent the rest of the day transporting supplies from the depot and getting to know each other better. Neither of us had been told much by our former commanding officers about what to expect when we were transferred to Captain Perrenot's command. The captain hadn't said much either. I did know that whatever we did now to obtain supplies would be to our advantage later.

When I inventoried the food supplies the quartermaster had issued us, I realized that things would be getting lean soon because he had given us only 900 meals. This meant that the thirty men Captain Perrenot was going to command would only have one meal per day for thirty days and the quartermaster had said the K-rations were over twenty years old.

*December 10 1941*

The next morning, when Brewster and I went to the supply depot, I told the quartermaster we did not have enough food rations for the number of men in our battery. "Hey, Chief, we're short 1800 units of rations for our artillery unit. What gives?"

"Everything is limited for the time being because the Japs have surrounded the island with a blockade and our supply ships are not getting through. Do with what you've got, and we'll re-supply you when we get more," he said gruffly.

"What about more .30-caliber ammo?" I asked.

"That too." he replied.

"Okay, we'll take whatever you can give us. Maybe the local native people who live in the jungle will give us bows and arrows or blowguns that shoot poison darts."

The quartermaster and Brewster looked at me incredulously. I was joking, but not completely.

"Yeah, it's true," I continued. "The native *Negritos* who live in the jungle can kill you silently with weapons they make out of wood and poisonous plants."

Both Brewster and the quartermaster curiously listened to the story of how I had met the native *Negritos* while out on a truck-washing detail. It had been another hot Philippine dry season day, the kind of day that one would rather spend by a cool, shaded jungle stream. Since our trucks were covered in the fine powdery dust from the unpaved roads, I suggested to the lieutenant that he authorize us to clean them up post haste. We were told MacArthur was a stickler when it came to cleanliness, and the trucks definitely needed a wash. There was a place I had spotted not far from the base that would be perfect for accomplishing our objective. We parked the jeeps and the GMC deuce and a half directly in the shallow stream and started to scrub down the vehicles with sponges and bars of army-issue soap.

Suddenly and silently, a band of small, black, muscular men emerged from out of the thick vegetation, carrying bows, arrows, and blowpipes. We were completely surrounded, our rifles were out of reach on the bank, and escape would have been impossible.

We smiled and whistled, and continued to clean the trucks as a show of non-aggression as the apparent leader and two of his men curiously approached my crew. They seemed less interested in us and more fascinated by the soap bubbles. I could tell by their smiling faces that they meant us no harm. None of the group of about twenty *Negritos* was taller than three-and-a-half feet. At five-seven, I felt like a giant.

"You like?" I asked as I handed the leader a soapy sponge. "Here. For you."

He squeezed the sponge and watched intently as the bubbles oozed out, some of them floating off in the breeze. I felt like one of the colonial settlers who gave beads to the Indians in exchange for Manhattan Island.

One by one, the other soldiers in my detail offered their rags and sponges to the *Negritos* surrounding us. Without asking, the little warriors crawled up on the fenders and began to scrub the trucks. I looked at the other soldiers, shrugged my shoulders and we all started to laugh.

"What a deal! They're going to wash the trucks for us," laughed Herman Tafoya, my high school friend and fellow New Mexican National Guardsman. Since the *Negritos* wanted to do the job, the rest of our guys kicked back and relaxed in the shade.

It was amusing to see them crawling all over the huge trucks with the cleaning rags in their hands and soap bubbles in their curly hair. After the trucks were rinsed, I took a photo of our new friends standing by the sparkling clean trucks with my Brownie box camera. When it was time for them to leave we gave our new buddies several bars of the army soap. With big smiles they reciprocated and gave us their tiny bows, arrows and some hand carved beads they wore around their neck.

"I believe they will be on our side if the Japs come," remarked Herman.

"I hope so. I think we're going to need all the help we can get," I replied.

Although the quartermaster seemed amused at the story of our new allies, he finished appropriating the supplies and said, " I got you as much as I can for now."

Brewster and I hauled the supplies back to our bivouac area to uncrate and organize them. When we were through stacking everything in order, we loaded our bandoleers with bullets and crisscrossed them across our chests. We then strapped on .45 semi-automatic pistols, mess kits, canteens, gas masks, backpacks with blanket rolls, and topped off the battle gear with steel helmets and Springfield rifles. We laughed at our loaded down condition remarking that for two artillerymen, the full infantry gear almost made our knees buckle.

I joked "Brewster, we look like Pancho Villa's banditos except for their ten gallon hats and beer bellies!"

*December 11, 1941*

The next day, Brewster and I continued to organize our bivouac area in preparation for Captain Perrenot's return with the rest of the men. It was hard to sleep because I couldn't stop wondering when the Japanese would return. I knew that all the training we had received at Fort Bliss was going to be tested any day now; the difference was that real lives were at stake this time.

*December 12, 1941*

It had been four days since Captain Perrenot left us with orders to set up the G-Battery half-track bivouac area with supplies. After a breakfast of canned rations, Brewster and I cleaned weapons, loaded ammo belts and set up tents in our sheltered compound. We were starting to get just a little nervous because we had not heard from the captain. Shortly, after cleaning up, we heard the deep rumble of a powerful engine and the low-gear whine of a heavy-duty transmission slowing down. We both stopped what we were doing and ran toward the entrance of the compound as the huge, angular nose and cannon barrel of the first half-track rumbled into the bivouac area.

Whoa!" exclaimed Brewster, astonished at the sight of the impressive fighting machines.

M-2 Half-track with French 75mm

The first half-track looked even larger and more awesome then we had imagined from Captain Perrenot's drawing. The olive-drab paint that covered every square inch of the half-tracks' outer surface was unscratched and still smelled of protective cosmolene grease. The 75-mm cannon was twice as large as the turret guns I had seen on the "General Stuart" M-3 Light Tank operated by the 194th Tank Battalion. Inside the large 75-mm cannon, deep spiral grooves twisted through a mirror-bright barrel lining that spins the fired projectile like a thrown football. This spinning motion keeps the deadly projectile on its intended target.

The captain had returned with four half-tracks and five Filipino Scouts that he knew from his previous assignment. The Scout officers were the elite fighting soldiers of the Philippine Army. They were highly trained in a variety of ground military activity and had a reputation at Fort Stotsenberg of being proud, disciplined leaders. Their expertise and knowledge of the territory in which we would be potentially fighting the Japanese would prove to be an asset later on. He introduced Brewster and me to them and then instructed us to load the trucks and half-tracks with the ammo and to familiarize ourselves with the machines. Captain Perrenot told us he had to leave again to get more men.

"Lovato, you and Brewster have done a good job setting up. The bivouac area looks great. It looks like you got all the supplies and more."

I replied and saluted, "I did what you told me to do, Sir."

He shook his head, grinned, and smiled, "I don't know about you, Lovato." I could tell he didn't mean it literally; rather it was one of those peculiar affectations people say when they are surprised.

*"Que paso?"* I asked one of the Philippine Scouts, who was surprised I could speak one of their languages, although in a different dialect. Filipinos speak Tagalog among themselves more frequently than Spanish or English. "We have a lot to learn together in a very short amount of time before the Japanese invade the Philippines," I continued. "We're going to be fighting for your country and for all of our lives."

"And the lives of our children," he added.

A Filipino Scout lieutenant said that he was well trained on all American infantry weapons but had had very little experience with artillery.

"Brewster and I will do our best to show you what we know about firing and maintaining the half-track's 75-mm artillery piece," I responded. "Our training has been predominantly in three-inch and 37 mm anti-aircraft artillery so we have a lot to learn together."

Brewster listened as the Scout and I communicated in both Spanish and English, trying to build camaraderie through common language and understanding. I'm sure that having a Spanish background in common with the Filipinos helped break the ice as we examined the mechanical workings of the half-tracks. The Filipinos indicated that they knew all of Luzon (a major Philippine island) like the backs of their hands. Their knowledge would be an indispensable asset in the field. After all, we were a mobile self-propelled artillery unit and probably would be traveling the back roads frequently. Upon careful examination of the half-tracks' engine, drive train, and weapons, I determined that the armor around the rear was too thin, and offered only minimal protection for the weapons operators.

"Captain Perry (he had told us to call him Perry for short), I've got to tell you Sir, the armor around the box couldn't stop a BB." The box is the area behind the cab where the artillery and machine gun are mounted. "When men are standing, loading, and firing the guns they will be exposed from above and only protected by thin walls of light-gauge steel." Although I had facetiously exaggerated the minimal protective capabilities of the box's armor, I was sure it would allow easy penetration by a .30-caliber or larger bullet.

The captain looked closely at the side metal, nodded and said, "You're right, Lovato, but what can we do about it now? I was lucky to get these half-tracks off the dock because they were originally scheduled to be delivered to Australia.

"Maybe we can get someone at the maintenance depot to weld some additional steel plates over the existing metal," I suggested.

The captain nodded again, then quickly said, " There's not enough time right now. We'll have to make do with what we've got."

The front end was well armored, and it was possible to open and close louvered shields on the windshield and radiator during heavy fighting. The White Company gasoline engines purred as smooth as kittens when accelerated and had shielded wiring for fording deep water. Because of the tank tread rear drive, turning the half-tracks at a standstill was possible. One tread went forward, the other backward, and rotated the heavy armored vehicle 360 degrees. The half-track's treads were made of hard rubber and were much quieter on the road than metal tanks treads.

Captain Perrenot called the scout officers, Brewster, and myself together and gave us a short directive: "We have all the supplies and ammo we're going to get until we can be re-supplied. We have only a few days to whip this battery of soldiers into a fighting artillery unit. "Lovato, I'm going to begin training on the 75-mm at 1400 hours. I want you to assist me when I go over the operation of the mechanicals. Captain Grimmer told me you were a squad leader in anti-aircraft and a good vehicle mechanic. That's why he said he recommended you to join my unit."

I had been trained at Fort Bliss, Texas, for anti-aircraft artillery, and the principles of field artillery were basically the same. One had to consider the coordinates of direction and distance, and take into consideration wind and target movement. Captain Perrenot began our half-track orientation with a walk-around explanation of the moving parts and the French 75-mm step by step operation. After a thorough question and answer period, Captain Perrenot left at nightfall to try and obtain more personnel.

*December 13, 1941*

Captain Perrenot returned with a mixed group of Philippine regular army, conscripts, and Scouts. G-Battery now numbered thirty-three men, some with no previous training, but we were united with one common purpose: we were going to destroy the enemy before he could destroy us. It was like boot camp all over again as we learned how to operate the half-tracks under every imaginable condition, from flat roads to jungle trails. Because we didn't know when we would be re-supplied, we only fired the big guns twice in practice. It was train, train, and more training. There would be no tomorrow if we weren't ready. I also removed the engine governors from the half-tracks and trucks so we could get the best top speed and performance from the engines. We knew the Japanese soldiers were experienced fighters because we had seen their ferocity and fighting prowess in motion picture newsreels. Predictably, they would need to invade the Philippines in order to establish a stronghold in the South Pacific.

Whenever they had the opportunity, the majority of the Filipinos preferred to congregate together and speak their own language, tell jokes and relate their viewpoints about all that was happening. I enjoyed those rare moments when we did have the opportunity to learn a little about each other. Those times were few and far between.

*December 20, 1941*

Twelve days after the Japanese attack, our practice and training was over. Captain Perrenot gave us our new orders, "Pack up, men! We move out at 1900 hours."

Our battery consisted of four half-tracks, two trucks, the captain, Brewster, thirty Filipinos, and myself. According to the captain our assignment was to proceed about eighty miles north to Lingayen Gulf, and conduct shore patrol.

"Use cat-eye shields on the headlights. We don't want to be spotted by the Japs," ordered the captain. Cat-eye covers allow only a slit of light forward and down. We were to leave our bivouac area under the cover of darkness for additional protection and secrecy. It was known that there were Japanese spies everywhere and because they often looked similar to Filipinos and other South Pacific islanders, they could infiltrate our ranks easily as civilian volunteers.

Before departing, Captain Perrenot called us together in the fading light of dusk. "We're on our own, gentlemen. A unit of tanks will join us later. We have no air cover or infantry support until we reach our destination. We can only count on each other until further notice."

"Follow my exact orders at all times or ask your officers [Scouts] if you have any questions." The Filipinos mumbled to each other in Tagalog and seemed surprised that we were going to be on our own, but they asked no questions. After a short pause the captain said, "Let's go!"

I leaned over to Brewster and whispered, "Some of the guys are looking like they're having second thoughts about heading north."

Brewster grinned and replied, "Nobody really wants to be here to spend Christmas on a battlefield. Worse yet, maybe die on one."

Almost in unison, high-pitched starter motors cranked the half-tracks and big trucks to life. We were not waiting at Clark Field for the Japanese to attack again; we were going out looking for them. From the lead half-track Captain Perrenot signaled the column to move out.

The deep rumble of the half-tracks blended with the whine of shifting gears and created a mechanical symphony. The hard-rubber treads made a clacking noise on the road that sounded like a theater audience clapping. Each half-track crew consisted of two drivers, four men to operate the 75-mm cannon, and two men for the .30-caliber machine gun.

As our convoy motored in to the dark, moonless night, I thought back to how all this all began for me back in New Mexico. In the summer of 1940, between my junior and senior year, my best friends and I, Herman Tafoya, and Arthur Garde joined the National Guard in Albuquerque because it seemed like the right thing to do at a time when the threat of war loomed on the horizon. We spent that summer training at Fort Luna near Las Vegas, New Mexico. In December, 1940 we had to leave school because we were notified that our Guard unit was being sent to Boot Camp. After New Year we were sent by bus to Fort Bliss, where we earned the title of the "Fighting 200th" on the training grounds as well as in the bars of El Paso, Texas, and Juarez, Mexico.

In September 1941, after nine months of training we were transported by train to San Francisco, boarded on to the USS Pierce, and set out to sea not knowing our destination until we were several miles out of port. During the journey our ship almost went under during a massive storm. One night while I was on watch I had to tie myself to the ships' railing to keep from being washed overboard. Our National Guard unit was officially activated into the US Army before we docked in Hawaii and spent two days in Honolulu before setting sail for the Philippines.

Another day while I was on watch between Hawaii and the Philippines, I saw a huge black shape in the water cruising a few hundred feet alongside the ship. I sounded the alarm because I thought it was a submarine. Everyone on board was relieved when the black whale raised out of the water and cleared its air hole.

We disembarked the old converted ocean liner at Caviti Naval Base on September 25th. The next day we were trucked and assigned to Fort Stotsenberg and nearby Clark Field airbase. For the next two and a half months we continued to train in the tropical environment of the Philippines, a stark contrast to the bitter winter cold and stifling summer heat of El Paso. And now here we are driving away from the base to some shoreline we've never been before to possibly meet the enemy face to face.

Captain Perrenot wanted to get to Lingayen Gulf before daybreak to avoid the possibility of being spotted by Japanese aircraft. Our convoy was leaving a dust trail that during the day would have been easily detected for miles. Without air cover we would have been easy targets for strafing planes or light bombers. The only defense we had from enemy airplanes was the .30-caliber machine guns mounted on the four half-tracks, our rifles and our handguns. Sometime during the night two of the Filipino recruits deserted.

CHAPTER 2

# Facing the Enemy

*December 21, 1941*

The red morning sun rose at our backs as we stood in silence, engines idling, overlooking a gently sloping beach in Lingayen Gulf near the town of Agoo. The long curved expanse of smooth beach, lined with palm trees and thick tropical foliage looked like a tan crescent moon dotted with mounds of green debris. Seawater turned from jade green by the shore to deep cobalt blue at the horizon where steely-gray storm clouds towered in to the hazy blue sky. A calm, warm breeze blew gently in from the South China Sea, stirring the palm fronds like little green flags. I took several deep breaths of the damp air to refresh my sore lungs after coughing all night from road dust kicked up by the half-tracks.

Captain Perrenot stood in the box of the lead half-track, surveyed the area, and then waved us forward to the edge of beach where the flat terrain met the sandy beach. From where I stood, the beach curved about five miles in an arc that faced west toward the South China Sea.

Captain Perrenot raised his hand and stopped the convoy. He stepped down from the rear of his half-track and reassigned Brewster and me, from our trucks to replace the deserters.

"Lovato, I want to position the first half-track here. Bury it part way in the sand and cover the rest of it with vegetation. I am going to position the rest of the half-tracks farther up the beach. If the enemy tries to approach this beach-head, they're going to have to go through us."

I replied, "Yes, Sir, I'll make sure they are well camouflaged. No one will be able to see us. We can cover the half-tracks with the vegetation from the surrounding area to look like those piles of debris on the beach."

What the captain didn't know was that I was the "camouflage king" at Fort Bliss. I earned that title during an exercise when I hid my vehicle and myself so well in a desert arroyo that no one could find me. Although most of the men spoke some English, I relayed the captain's orders because I could explain them more clearly in Spanish to the Filipinos. I nearly got into trouble because Lieutenant Shambling, the officer who told me to hide the Jeep said, "Under no circumstances, do not, I repeat, do not, come back until the men find you. Understand?" Following orders, I hid and waited. Early the next morning, after spending a chilly night in the Jeep, I figured that they had forgotten about me. I was extremely hungry since I had missed both lunch and dinner. So I returned to the base to a very upset Lieutenant who in turn ordered me to show him exactly where I had hidden. Since nobody had been able to find me, the officer had assumed I took the Jeep and went AWOL to El Paso. I explained that once I wedged the vehicle into the crevice, I brushed out my tracks and covered myself and the open Jeep with a canopy of tumbleweeds. Clearly embarrassed or irritated, Lieutenant Shambling nodded his head and walked away without saying a thing. The captain broke his somber gaze at the beach, turned and looked at me with a grin and said, shaking his head slow, "I don't know about you, Lovato!"

I described to the Filipino soldiers, who wielded long bolos (machete-like swords), the plan we would use to cover the half-tracks. They understood completely and began to cut the palm tree fronds, bamboo, and jungle brush with their razor sharp bolos.

Camoulflaged and waiting for the enemy near Agoo
*Drawing by Francisco Lovato*

First, we partially buried the half-tracks in the sand facing seaward (west). Next, we built bamboo and driftwood structures that we lashed together to provide a framework to attach the palm fronds, brush, and foliage. All the exposed metal was smeared with mud to reduce glare or reflection. We also made dummy emplacements that resembled the actual emplacements to complete the deception. The half-tracks now looked much like the other piles of vegetation on the open beach.

Occasionally a native fisherman paddled by in his colorful canoe-like boat, looking curiously at our activities on the beach. Even the walkie-talkie wires were buried between the half-tracks. Before crawling into the emplacement we swept smooth our wheel, tread, and foot marks leaving no trace of our presence in the sand. G-Battery could not be seen from the air, land, or sea.

By late afternoon our half-tracks and dummy emplacements were ready. The palm fronds provided shade from the sun as we climbed into our respective half-tracks and began to wait for our date with destiny. If the enemy planned to land on this beach, we were in the perfect position to stop them.

While we sat and waited, Brewster asked "I wonder if any Japs will be coming this way, Frank?"

I answered, "How do I know? We have no communication with HQ. We're just a shore patrol on a remote beach. The captain's just following the orders he was given."

"Do you think we're going to see any action all the way out here? The Japs are probably going to attack Manila. I mean, why would they start all the way out here in the middle of nowhere and then have to march all the way down the island?" Brewster reasoned.

I thought about it for a while. "If the Japs go into Manila Bay they're going to have to face the huge fixed cannons on Corregidor and Bataan. And, if any of them come this way, we're going to welcome them with our 75-mm cannons. If they do come, I hope they come in the morning hours."

"Why's that?" asked Brewster.

"Because we're facing directly west. The sun will be in their eyes. When we face the open water, the morning sun is to our back. Approximately six or seven miles to the east and directly behind us, the morning sun's brilliant rays will break over the mountain range and provide us with additional cover until late morning."

By dark we were thoroughly exhausted and hungry. After eating a small ration of canned meat and crackers I climbed into the front seat of my truck hidden in the trees and fell asleep.

*December 22, 1941*

With the first light of daybreak answers to our questions revealed themselves ominously on the horizon. I woke on the front seat of my truck that was backed into the trees behind the camouflaged half-tracks. Brewster was sleeping in the rear of his truck. I squinted through the early morning haze and spotted several angular objects in the water. From our perspective, the horizon was filled with anchored warships, each a dark shadow floating in the mist.

"Brewster! Wake up! Look!" I yelled as I shook him awake.

"Oh my God! It's got to be the entire Japanese Navy!" Brewster gasped.

I jumped out of the truck and ran across the short expanse of sand to Captain Perrenot's half-tracks, and yelled, "Captain, Captain!"

"I see them," he said.

By now everyone in G-Battery was awake and staring in stunned silence at the enemy armada anchored on the dark water about two miles offshore. *Maybe they're anchored out there for regrouping purposes. No, they're coming our way. Where in the hell are those tanks Captain Perry said were coming?*

I mumbled to Brewster, "My God. We're going to need a hell of a lot more firepower."

As the first light of day slowly emerged, we could see smaller boats filled with Japanese soldiers beside the mother ships. The invasion troops were waiting to begin their attack. I shuddered at the thought of how many soldiers all those Japanese ships could carry. An armada that size could deliver several thousand troops.

Captain Perrenot calmly picked up his half-track's radio and gave the first orders to the other three half-tracks. "This is it, gentlemen. The enemy will come in small landing crafts carrying thirty to fifty men. Those will be our targets," he said flatly. Raising his voice, he emphasized, "Stay completely covered! We will fire on my orders only! I will give the coordinates and the order to shoot! We must make every shot count. There is no telling when we can get re-supplied. Got it?"

Some of the Filipinos began to pray and made the sign of the cross over and over. We hurriedly checked and re-checked our weapons, ammunition, gun sights, and opened crates of the 75-mm ammo. We cleared out some of the frontal camouflage for better visibility. By all indications the Japanese would attempt to land at least part of their troops in our sector. I never imagined that I would be one of the first to encounter the enemy on the shores of the Philippines when I signed up with the National Guard in Albuquerque. I asked, "Captain, how in the world are we going to take on all those boats?"

Captain Perrenot kept looking seaward at the flotilla and answered without emotion, "One at a time."

"Okay, Sir! Got it. Will do."

I could see that he was thinking, calculating, and trying to figure out the best move for the circumstances. His command decisions would affect the lives of thousands of soldiers on both sides. Still staring out to sea, Captain Perrenot said in his low monotone, "They'll probably send out reconnaissance aircraft to survey the beach and the area behind us."

We had camouflaged everything sufficiently to avoid detection, but then I remembered the footprints Brewster and I had made running to Captain Perrenot's half-track. I quickly jumped out and smoothed the sand leading to my truck before a plane could spot me. Just as I finished brushing out the footprints and got under the camouflage of the half-tracks, I heard the steady drone of a small aircraft engine approaching from the south. We all peeked through the cracks in the camouflage for a glimpse of the approaching airplane. A few short moments later, the enemy reconnaissance plane followed the contour of the beach northward less than one hundred feet over our beach emplacements. Captain Perrenot was correct about the enemy's next strategic move. It appeared that the pilot didn't spot us under our thick layers of vegetation. When we were certain the plane was out of sight and we had avoided detection, Brewster asked, "What's next Captain?"

"Well, their battleships, cruisers and destroyers will probably pound the shore with big artillery. I pray they can't see us." The captain stared out at the big ships coming in to clearer view as the morning mist lifted. The sun had not yet crested the mountains behind us.

*What are the Japs waiting for? When are they going to attack?* Tension built with every passing second. We were in for the fight of our lives, and everyone knew it.

I asked the captain, "Does headquarters know the Japs are out there? If those ships are filled with soldiers, there's got to be thousands of them coming at us. Where are our tanks and heavier artillery?"

Captain Perrenot paused. "I don't know," he said. "We'll do our job and they'll do theirs." We stared through the cracks of camouflage branches at the flotilla of ships, realizing that we were probably going to face the enemy all alone on this isolated beach because we hadn't heard from any other units since we arrived.

The smell of sweat and fear filled the air of our half-track and I suspected that everyone in the other emplacements must have been feeling the same tension. Thoughts of my family raced through my mind. There is no other life experience that can approximate what a man feels when he sees a huge enemy armada amassing right before his eyes. I felt the same way General Custer must have felt at Little Big Horn. They can teach us to shoot straight, dig holes, master the use of unfamiliar equipment, but they can't teach us to face the enemy in combat. We only learn that on the battlefield. I prayed our outcome would be better. *Surely headquarters knows by now about the huge armada. How can they not see a hundred ships? We can't be the only ones who see this. Damn it! We don't have radio communications with anyone!* Our telephone-type radios only worked with hard wire lines, and we didn't have a wire to field headquarters.

Without warning, a collage of bright yellow flashes and smoke-ring puffs emerged out of the big ships' guns followed seconds later by their thundering, staccato reports. Within seconds several large-bore naval projectiles exploded somewhere behind the half-tracks emplacements. Everything shook each time they struck nearby. Between the deafening blasts, one could hear the high-pitched whistling sound as the steel projectile ripped through the air. As powerful as the concussions were, it would seem that even a close hit might destroy us. *Either they don't know where we are on the beach or they are very bad shots.* The Japanese warships bombarded the terrain behind us for about fifteen minutes. Everyone but Captain Perrenot cringed at the high-pitched whistle of the incoming projectiles. He grinned in amusement and said, "You don't need to worry about the shells you can hear, they're already past. It's the ones you don't hear that'll get you." Somehow his revelation, although technically correct, wasn't reassuring. After another ten minutes or so, a time period that seemed like eternity, the shelling stopped. The still silence that followed the explosions and shrilling contrails was eerie.

The men sat and I'm sure wondered, like me when our time to fight would come. The ships were much too far away to hit with our 75-mm guns. Captain Perrenot told us that our primary targets would be the landing crafts and we would have to wait for them to come into range.

Growing out of the utter stillness, we heard the distinct drone of Japanese airplanes approaching. One after another the powerful light bombers flew over our positions, so low we could see the faces of the pilots and tail gunners. Bombs dropped from the planes bellies, landing somewhere behind us in the trees. All I could guess was that they were flattening the terrain to make it easier for their infantry troops that were soon to land. Without warning, a bomb suddenly exploded near us that viciously shook our half-track. My eyes rattled out of focus for a brief second.

Captain Perrenot looked at his map. "There might be a Philippine army unit and the 31st Infantry in the jungle behind us. The planes are probably shooting at them." We then heard a thunderous artillery report come from behind us. Its projectile sounded like a freight train tearing up the sky. "It must be one of our big artillery pieces firing on the enemy ships," said Captain Perrenot.

"All right! It's about time some of our big stuff got on the job!" cheered Brewster. He appeared excited to know that others on our side had joined the battle.

Two enemy attack planes flew over us and headed inland toward our big guns. Less than a minute later several large explosions interrupted the steady drone of the aircraft engines. The planes made another pass, but our big artillery was silent. We looked grimly at each other, suspecting the tragic fate of our fellow soldiers. The big artillery guns were easy targets for the low-flying aircraft. Our fate was nearly at hand. Thanks to the skilled hands of the Filipino men, we had remained undetected under the camouflage. The once-beautiful beach was strewn with broken and splintered trees. Smoldering brush blackened the sand and made our four camouflaged half-tracks blend in even better. Paradise had turned into hell, but we were still alive with no casualties. Brewster and I had hidden our trucks in the trees behind the half-tracks. I hoped they had not been hit.

The Japanese ships had ceased firing during their airplane attack and had not resumed for over ten minutes. We waited for their next move.

White bubbles burst from the prows of the landing craft and signaled that the invasion had begun. The sun had finally crested over the small mountains to the east, and we could see boats with red and white bulls-eye flags headed straight toward our beach. "Good! The sun will be in their eyes as they approach us!" yelled Captain Perrenot. With his eyes fixed on the oncoming boats, he held his radio handset ready to order us to commence firing. "There will be no tomorrow if we fail!" he shouted. "Fire only under my orders! Keep the gun barrels covered until then!"

From our vantage point at water level, we saw a wave of six enemy boats packed with soldiers heading directly towards us. A second wave aimed at us and slowly plowed through the jade colored water, white foam breaking across their prows. Dozens of other boats headed farther north on the bay beyond our effective firing range. No boats appeared to be headed south of our emplacements. Sweat poured down our foreheads like hot rain. We waited for the boats to come within range and to hear Captain Perrenot's order to fire. My heart was pounding so hard, I thought it was going to burst out of my chest. Captain Perrenot stared over his cannon's long barrel, never taking his eyes off the approaching boats as they lumbered forward.

Dec. 22, 1941 — Japanese General Homma's Invasion Force begin beach landings at Northern Lingayen Gulf between Damortis and Bauang.
*By Francisco Lovato & Colleen Greene*

His order thundered over the radio handset, "Unit 1! Take the left two targets! Unit 2! Take the middle two targets! Unit 3! Take the two on the right! My unit will cover all targets!"

As the boats neared my senses became keener as I waited for the chance to do battle with the enemy. It seemed that when the boats were about one thousand yards away, the sound of our panting was louder than the boat motors. Our eyes were fixed on the incoming boats, like a hawk's eyes as it focuses on its unsuspecting prey. I wanted more than ever to avenge their sneak attacks on Pearl Harbor and Clark Field. Shooting at their airplanes with my Springfield rifle back at Clark Field was hardly enough. Now I felt we had a chance to do some serious damage to their invasion plans. The enemy boats were about 750 yards away. I could see sweat pouring off the brown, boyish faces of our Philippine recruits. A chorus of voices whispered prayers in Spanish and Tagalog. Through binoculars I could see each of the helmeted Japanese invaders was holding a rifle pointed upward. Each advancing boat was loaded with forty or more soldiers. The wooden boats were so low in the water that the waves were splashing the soldiers. *A close hit would sink them.* When the boats were 400 yards away I thought, Oh, my God, this is for real! It's them or us. The radio crackled: "Get Ready! Set distance for three hundred yards. Fire!"

The big 75-mm cannons thundered almost in unison as the roar of our big guns broke the tense quiet. The recoil shook the half-track, our bodies and our brains. As the exploding projectiles struck the sea, tall waterspouts gushed upward beside the nearing boats. "Load! Aim! Fire!" The boats were helpless to do anything but to continue their approach. This was our chance to take the advantage because they were vulnerable. "Load! Fire!" Each shell hit the water closer as we zeroed in on their plodding vessels. The sun was still low on the horizon and was shining directly in their eyes and prevented them from seeing us.

We were still cloaked in our camouflage, and our nostrils burned from the strong, pungent gunpowder smoke. We loaded and fired in rapid succession at the oncoming boats. After each shot, the breach lock was opened by hand with a counter-clockwise twisting motion. One man ejected the spent shell casing; a second man shoved in a fresh round. A three-foot long projectile sliding into the breach made a shrill metallic sound. The first man then locked the handle in a clockwise position. The heavy clank of the breach slamming shut was followed by a brief moment to adjust the aim. Captain Perrenot called out new coordinates and signaled when to pull the lever. My ears rang from the repeated explosions from our cannons. Unfortunately two out of ten shells were duds.

The enemy boats exploded into pieces of wood and bodies. "God forgive me," I whispered as I saw Japanese soldiers in the water, their arms flailed as they screamed in panic and pain between volleys of our cannon fire.

Captain Perrenot continually radioed the other three half-tracks new coordinates. Another hit! Our four cannons pounded the oncoming boats, blasting one enemy boat after another as they pushed ashore from the Japanese transport ships. The once peaceful, crescent moon bay was now strewn with pieces of boats, canvas packs, and screaming, drowning soldiers. Those who could swim went toward other boats. The rest of the Japanese soldiers splashed and floundered in the water and tried to grasp any floating parts from the destroyed landing crafts. Even the near hits were causing their boats to sink because they were so heavily loaded.

The Japanese kept coming in waves of five or six boats. We remained under our camouflaged shelters. Packed like sardines in a can, the Japanese were slow and easy targets in the water. There were no artillery or machine guns returning fire. It was like shooting ducks on a pond. I kept wondering when the big ships would fire on us, now that we had revealed our position.

The captain's directions and coordinates were right on target. We were sinking every enemy boat before they could reach the shore at our sector; but there seemed to be an endless stream of boats coming from those transport ships. We wouldn't have enough ammunition to keep firing at them much longer at the rate we were shooting.

*Hadn't the big ships seen us by now? What about the boats that were heading farther north? What will they do when they land? Surely they'll spot us. Where were those tanks we were promised? They should be here by now, because this is where the action is.*

The water was murky from the landing crafts churning the muddy bottom of the bay. *How quickly heaven had turned into hell.* Our cannon barrels were burning hot from the continuous firing. The Filipinos in the other half-tracks were taking rifle fire from the enemy until they could blow the boat out of the water. Some boats made it as close as fifty yards from the shore. Our men never faltered in their duties. The Filipinos blessed themselves in the name of the Father, the Son, and the Holy Ghost between loading and firing the French 75 cannon.

The wooden crates of ammo were quickly being depleted. The water around the sinking boats churned with screaming enemy soldiers, splashing to stay afloat before sinking into an ocean grave. There was no time to think; the enemy kept coming in waves; boat after boat. "Load! fire!"

Suddenly an explosion shook the ground and rocked the half-track. We began to take artillery and rifle fire as bullets ricocheted off the half-tracks' steel armor. Enemy soldiers, who had landed on the beaches farther north, were taking shots at us. They were throwing the big stuff at us: cannons or mortars.

"We're going to pull out before we get surrounded," Captain Perrenot called out over the constant gunfire. Bamboo, palm fronds and sand flew everywhere as the half- tracks crashed out of the cover onto the open beach. Philippine Scouts manning the .30-caliber machine guns hammered a staccato barrage at the Japanese soldiers running toward us on the beach. Exploding mortar fire landed all around us as we backed our half-tracks into the trees away from the advancing horde of Japanese infantry soldiers shooting at us from our right. "Man, I wish they had build the sides a little thicker," I said to Brewster. "The armor won't stop it if we get hit by one of those heavier slugs."

Captain Perrenot yelled over the noise of our half-track's engine, "Lovato and Brewster, get your trucks and follow us out to the road. We need to re-group with the others."

Brewster and I jumped off the half-track and scrambled to our trucks that had somehow survived the Japanese artillery and aerial bombing. We roared over broken, smoldering trees as fast as our trucks would go and we followed Captain Perrenot away from the beach.

"Hey, look! It's one of our guys!" yelled Brewster as a US GI stepped out of the trees onto the road followed by a group of other soldiers. "All right! Man, are you guys a sight for sore eyes!"

"We're from the 31st" one of the soldiers shouted. "We've been fighting Japs farther north," he said. "They're infiltrating south and are trying to cut us off."

The captain warned the soldiers about the huge invasion force that had landed and was headed our way. Gunfire could be heard in almost every direction. *Thank God the 31st have joined us in the fight.* They were tough, seasoned US Army infantrymen who had been in the Philippines years before we in the 200th had arrived. Shots were coming from behind us as Japanese troops advanced through the trees.

Although not a single Japanese boat reached our sector of the beachhead, there were apparently no other defenders to stop the enemy who had landed north of us. I kept wondering where the rest of our beach defenses were.

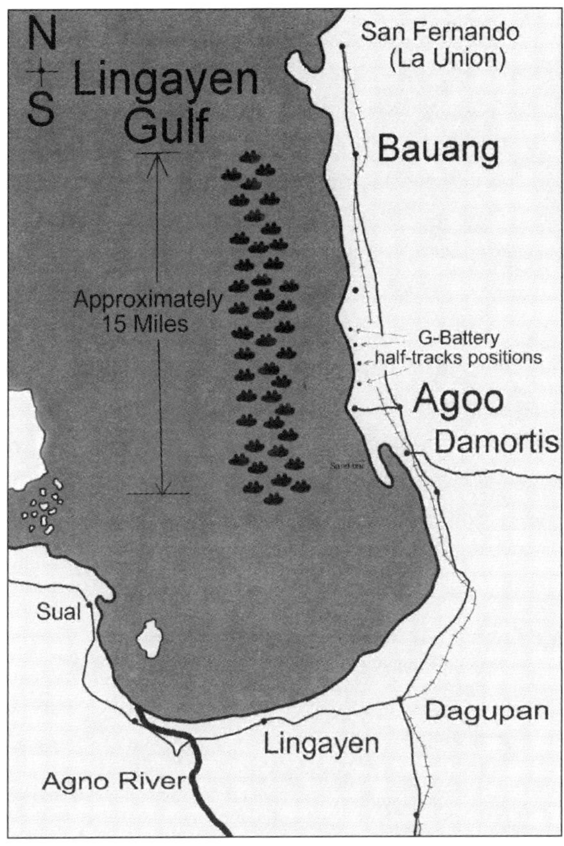


Japanese Philippine invasion force landings December 22,1941
*By Francisco Lovato*

CHAPTER 3

# Message from the Front

We were low on 75-mm ammo, under-manned, under-supplied, with no plan but to stay alive and destroy as many Japanese soldiers as we could before they could get us. It was clear we would have to retreat. At least we had the terrific Philippine scouts who knew the terrain. We drove into the interior on the main road ahead of the advancing Japanese infantry. *Thank God for the incredibly well built White engines that propelled the half-tracks, because they never fail to start.* And, they were even faster since I had removed the engine governors that restricted the overall top speed in each gear.

After a few miles, Captain Perrenot pulled over and signaled me to stop. He called out to me, "Lovato! You've got the fastest truck. Take this envelope and deliver it to the highest commanding officer at field headquarters. We have no other means to let them know what the hell is going on here. And don't stop for anything!" I could see it in his eyes the captain was dead serious.

"Yes, Sir! Is there anything else, Sir?"

"Yes, You and Brewster take these six (Filipino conscripts) men with you. Don't come back looking for us. There will be Japs everywhere. We'll regroup in a couple of days behind our own lines." With one of his rare grins, he whispered, "Good luck Lovato! Don't stop for anything, not even for a *maganda laga* (pretty Filipino girl)." Although he smiled at me he looked worried. I thought it was peculiar that he was joking with me at such a time. He had never joked about anything before. We had been through a lot together in a very short time.

"I got it Captain. Not even a *maganda laga*, Sir!" I took the orders, secured them in a buttoned pocket, loaded the Filipinos in the canvas-covered rear of my Chevy ton and a half, and headed toward the field command post which, according to Captain Perrenot, was about thirty miles south on the main road. I figured the captain would have told me what was in the orders if he wanted me to know. All I knew was that he wanted them delivered as soon as possible, and it was my job to get them there. One Filipino sentry rode on top of the rear cover to search the sky for any low-flying enemy aircraft as I charged down the road as fast as I could. I didn't like the idea of leaving everyone behind, but orders were orders.

Less than ten minutes from the beach the sentry yelled "Jap plane! Jap plane!" as he banged in panic on the top of the steel cab. "Hang on to your butts. The nearest cover is almost a quarter mile ahead!" I yelled as I floored the Chevy. In the rear view mirror, I could only see a trail of dust in our wake, making us an easy target for aircraft. Then came more banging and frantic cries in Tagalog that I couldn't understand. I hung on to the steering wheel for dear life, as we bounced up and down along gaping potholes and bumpy ruts. I kept my eyes focused through the dust-covered windshield on the dense tree cover, less than a hundred yards ahead.

At first I couldn't see the enemy aircraft but I could hear the hysterical cries of the five other men in the back of the truck as it swooped down to attack us from behind. Bursts of machine gun fire and the loud exhaust of the warplane drowned out their panicked voices until it passed overhead. A shower of enemy bullets slammed into the dry, dusty ground all around us as the plane missed, arced upward, and banked to the left for a return attack.

"Damn! It's one of those long-fuselage attack planes with the rear mounted machine gunner!" Brewster hollered over the revved-out Chevy six cylinder engine. The Mitsubishi Ki-30, nicknamed the "Ann", could fire wing-mounted machine guns as it approached, drop a bomb, and shoot from a rear-mounted machine gun as it pulled away. We feared encountering an "Ann" more than the fast "Zero" fighter plane because of its firepower. The rear gunner aimed his machine gun at us and fired a short volley, but missed again. "Thank God they can't shoot!" he cried out. By the time the Japanese plane could make another pass I pulled the truck under a thick overhang of dense trees. The mottled green attacker made two more passes then departed without firing another shot. When we couldn't hear the plane's engine anymore I sent one man to the edge of the grove to check the sky.

"Whew! That was a really close call. Man, I thought that Jap had us for sure." remarked Brewster in his typical low key voice. All of us were terrified at the prospect of being caught out in the open again. One fellow had to be cradled in his buddy's arms as he whimpered like a baby.

The scout came back and reported he didn't see anything, so I said another Hail Mary then crept slowly out of our protective umbrella to proceed on our mission. *The enemy airplane must have had bigger game in mind than our solo truck.* From then on we had to assume that any plane was an enemy aircraft since most of ours had been destroyed at Clark Field.

About twenty minutes after the first attack, one of the Filipinos riding in the cab with us slapped my shoulder and pointed out the passenger side window at a low-flying attacker approaching fast. I cranked the steering hard right and crashed into dense shrubbery trying to avoid the trees. Branches snapped and slammed against the windshield as I stopped, turned off the engine, and prayed the warplane couldn't see us.

Again we waited under the umbrella of trees, like a field mouse frozen still after seeing a hawk's shadow. I turned and saw the men huddled in the rear of the truck, praying for safety and deliverance. Beads of sweat rolled down their dust-covered faces as they cowered from the noise of the approaching plane.

The muffled sound of our prayers were drowned out by the plane's blaring motor and blasting machine gun bullets ripping through the foliage around us. The plane made a third strafing pass, then disappeared as swiftly as it had appeared. No one talked as we listened for the aircraft to return. After a few minutes we gasped sighs of relief that he was gone and miraculously the truck and men had not been hit. After a few more signs of the cross we inched out of the overhang and headed to our destination.

Each time I fired up the Chevy and crept into the scorching sun, I prayed for protection. I didn't think it likely that we would encounter Japanese infantry this far inland since we had left the beach before they did and they didn't appear yet to have any ground vehicles. We were vulnerable to aircraft and I knew it was time to forget about everything else and get this truck, the men, and these important orders to the command post. We were a mobile unit and didn't have a radio transmitter that could reach the field command post. I was sent to carry the message by hand because I was the only means of communication our unit had.

So far we had encountered only one friendly unit on our mission. I suspected that most of the Philippine and American defenders didn't know that the Japanese had landed at Lingayen Gulf, or we would have had additional support. It appeared to me that my sealed orders were bearing the news to the nearest command post to alert them.

At about 1500 hours we saw Old Glory rippling in the light breeze. The sight of our flag signaled that we had found our destination. "Thank God we made it in one piece," sighed Brewster. Our army was using the mansion of a sugar cane plantation as our field command post. A long, shiny, black Buick Roadmaster was parked in the center of the circular gravel driveway of the mansion. Bumper-mounted flags with stars indicated that it belonged to a general.

"What do you need, soldier?" asked the guard at the entrance to the mansion.

"I have sealed orders to give to the highest ranking officer," I replied.

He looked at my unshaven face and my uniform shirt that was covered in dust and week-old sweat, and then proceeded to take a wary look at the truckload of battle-weary Filipinos. He snapped back authoritatively, "Hand them over. You can't go in there yourself."

Obviously he had no idea what we had been through. Nor did he realize what an important message I was carrying for his commanding officer. The mood around the mansion was calm. There was no evidence of war at all. *Boy, do I have news for them.*

"I have sealed orders from my commanding officer and I have been given strict orders to only give them to the highest ranking officer immediately," I barked at the cleanly-shaven, freshly uniformed guard.

Without a word he accompanied me to the door of the mansion where a major ordered me to turn over my envelope.

"Sorry, Sir, but I have been ordered to give these to the highest commanding officer, and that person is the general," I replied.

"Come with me," the major responded. We went to a doorway that adjoined the general's office. "See the general? Now hand me those orders, soldier."

I stood at attention and reluctantly handed the major the envelope and yelled across the room, "General, Sir, this is information you should see right away, Sir." From the open doorway I saw the major hand the general the orders. The general opened the envelope and silently read the message. He immediately told the major and the other officers about the invasion. While the major began gathering up papers as if packing up shop, I stood in the doorway awaiting further orders.

As everyone rushed out of the general's office I asked the major, "What's going on, Sir?"

"You've got to go now," he yelled.

I answered, "Sir, I have six Filipinos and one GI who have been fighting with us at Lingayen. Who are we to report to now?"

The major snapped, "Your outfit has probably been annihilated by now, so go find yourselves a home. We can take you two GIs, but not the Filipinos. We don't have enough supplies."

"What?" I yelled back. *I thought we were all in this together.* "Well then who should we report to, Sir?"

"You're on your own, soldier," he said and continued frantically to gather up his maps and papers.

I couldn't believe my ears. *Weren't we on the same side?* Only a few hours earlier we blasted the Japanese invasion force with everything we could: we took artillery and rifle fire, and we had been strafed by enemy aircraft on the way to deliver this message. And all he had to say to me was "Find yourselves a home." I turned around and looked back through the long hallway leading to the general's office. I saw Brewster and the Filipinos standing outside in the driveway with blank stares on their dust-covered faces.

"What the hell am I supposed to do now?" I mumbled as the officers and guards scurried past me through the door toward the Buick Roadmaster.

The major said, "Don't follow us! Your truck will make too much dust!"

Brewster and I looked at each other incredulously and wondered if he had really said that. In less than ten minutes from the time I had handed the sealed envelope to the general, he, his staff, and the guards were leaving us. I felt abandoned by my own command. We hadn't eaten since the night before. We certainly didn't eat during the battle or on the journey to this outpost. Now we were being left behind to fend for ourselves in no-man's land. "Man, this is a hell of a way to fight a war" I grumbled as I gazed at my weary bunch of fellow soldiers.

I walked back outside to the truck and wondered what I would do with these very hungry men. I couldn't feed them. If it hadn't been for them, we wouldn't have been able to hand the general the valuable information that would save his troops.

The decision of what to do next made me realize how difficult it is to be a good commanding officer. It looked like I was going to make the next decision for the wellbeing of our outfit. *No wonder Captain Perrenot hardly ever talks much. He's always thinking about his next move.* It's not easy to be responsible for the lives of so many human beings that are looking to me for answers. I figured there must be other units out there we could hook up with until we'd be able to communicate with Captain Perrenot. There was no one I would rather fight under than Captain Perrenot. He had guided us well enough to knock out every one of those oncoming Japanese landing boats. And, he led us off the beach in time before any lives or machines were lost. He would be my commander until I heard otherwise.

"Ok guys, this is what we're going to do," I said. "We're going south, down the main road toward Manila and Clark Field. Once the dust settled, we loaded up and headed south in search of another unit to which we might attach ourselves. The men looked dejected. *If those officers could have seen these men during the invasion bravely firing and sinking hundreds of the enemy, they would have taken our whole unit with them and found the provisions for us.*

About five miles down the road, we encountered a communications unit. "We're from G Battery, Second Provisional Group, Self Propelled Artillery. I want to speak to your commanding officer," I told them through the window of the truck.

A burly seasoned sergeant stepped forward as I got out of the truck. "What do you need soldier?" he asked.

"We've been temporarily separated from our outfit and need to attach to another unit until we can get back to our guys," I explained.

Before he said a word the squinty-eyed sergeant stepped around the truck and looked over the six Filipino soldiers. "We can take you and the other American but not the rest," he yelled back, loud enough for everyone to hear.

The Filipinos who spoke English translated into Tagalog so everyone knew what the sergeant had said. I was ready to explode. I wanted to scream out to him exactly what I was feeling, but I kept my cool and held it down to a rumble.

"Damn it Sergeant, these men fought bravely and courageously for their lives and yours. All we're asking is to join you and your men in this same war until we can reconnect with our unit."

He turned around, faced me squarely, and in an apologetic tone of voice said, "I don't have enough food for all the men I have."

I wondered what Captain Perrenot would do in a situation like this. *Why did the captain send them with me in the first place?* I certainly didn't need that many men to help me deliver the sealed orders. I didn't think to ask him then; I just followed his orders. He had entrusted me with the lives of seven other men, he must have thought I would do the right thing.

He had kept the Scouts and the rest of the soldiers to man the half-tracks until we could reunite again. Only two weeks earlier, the two of us had met out at the baseball field and Captain Perrenot had shown me a pencil drawing of a half-track and a plan to form G-Battery. On a wing and a prayer Captain Perrenot had planned and I had implemented whatever there was to be done. He was the coach, I was the quarterback. This war was fought one play at a time. I never questioned his decisions, and he trusted me to carry them out the best I could.

I stepped away for a moment to weigh all the possibilities, and after painfully considering the options, I returned with the only conclusion that made any sense to me. Three weeks earlier the Filipinos had been civilians. I figured the best thing to do was to allow them to get reconnected with their fellow countrymen where they could get food and shelter. They stood a better chance of survival on their own than with these units of poorly rationed troops. I figured Brewster and I would get by until we could catch up to the captain and G-Battery. I went to the back of the truck where the men waited. I said sadly, "Soldiers, the time we have spent together has been short. We are all in a battle for our lives and your country. It's been an honor to fight alongside you. We did some serious damage to the Japs back at Lingayen. You fought bravely and without complaint, but now I must release you to go on your own and join your people's army where you can be the most effective. Good luck and *vaya con Dios.*"

Following handshakes and well wishes the Filipinos said they were going to a nearby village where a few of them had relatives.

The sergeant turned to me and told me his group was a communications unit. He asked Brewster and me if we had any experience in communications. "Sarge," I said with a grin, "we have plenty of experience in lack of communications."

"What?" he barked. He didn't look amused.

Quickly I told him of our difficulty in establishing communications because of the lack of wireless equipment.

"Sarge, we were at Lingayen when the Japs landed. We were in a half-track unit, but our captain ordered us to deliver a message about the invasion to the command post. We want to get back to our unit as soon as possible. Have you heard anything about G-Battery, Second Provisional Group, Self-Propelled Artillery? Our commanding officer is Captain Travis Perrenot."

"Sorry soldier, we have no word about either," the Sarge stated with a hint of concern in his gruff voice. "You guys can lay wire until you find your unit. We're low on food and supplies here like everywhere else, so I hope you find them soon."

I told him, "Hell, Sarge, in the past twelve hours we were bombarded by naval artillery, we took mortar and machine gun fire, and we were attacked by two Jap fighter planes while racing here to warn everyone. Hell, up until now, I was too excited to think about eating."

As we turned toward our roll of wire, I grumbled to Brewster, "But now I'm beginning to get really hungry."

The rest of the day Brewster and I strung wire wherever they wanted it. We were tired from carrying the heavy spool of wire from unit to unit. We had to roll the wire from the spool so it wouldn't get kinked. We used a stout pole through the center to create an axle for our wheel of wire. Around sunset we headed to the bivouac area for another meal of canned rations and then headed to our truck for some sleep.

*December 23, 1941*

Bombs exploding and the low chuckle of machine gun fire north of our position woke us early the next morning. We quietly tended to our new job, and saw the American and Philippine Scout officers pointing at crude maps and discussing their next action. Brewster and I carried the heavy wooden spool of telephone wire to a location and a soldier would cut it and connect the communication devices to it. The wire phones were the only means of intra-unit communication. As we rolled out the wire we saw soldiers fidgeting nervously with their Springfield rifles, sharpening their bayonets, and loading their ammo belts as they prepared their weapons and their minds for the fight ahead. None of the American and Filipino soldiers we encountered had ever seen a Japanese soldier. They did not realize the massive size of the invasion force we had seen at Lingayen Gulf.

While stopping for a quick break, Brewster squatted down and put his head between his knees and moaned, "Frank, I'm so sick of stringing this blasted wire. I wish we could get back to Captain Perry and our unit."

I nodded in agreement. I missed Captain Perrenot and our pick up team of Filipino soldiers. Aside from the two conscripts who had deserted on the way to Lingayen, the majority of them had done an exceptional job under fire on the beach. I thought back to Lingayen and all the excitement of the first blasts from our cannons and the artillery shells exploding around us. "Man," I said to Brewster, "these guys here wouldn't believe what we went through back at the gulf. The war hasn't gotten here yet."

Brewster lifted his head and looked at me from beneath his helmet and spoke only three words, "It will though." I remembered what Captain Perrenot said after the Japanese attacked Clark Field on December 8th: "That was just the beginning."

Our sweat soaked shirts never seemed to dry out completely in the thick, humid air. How I longed for a long, hot soapy shower to scrub off the sticky dirt and grime that never seemed to come off no matter how hard I wiped it. Whenever any of us would complain about the heat back at Clark Field, the Filipinos would laugh and say, "If you think it's hot now, just wait until the hot season." When I arrived in Manila in September, it took me several weeks to adjust to the humid tropical heat. Cool showers and fans in the barracks had helped, but now I was living out of the front seat of my truck. Every discomfort increased with each passing day. We no longer had netting to protect us at night from the ever-present mosquitoes whose voracious appetites left itchy dime-sized welts and worse, infected our bodies with the dreaded dengue fever and malaria. I had only one week's supply of quinine left.

I stared at the waiting roll of wire and joked, "Hey, Brewster, I felt a heck of a lot more secure in the half-track with its big 75-mm cannon and machine gun than I do wandering around out here with this spool of wire."

"Yeah," he replied as he got up and stretched his arms wide in preparation for our monotonous but physically draining job. "Let's go, Frank. We still have a few hours of daylight left," he said with a sigh. It was difficult to leave the shelter of shade and venture out into the intense tropical sun that beat down on our tired backs. We worked until dusk, and had probably lain over a mile of wire.

The communication unit bivouac area was about a mile south of our job. After a meal of canned meat and crackers, I sat in the front seat of my truck. The sun had just set below the horizon when, from out of the darkness, emerged a tall, solitary figure, walking slowly up the path with a bouncy gait. At first I thought I was hallucinating from the heat. There was only one man I knew who walked that way.

"It's Captain Perry!" I shouted to Brewster, who was leaning against a tree half asleep. I jumped out of the truck and ran down the road toward my captain and what remained of my battered unit. Only two of the original four half-tracks rumbled into view.

"Hey Lovato! Brewster! Great to see you guys made it!" he called out, with a smile.

"It's really great to see you and the men, Captain," I replied. "Brewster and I were worried about you making it out of Lingayen. What happened after you sent us, Sir?"

Captain Perrenot's smile melted into his typical serious and penetrating stare. "Before I say anything else, I need to know whether you delivered the orders to the highest-ranking officer."

"Yes, Sir, I made sure the general got them himself. The general read them silently, said something to his major, packed up his papers and maps, and took off like a bat out of hell with his staff."

The captain never took his piercing blue eyes off me and replied with a half grin, "Good job, Lovato. You might have been the first to notify them that the Japs had landed. You're a real Paul Revere."

"Thank you, Captain."

"Where are the rest of the men?" he asked next.

"Casualties, Captain," I replied feeling disappointed. I relayed our travails since I had left to deliver the invasion news. "I couldn't feed them. None of the units we tried to hook up with after the major told me to find us a home could take all of us on. They all said that there wasn't enough food to feed all the men that were already in their units."

The captain looked down at the ground and shook his head. We both agreed it didn't seem right, but this was war and everything was wrong.

"Captain, we had to take some back roads on the way to the field command post after the Jap fighter planes spotted us and fired. Thank God the Filipinos knew the lay of the land so we could travel on trails that had a canopy of trees for cover. I figured they knew their way around the territory and could get food from the locals. If the infantry units we approached couldn't feed them, I thought the best thing to do was release them to attach to a unit that could. What did happened after you sent us to deliver the orders, Sir?"

The captain's face darkened. In a deep and shaky voice he slowly related the tragic fate of the other two half-tracks and their crews. "The Japs kept coming in droves from the north. Their landing force is huge and well armed with tanks, artillery and heavy machine guns. According to the guys from the 31st, the Japs landed continuously from our position on the beach to about fifteen miles north. Thank God we were at the southern end of their invasion force."

That explained why the enemy kept coming at us either from straight ahead or from our right.

Captain Perrenot picked up a stick and mapped the territory in the loose dirt. He drew where we had been on December 22 and the locations of the Japanese invasion army and our defense forces. He pointed to a place inland from the beach and said, "We took a lot of the approaching enemy infantry out, but there were so many of them and so few of us. When they brought their artillery and tanks ashore, all hell broke loose and they hit two of the half-tracks." Captain Perrenot bowed his head and paused for a moment of silence. "We lost eight men back there." He paused again and his voice choked, "Eight brave men. I can hardly pronounce their names, but I'll remember their faces the rest of my life." He cleared his voice and told the rest of the story of their escape from total annihilation. "You could hear the gunfire increase between the Japs and the 31st infantry. The Japs were about to cut us off from behind so we withdrew according to the original plan. If it had not been for the Filipinos and their knowledge of the back roads, we wouldn't be here today."

I felt the captain's pain as he paused again. "The general at the field command post advised me not to go back to find you because he figured all of you had been destroyed," I told him.

Captain Perrenot never looked more serious than at this moment, as he slowly described the immediate plan of action. "This is the real thing. The Japs are throwing everything at us in huge numbers. They want the Philippines badly. I hate to say it, but we're not prepared for this. My orders are to engage the enemy and retreat. When we are out of ammunition for the 75-mm we'll have to fight with what we have."

"Captain, did our tanks ever make it to Lingayen?" I asked.

He shook his head no and mumbled something.

"Why wasn't there anyone else, Captain?"

"Lovato, G-Battery was assigned to provide shore patrol north of where the main Jap invasion force was expected. Most of our main forces, tanks, artillery and infantry were positioned about thirty-five miles south of us at Lingayen City. Either the Japs got wind of our plans to defend the beaches farther south, or they had always planed to land where they did. Who knows? A-Battery was positioned in San Fernando and they might have engaged the enemy north of our position. I haven't heard about them so I don't know. What I do know is our thirty men and four half-tracks took out at least twenty-five landing crafts before we had to withdraw."

"That's right, Captain. We did some serious damage, Sir," I confirmed.

"We might have been the only American and Filipino artillery unit to attack the Japanese invasion forces on the beaches at Lingayen Gulf," the captain speculated. "How's your truck?" he asked.

"Good as ever Sir. Only a few bullet holes in non-critical places," I answered.

"We're going to join with another battery and I'm going to get a couple more half-tracks from another battalion that lost a couple of theirs. We'll patch together a complete battery.

That night as I laid outstretched on the seat of my truck gazing out the windows, I had the time to think about something other than the war. I remembered the first time I'd seen the sunset in Manila. It rivaled the ember-red New Mexico fall panoramas. In all the ugliness of war I needed beauty to keep some peace and calm within me. Music and nature's beauty had calmed me since I was a little child. Memories of Mother playing the piano and singing Spanish songs *La Paloma* (dove) and *La Golindrina* (swallow) with passion and love made my heart smile. Colorful memories of when Dad used to drive us in the open touring car on Sundays after church along the banks of the Rio Grande to see the fall's changing colors, all made me long to return to my beautiful homeland. But the heartfelt love of my family was what I missed the most. I prayed that I would get home to enjoy that peaceful life again.

*God, I love America. God, please get me home, I prayed. If I am going to get back to all that I love, we will have to win this war. I took out my harmonica, closed my eyes to picture the faces of my family, and played "God Bless America" before I fell asleep.*

CHAPTER 4

# Enemy Spies

The new troops Captain Perrenot had assembled were experienced Filipino Scouts from the A-Battery half-track unit. Their battery had been almost surrounded by the invading Japanese Army farther north near the town of Bagio. The A-Battery commander concluded their only chance for escape was to destroy their half-tracks and cross over steep mountain trails under the cover of darkness. After setting the half-tracks on fire they pushed them over a cliff into a deep ravine then began their journey to meet up with friendly units along the strategic withdrawal route.

A few days later I was laying wire when Captain Perrenot complained, "What's wrong with this phone? Lovato, I thought your crew put this line in this morning. It's dead as a doornail." The strategic withdrawal plan was to slowly move south. That also meant keeping the enemy at bay for as long as possible, to allow the evacuating Filipino civilians time to get behind our lines of defense. The only means of communication that was available from the quartermaster were telephones that required hard wire between handsets. No line, no connection. No connection, no communication. No communication equaled disaster. We were constantly retreating from the advancing Japanese. Every night, we moved a mile or so south to set up a new defensive line and had to re-wire them all over again.

"Sir, we just laid that line this morning and it was all good wire," I said.

"Lovato, the Japs are going to be here soon with tanks and infantry and we've got to stop them before they get to the main bridges. I need these phones working now!" shouted the captain in a rare outburst of emotion. He had an unusually worried expression on his face.

"Don't worry, Captain. We'll find the problem." I assured him. I got my crew together and informed them that we had a break somewhere along the line and that, come hell or high water, we had to repair it right away. My crew of five was made up of three men from our original half-track battalion and two new Filipino conscripts. We needed every able-bodied man who could shoot a rifle, dig a trench, scrounge for supplies, and lay communication wires. It was hard to keep track of everyone. Those not officially assigned to a specific unit posed a security problem that was difficult to correct. We were moving through ever-changing geographic locations and there were groups of civilian refugees constantly moving through the front lines.

After about fifteen minutes of visually checking the wire, we found the source of the problem. Clean, sharp cuts severed the connection on both ends. No animal could have chewed through the wires that cleanly. The cuts had to have been done by someone with a knife or wire cutters — someone working for the enemy. An enemy soldier dressed as a civilian could easily appear to be a Filipino refugee, slip behind the lines, and sabotage our effort. There was a constant stream of refugees fleeing south with us. I assumed that the Filipinos who stayed in their homes were Japanese sympathizers. As we retreated we came to abandoned farms, homes, and villages. The Filipinos took as many of their belongings as they could carry, which included their food and firearms.

I called Brewster over and showed him what I found. "When could anyone have done this, Frank?" asked Brewster. "We laid this line a couple of hours ago."

"I have no idea. Let's just splice it and get it operational. We'll figure out who and why later." We re-connected the wire and returned to tell Captain Perrenot what we had discovered. I told the captain that in the future we would double-check the line as we laid it to be sure it was intact.

He just nodded his head and walked away with other problems on his mind. He always turned to me to solve the practical and mechanical problems of the unit, which were ordinarily done by a sergeant. He and his superior officer, Colonel Babcock, concentrated their efforts on strategies to defeat the enemy.

"Hurry up guys, we've got to get this line set up pronto," I urged. Two men carried the heavy spool and unrolled the wire, while two men in front cleared the way with bolos. Another soldier helped pull the wire off the roll and checked to make sure there were no breaks or kinks. We were taking a short break when one of the Filipino civilians said he was going to check the wire in the brush to be sure that it hadn't gotten tangled or torn. I had a feeling something was wrong in light of the recent sabotage. The conscript disappeared into the thick foliage. I gave him a minute, and then I summoned the rest of my crew to join me to see what our new guy was doing.

We proceeded quietly. Our eyes slowly adjusted to the darkness under the tropical leaves. Thirty or so feet away we could see the conscript looking under the brush. "What the hell is he doing?" whispered one of the Filipino Scouts.

"Let's go find out," I said out loud. He looked surprised when he saw all of us headed his way. He stood up and started walking back toward us.

"What are you doing?" I asked, as I pointed my .45 semi-automatic pistol at him.

He stammered an answer, " I ah, was ah, I ah found a break. Back there." He pointed to the spot where he had been squatting.

The break was cleanly cut. It was not a rip or split which might be caused by a sharp rock. Surrounded by scowling faces he trembled as the angry crew searched him for weapons. The would-be saboteur almost fainted from fright when the telltale wire cutters were taken out of his pocket. "Take him to the rear echelon and let them deal with him," I said. "They'll want to question him. He might be persuaded to turn over some information. *"Comprende?"* The men would have killed him on the spot if I hadn't stopped them. We had been instructed in boot camp to turn over spies whenever possible to those who could extract valuable information from them. A dead spy cannot give information.

When I told the captain we had found the saboteur he surprised me by saying, "Good job, Lovato. I want you to know that I'm putting you in for sergeant at field HQ. Can't tell you when your promotion will go through though."

I was stunned by his sudden announcement and all I could manage to say was "Thank you, Sir." In my heart, I also thanked Captain Grimmer back at Clark Field for transferring me to Captain Perrenot's unit. In less than one month with Captain Perrenot, I had been promoted to sergeant.

*Christmas Eve 1941*

As the sun descended on the night before Christmas, the bright half moon lit our camp like a giant search beacon. The full moon rising over Manila, the Pearl of the Orient, had been one of the most beautiful sights I'd seen in the Philippines. Now the approaching full moon provided us a chance for us to do some recon without telltale flashlights.

"Lovato, I want you to go out and see if you can locate any advancing enemy units," ordered Captain Perrenot. "We need to know which way they're approaching so we can plan our defenses in the most efficient manner. We don't have the ammunition to confront them head on. We'll have to rely on outsmarting them when we can."

"Yes, Sir," I replied.

The captain picked me for reconnaissance because I had a good sense of direction and I could camouflage myself. While hunting game, Dad had taught us to move stealthily. We watched each step so we didn't snap a dry twig. We kept in the shadows, and stayed downwind when possible.

The enemy knew they outnumbered us and we were retreating from their advancing front line. The Japanese moved during the day and established bivouac positions at nightfall. They were not afraid to build fires because we didn't have air-recon; most of our aircraft was destroyed on December 8th. The only way to locate their camps was on foot.

Captain Perrenot wished me good luck as I headed out into the night north toward the approaching enemy. I stayed in the inky shadows of the trees and dense bushes that bordered the glistening rice paddies which were the only open areas. I planned my route so that I would make no shadow and could keep out of the brilliant light of the moon. Getting lost in the dark on the wrong side of the line could be fatal. I used directional skills that Dad also taught me in the field while hunting. "When there are no roads or paths to follow, pay attention to the landmarks: stars, moon, mountain peaks, rivers, and other fixed, natural objects." I knew I wouldn't get lost if I made a map in my mind of the path I took on the outbound journey. *Hopefully, I would come across some wild fruit or hidden caches of food,* I thought as I ventured in to the darkness. *How could a country as great as ours, with a smart president like Mr. Roosevelt, allow us to be so short of food, ammunition and equipment?* Our food supply had run so low that men were eating anything, including the wild pigs that we caught when they came in at night to eat our excrement from the open slit latrine trenches.

As I walked through the quiet moonlit night, I thought of my family and wondered if I would ever see them or my beautiful New Mexico again. The captain had said that our retreat was part of a bigger plan to defeat the Japanese. I still could not understand how going backwards was going to defeat anyone, but I hoped the generals knew what they were doing.

After almost thirty minutes moving northward, there was still no sign of any enemy encampments. I couldn't hear any noise, see any lights or smell any cook-fires. As I walked along the trees that bordered an abandoned rice paddy, I must have been mesmerized at the beauty of moonlight as it glistened on the dead-still surface of the paddy. For a moment, I forgot about war, hunger, and about the enemy. Captivated by the beauty of the night, it seemed that I was alone with the moon.

As I came around a dense patch of brush at the far end of the rice paddy, I looked over my shoulder at the snow-white path of moonlight following me across the black water. Suddenly, without warning, I smashed into someone that hadn't been in the path a split second earlier. I turned and looked to find I was face to face with a Japanese soldier. Startled, I yelled, "What the hell!"

Almost in unison he shouted out something in Japanese.

We both stumbled to recover our balance, like two Keystone Cops bouncing off each other we reached for our respective rifles. I was startled and shaking uncontrollably. My heart pounded and my senses were so acute that I could smell his body odor, even the oil on his rifle. I recovered my footing, lifted my rifle, and pointed it at his chest. He did the same. God is this really happening? We stood less than six feet apart and stared at each other down our rifle barrels. Up until to this point the Japanese were a faceless enemy. Now I saw the face of my enemy. It was as though we were mirror images of each other; one of us was Japanese and the other American. I waited and watched the bizarre scene unfold before me as if in slow motion. Time seemed to stand still, frozen in the brilliant moonlight. A voice inside me told me not to pull the trigger.

We both backed up; one step at a time, until we both disappeared into the bushes.

For a moment I stood there pointing my Springfield at an empty space, like waking up from a dream and finding everyone gone. My counterpart was as silent as a ghost in his retreat. Moving backward, I still pointed my rifle in the direction of our standoff in case he changed his mind and returned. I looked around the bushes cautiously and realized he had gone north, into an area thick and difficult to negotiate in the dark.

*Perhaps he was out on recon, just like I was?* I made the decision to return to camp and tell Captain Perrenot what had happened and what direction the Japanese soldier had taken. I made my way through the shadows, circling back twice to be sure I was not being followed.*We might meet again in battle. The choice to whether or not to kill each other will not be an option.*

## CHAPTER 5

# The Chillicothe Kid

*December 26, 1941*

Christmas day passed uneventfully as we shored up our defensive positions. I didn't realize when I saw a stranger in western garb talking to Captain Perrenot that the Christmas Angel of 1941 had arrived, cleverly disguised as a six-foot-seven cowboy. When I first saw the tall, curly blonde Texan in his white cowboy hat sporting a pair of mother-of pearl Colt revolvers in leather holsters, I knew immediately I was going to like him.

"Where in the heck did you come from?" I asked the man, who looked as if he had just stepped out of a western movie.

He looked at me with a smile and then retorted, "Manila is where I was yesterday. But I'm from Chillicothe, Texas."

Jokingly I shot back, "I guess you must be the Chillicothe Kid."

He paused for a moment, tipped his hat back and with a smile, drawled, "Yeah, that's right. By way of Manila, Philippines."

"Pleased to meet you, cowboy," I reached out to shake his hand.

"Likewise," answered the Kid.

Captain Perrenot seemed amused that the Kid and I hit it off from the start. "Lovato," he told me, "I want you to take him with you on recon. Mr. Cowboy has offered to give us a hand until he can get a boat off the island. He said he's pretty good with those six-shooters."

"Sure, Captain," I agreed. "I can always use company now that the sneaky Japs have snipers in the trees."

Nearly everybody owned guns when I was growing up in New Mexico, and we all knew how to use them. According to the Kid, it was the same in Texas. The Kid told me that he had started shooting as soon as he could hold a gun.

Earlier that morning I had found a Jeep abandoned in a ditch. It wouldn't start until I repaired a short in the wiring. Captain Perrenot reassigned my truck to a Filipino regular to haul our supplies. Having the Chillicothe Kid ride shotgun with me was reassuring.

"I'm ready when you are," announced the Kid, as he sat down in the passenger seat, his long legs rubbing the metal dash. "Let's go find us some Japs!"

I don't remember his real name, because once he told me that he was from Chillicothe, Texas, he became the Chillicothe Kid to everyone. The Kid had been a businessman in Manila when the air attack on Clark Field signaled the beginning of hostilities. Caught in the war and unable to find passage out of the Philippines, the Kid had hooked up with our unit as a fighting civilian. So here we were stateside neighbors, fighting for our lives with every possible means.

"Hey! Look who we got here. It's Mutt and Jeff," joked an infantry soldier as we stopped at a checkpoint on our recon patrol. The Kid stood at least six foot seven and had blonde curly hair, and I was barely five foot seven with straight black hair. "What the hell you guys doing here anyway?" barked the sergeant.

"Looking for Japs! Seen any?" joked the Kid as he pulled on the corners of his eyes, giving them a slant.

"There's plenty of them the way you're headed," remarked the sergeant.

"Good, then I best get out and sit where I can see them better," answered the Kid, as he moved to the hood of the car.

"Better put on a helmet, Cowboy. That white hat would make a big target for one of those Jap snipers," added the sergeant.

The Kid just smiled, and tilted his hat down to keep the sun out of his eyes. We drove off with his cowboy boots wedged on the steel bumper for support. The bumpy road led through thick trees that made visibility difficult. Less than five minutes from the checkpoint, the Kid motioned with his hand and in a low voice said, "Frank, stop. Two o'clock." Then in a flash, like Tom Mix fast-drawing on a bad guy in a Hollywood western, the Kid fired one shot from each of his Colt pistols at a sniper high in the tree.

The sniper crashed down through the branches. The Kid blew on each smoking muzzle acknowledging his success. Quickly I grabbed my .45 and pointed it at the fallen sniper. It wasn't necessary. The Kid had finished the job in two shots.

"How's that for protection, Frank?" asked my new partner.

I nodded and said, "I'll tell you what, Kid. I didn't even see the sniper."

He just laughed and retorted, "Frank, you do the driving and I'll do the shooting, okay?"

"A-okay!" I answered enthusiastically. It didn't take any more to convince me that his was the best plan.

The next day Captain Perrenot told me to go north, back to a small village we had passed through to see if I could find any food. The enemy would be coming through the village shortly, and this would be our only chance.

I asked the Kid if he'd like to join me on this short jaunt. He was most agreeable.

"*Vamanos amigo.* But how about putting on a helmet? Your big white hat is not going to protect you from much, and it's a mighty big target," I pleaded.

"No way in hell," was his simple response. He put his long arm over my shoulder and gave a whoop. "Let's scoot. I like you, Frank. You're not like the others. We understand each other." Knowing Captain Perrenot could hear, he said, "And you don't try to order me around, like some others around here."

The captain was listening. He shook his head and uttered his familiar endearing comment, " I don't know about you two."

The Kid was often the brunt of a good deal of joking. Most Filipinos were about my height, five feet to five foot eight. His six foot seven frame plus the nine-inch crown on his ten-gallon hat towered above everyone. The others had no idea how deadly this man was with his six shooters. They hadn't seen him shoot that sniper out of a tree. He was an answer to my prayers: my guardian angel.

CHAPTER 6

# Tank Hunters

*New Year's Eve 1941*

When a soldier is in a kill or be killed situation holiday celebrations receive no priority. New Years Eve 1941, began like any other day. We were moving our position south ahead of the advancing Japanese forces. The captain called it "strategic withdrawal." Before my military days, my experiences in football, boxing and wrestling had taught me that in order to win, the best strategy was to take the battle to the opponent.

I asked, "Captain, why do we keep withdrawing? He looked at me silently for a moment then asked, "Lovato, how many rounds of ammo do you have? How much food and quinine do you have? How many gallons of gasoline and oil do we have?" He paused giving me time to answer in my mind that we were low on everything. "Lovato, do you know when we'll get more of everything we need?" He turned away and looked south to the heart of Bataan where we were headed. His stoic answer had an edge of anger and frustration, "Because I don't." He raised his voice; "We can't fight and advance our position when there are no supplies to support it. We don't know what the high command is up to. We don't know how or when they're going to re-supply a us."

Moments later, Captain Perrenot gathered his composure, changed his tone of voice, and in his usual commanding manner said, "We can fight and inflict damage if we strike and retreat. We must stay ahead of their advancing ground soldiers and artillery. We'll take them out when we gain a strategic advantage."

"Okay, Captain," I answered. He was correct as usual. "It just doesn't feel right having always to retreat, Sir," I grumbled.

"Cheer up, Lovato. I think we're going to have our hands full tonight. Our Scouts' recon patrol spotted the Japs advancing their tanks last night. We might have to give them a G-Battery welcome if they move again tonight."

It had been nine days since we had destroyed several of their landing boats on the beach. Now we had a chance to see if our half-track's big 75-mm would be able to destroy a Japanese armored tank as easily as it had sunk their landing boats.

Captain Perrenot called us together for a briefing on the plan of attack. He pointed to two X's on a hand-drawn map that marked where he wanted us to intercept the enemy tanks. "These are small bridges where the Japs will have to slow down in order to cross. We're going to position the half-tracks next to the bridges. Two units here by this bridge, and two by this one," he continued. "We'll set up before dark, camouflage the half-tracks and wait for them. If they come like we expect, they're ours." Captain Perrenot looked up. "We'll be firing at point blank range." He assigned the half-track units to their respective bridges, and indicated a point on the map where we would rendezvous at midnight. "Any questions? No? All right. Move out."

We were somewhere in the vicinity of the Calumpit Bridge, a major crossing point. When the Filipino reconnaissance scouts saw the Japanese moving light tanks on side roads, the smaller bridges became our responsibility.

Nightfall gradually veiled our camouflaged half-track emplacements. At Lingayen Gulf we learned to camouflage our equipment enabling surprise, and surprise provided us with our best advantage, maybe our only advantage. The dirt road approaching the bridge was the perfect location for an ambush. There was no need to use the range and distance sights on the cannons. All we had to do was look through the cannon barrel to see the enemy.

We waited beside the road and listened for the first telltale sounds of an enemy tank. In the deep silence of the tropical jungle night, every snap of a twig, stomach rumble, or bump against the steel half-track echoed in my head. We could be the victims if they saw us first.

The rumble of a Japanese tank, barely discernible at first, broke the eerie silence of the night. My heart began to pound so loud I thought the guys around me could hear it. We stared into the trees where our unsuspecting enemy would emerge into the clearing by the bridge. None of us had ever been this close to an enemy tank before.

We first saw Japanese infantry soldiers using flashlights to scan the bumpy road and guide the tank to the bridge. Like hungry cats we waited silently, eyes frozen, every muscle poised and ready to pounce.

Less than 50 yards directly in front of our half-track, the tank stopped. The lead foot soldiers examined the structure for strength with their flashlights. I looked through our cannon barrel and saw the enemy tank, framed by the circular muzzle. They were dead in our sights. Captain Perrenot nodded the signal to fire.

Tony, a Philippine Scout formerly from A-Battery, quietly loaded the round of armor-piercing ammunition into the breach and pulled the firing lever. Orange-red flames belched out of the barrel. The direct hit must have penetrated and ignited the tank's artillery shell magazine. Fire from the rear-mounted .30-caliber machine gun on our second half-track mowed down the enemy infantry. It was over in a matter of seconds.

When the smoke from the explosion cleared, all that remained were chunks and twisted fragments of the Japanese tank. The direct hit from our 75-mm round pulverized the tank as if it were a tin can. Most of the tank and its occupants were blown into the ravine. What remained we covered with stalks and branches. We waited for the next unwary tank to arrive. One hour later the second tank's fate was the same. Following the destruction of the second tank Captain Perrenot ordered us to withdraw to another position. There was no need to clear the burning wreckage. " Good work. We've done enough damage here tonight, gentlemen. We're moving out." He had planned a midnight rendezvous with the other two half-tracks on the main highway.

It was the foresight of the Filipino scouting party who predicted the routes the enemy might take. Apparently, the Japanese were never certain that their tanks could cross the lightly constructed bridges. Their hesitation was to our advantage. Perhaps they also thought that the Americans and Filipinos would be celebrating New Year's Eve rather than preparing for battle the following day.

The feeling of defeating the advancing enemy lifted the morale among the men and strengthened our confidence in Captain Perrenot. So far under his command our unit had successfully inflicted severe damage on the enemy. I still didn't understand why we couldn't get re-supplied from the rear echelon to wage a battle that we could win.

The four half-tracks met in a small clearing adjacent to a grove of huge mahogany trees. Each group had a story to tell of their night's success. Each of the other two half-tracks had destroyed one tank by the bridges that traversed the rutted ravines.

After a brief interlude for a celebration, Captain Perrenot interrupted the bragging and stated, "The night isn't over yet. The Japs are obviously moving their tanks tonight for a reason. We're going to hold this road until daylight. After sunrise we'll cross Calumpit Bridge and defend it front from the other side."

Our four cannon barrels faced north and were partially covered with tree branches. We waited patiently as the minutes turned to hours and to the morning of New Years Day, 1942. Captain Perrenot stood and stared up the twisted stretch of road. He felt something was coming, even though more than three tense hours had passed since our rendezvous. Except for some sporadic machine gun fire in the distance, it remained relatively quiet until about 0400 hours. Then, the familiar mechanical whine of a medium-sized Japanese tank broke the silence. Not yet visible on the winding road, the tank's steel blade treads signaled its lumbering approach less than forty yards away.

Captain Perrenot quickly adjusted the barrel and signaled to hold fire until the tank rounded the bend. If the Japanese tankers saw us, we would be the target.

*Not yet, hold on, Oh God, this one feels different.* I was ready to explode from the tension when suddenly the captain clenched his fist and lowered his arm, signaling doom for the unsuspecting tank. Our French 75-mm projectile smashed into the tank. The second half-track hit the tank broadside. A split second later numbers three and four slammed rounds into the hulk of the tank, igniting it into a fireworks display that would rival any Fourth of July finale.

"Happy New Year, Tojo!" shouted the captain, referring to the Japanese Prime Minister, Hideki Tojo.

For a moment we stood staring at the glowing molten steel remains of the tank. There were no traces of human bodies in that burning inferno; they must have been blown to smithereens in the multiple barrages.

The captain called the men together and, after congratulating us, stood on his half-track's hood and yelled out to the others, " Let's go! We're moving out!"

"Why are we withdrawing, Captain?" I asked. "We're kicking their butts! Why can't we stay and keep given them the business?"

Captain Perrenot nudged his helmet forward almost covering his piercing blue eyes and replied prophetically, "Lovato, you're going to have your fill of Japanese infantry, tanks, artillery, and airplanes soon enough. I pray we get more ammo, more food and more supplies soon. We're lucky the Filipino's are such good scroungers. We can't keep running on close to empty indefinitely."

"Okay, Captain, you know what you're doing. It just doesn't seem right, having to go backward all the time."

Captain Perrenot knew that if we met a battery of Japanese tanks and infantry, we didn't have the firepower to defeat them. Hit and run was our tactic: survive to fight another battle. His mind was always churning out decisions that would affect the big picture in this war. All his orders resulted in success.

"Where exactly are we headed, Captain?" I asked.

"Our orders are to meet with some other self-propelled units and to set up a major line of defense farther south along the east coast of Bataan," he replied.

"Once the Japs get to us, they're going to hit us with everything they've got." The new plan meant we would be fighting alongside other batteries of artillery as a combined force.

The captain turned and looked at me and said, "Keep what I told you to yourself, Lovato."

"I got it, Captain. Whatever you say, Sir."*I trust him with my life. I don't even know what state he's from.*

*Everything was moving so fast. We've never had time to chat about our personal lives back home. Someday before this war was over, I hope we get the chance.*

## CHAPTER 7

# Defense of Bataan

*January 8, 1942*

G-Battery, together with two other batteries of half-tracks, was assigned to a position in Abucay, a small village on the eastern coast of Bataan. Our forces had built a defensive line from the village westward up the cone-shaped volcano of Mount Natib, through narrow jungle trails and thick undergrowth impenetrable by mechanized equipment. Positioned along the line were 110-mm Howitzers and 155-mm cannons. If the Japanese planned on advancing south with their tanks, they'd have to go through us.

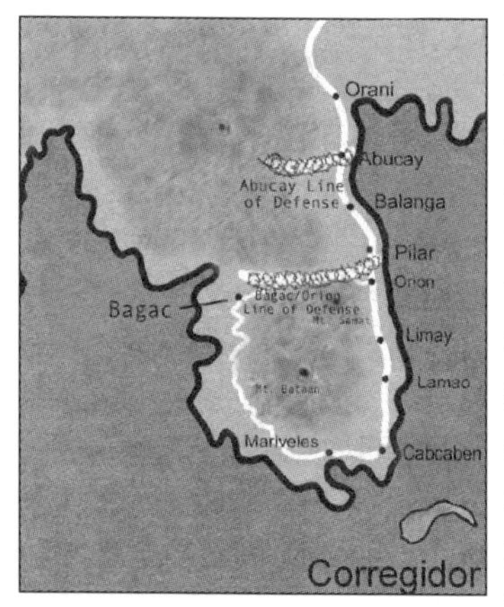

Main Defense Lines in Bataan Peninsula
*By Francisco Lovato*

I woke up soaking from a fever sweat on the front seat of my ton and a half. I stared at the muddy-green painted steel cab roof and my army-issue boots rested on the open windowsill. My dengue fever flared up with no warning. By now many of our men suffered from dengue fever or malaria in varying degrees of severity. Instead of awakening somewhat refreshed, I felt more fatigued than when I laid down. I still had not seen any medic tents, but I heard there were casualty stations at the rear echelon. The cone-shaped volcanic mountains, jutting up into the low-hanging, morning clouds, reminded me of the snow-capped mountains and the Three Sisters volcanoes at my home in the

Rio Grande Valley. Dad and I always got up before Mother and my other brothers and sisters and started the day before the sun crested on the soft purple Sandia and Manzano Mountains. I remembered our breakfasts of fresh eggs, toast, bacon, and a bowl of oatmeal. The thought of food made my stomach growl and my mouth water. If we were lucky, we'd have some hard tack biscuits, a couple of canned sardines and a green banana to hold us until the next meal of scrounged rations, iguana, or snake.

I gazed into my truck's mirror and saw my drooping, tired eyes, my scruffy, three-day-old beard, and my sunken cheeks. I wondered if I'd ever make it back to America. I felt physically weak and mentally foggy, and I looked like death-warmed-over from the debilitating effects of the dengue fever. I looked bad, felt worse, and smelled like a sewer. *Only death could be worse than this.* Dad had said, "War is hell on earth, and in order to survive it, one must have the desire to survive, to do the right thing, and be lucky." So far I was still alive, even though many others had taken a bullet, mortar round, or bomb blast. The wounded were sent back to the rear echelon to receive treatment at an aid station. Between we defenders and the Japanese invaders lay a zone of trees and vegetation a few hundred yards wide. We made our stand with the volcanoes to our left and the rice fields and ocean to our right. Here on the east coast of the Bataan Peninsula we were joined by small units of American, Filipino, Australian, British, and Canadian infantry who had been on Luzon Island when the Japanese attacked. Apparently the plan had always been to retreat to this point if the Japanese invaded the island.

I heard a shuffling in the back of my truck as the Chillicothe Kid awoke and stumbled out the tailgate. As he stretched his long arms upward, I thought he made the biggest "Y" I had ever seen. While yawning and stretching his lanky body he groaned, "Frank, I'd give ten bucks right now for a fresh, hot cup of coffee."

I looked at him standing there in his soiled, twenty-dollar shirt and hundred dollar cowboy boots. I couldn't keep from laughing. The only time I saw the Kid without his ten-gallon hat was for about thirty seconds after he got up in the morning. The brim of his hat creased his wavy hair all the way around his head, where it rested ninety-nine percent of the time. He even covered his face with his hat when he slept. I said, "Sorry, Kid. No coffee in these parts today. Maybe tomorrow one of the scrounge specialists will come up with some."

Some guys were better at "liberating" supplies from the more abundant sources than others. My specialty was keeping vehicles in working order, while the Kid was a natural-born marksman. Every man had his job, but it was getting harder with each passing day to hold it all together. The hungry war machine gobbled up resources at an alarming rate.

CHAPTER 8

# "There are times when men have to die."

*Secretary of War, Henry L. Stimson*

*January 3, 1942*
*Washington*

Stimson said following reading a report from General Dwight D. Eisenhower's War Plans Division that stated it was "entirely unjustifiable" to send a support convoy of reinforcement soldiers, ammunition, food, medical supplies and equipment to reinforce the American/Filipino forces battling for their lives in the Philippines. Eisenhower's planners continued to recommend a "Europe First" priority essentially dooming the fate of all the American/Filipino defenders of the Philippines and Allied bases in the Pacific west of Pearl Harbor.

*Second week in January 1942*

"Here comes Photo Joe!" shouted a sentry positioned in a treetop. "Photo Joe" was the nickname we gave the Japanese reconnaissance aircraft pilots who routinely flew over our defensive positions attempting to determine our size and armament. He hung his camera out of the side window and took photographs of the terrain where we had positioned our emplacements. Because of the destruction of our bombers and fighter planes at Clark Field, the Japanese owned the airspace over Bataan. Photo Joe and all other Japanese pilots flew at will over the peninsula and dropped an occasional bomb. The main line of defense was between Mount Natib and the coastline in a thick jungle that provided a sheltering umbrella of camouflage that made it difficult for the enemy to see our positions even from a low flying reconnaissance plane.

If Photo Joe found where we hid our tanks, half-tracks, field artillery and machine gun nests, the enemy artillery and bombers would shell us with precision. Official orders were to not shoot at him because it would reveal our position. It was very tempting to take a shot at the clearly visible pilot. He made treetop passes lower and lower each day, and tried to provoke us to reveal our location. Captain Perrenot said, "The less the enemy knows, the better our chance of catching them off guard. And as you know, that is exactly when we can do the most damage." G-Battery was fortunate to have Captain Perrenot who understood how to motivate and maintain morale among his men.

Lieutenant Williams, a black American officer and gentleman, brought cigarettes, candy, gum, and best of all, positive and congenial support to the front-line soldiers. It was difficult for us to stay upbeat and focused while medical supplies, ammunition, and food rations continued to diminish. Everyone's spirit perked up when the lieutenant appeared with his goodie bag and the right words of encouragement for each individual soldier. "Hey, Lieutenant, over here. Over here," shouted the men from the trenches and emplacements. His smiling presence brightened the day as he moved from soldier to soldier, handed out goodies, and asked about hometowns and other personal things. He had an uncanny ability to remember everything about each soldier as if he had known him for years. At a time when doubts were surfacing as to whether we were going to get reinforcements, the lieutenant took the time to encourage each man, like a chaplain, a coach and a good friend all wrapped up into one.

Behind the front line of trenches and artillery emplacements, we dammed a fresh water stream with rocks and created a small pool where we took baths and washed laundry. A naturally smooth rock formation affectionately named, "Hedy Lamarr," protruded out of the pool's glassy surface. Its flowing curves and bumps resembled a voluptuous woman's body — especially to young soldiers deprived of such earthly delights. When I saw a naked soldier crawl up and cradle himself in the wet bumps of our sexy Hedy, it was the first real, belly-aching laugh since before the war started. Not to be outdone in the ways of amorous lovemaking, more young soldiers scrambled onto the stone goddess and caressed, kissed and feigned sex to the cheers and applause of everyone. Before long, the water hole was simply referred to as "Hedy's". Watching others look at the curvaceous rock, tilt their heads slightly, change their angles for the best possible views of her well-placed curves, always made me smile.

We used "Hedy's" as a place of respite from the war until the day our ambassador of morale was ripped from our ranks by a burst of machine gun bullets. Photo Joe had already made his pass over the water hole and was methodically flying back and forth over the treetops, moving farther away from our position with each pass. His engine's humming sound seemed to be a safe distance away when Lieutenant Williams walked out into the open, took off his shirt and knelt down at Hedy's to wash off some of the smell of war. Without warning Photo Joe swooped down from out of the noonday sun fired a machine gun out an open window. The ebony giant's half-naked muscular body twisted violently as the bullets ripped gaping holes in his body. He fell face first into the stream. We were shocked at the surprise attack by a photo reconnaissance plane. A few of us ran from our cover to his body and didn't care if Photo Joe saw us. Curses screamed out from the thicket of trees as the whine of Photo Joe's propellers faded.

"No! Not the Lieutenant!" wailed the men, many almost in tears.

"God Damn Photo Joe!" boomed a voice from the thicket. Branches rustled as the men slowly emerged into the stream clearing to stand with our fallen friend.

The army lost a good soldier; his family lost a good son; and we soldiers lost a best friend. Sadness gripped our hearts. The lieutenant had touched every one of us with his compassion, generosity, and good will. A quiet burial by the stream was followed by several brief eulogies that ended another day on Bataan. No one talked as we walked quietly back to our positions

The next morning I awoke at dawn and walked to the latrine. The faces of the men I met revealed anger I hadn't seen before. No one said anything, but I could feel the lingering presence of the death and burial of Lieutenant Williams. The war had become a personal vendetta between Photo Joe and us. I tried to keep my feelings about soldiers killed in action impersonal, because when a man was killed it served as a reminder of my possible fate. I tried to concentrate on what it took to stay alive

Later, at about noon, the distant droning of a small engine airplane signaled the approach of Photo Joe. He was making his regular passes across our emplacements, cruising back and forth like a crop duster spraying a cornfield. Like so many times before we sat huddled under the thick tree cover as his reconnaissance plane buzzed overhead. His next pass would be directly over our unit. Eyes and rifles pointed upward, through the dense leafy umbrella that revealed only fragmented patches of hazy blue sky.

"Here he comes!" someone yelled. "Damn the orders! Photo Joe is going down!"

Suddenly, bursts of gunfire ripped toward Photo Joe's single-engine plane. His plane's light-gray underbelly appeared for less than three seconds, about fifty feet above the treetops. I only had time to fire one shot at him, but so did everyone else. I don't know whether my bullet hit its mark, but enough of our bullets did. Photo Joe's plane crashed into the treetops. Cheers roared from under our dense canopy of trees. We avenged our fallen buddy. People say that revenge is sweet, but I remember the stronger feeling of loss. Lieutenant Williams reminded us all of our humanity in the ugly face of war.

CHAPTER 9

# Holding On

*February 1942*

"Captain, we're almost out of 75-mm and there's none back at Mariveles Depot. We're low on .30-caliber. What do we do if we run out?" asked Brewster.

"We'll fight with what we've got as long as we've got it. After that," he bowed his head, closed his eyes, and didn't finish speaking what he knew was inevitable.

The Chillicothe Kid paced back and forth and asked sarcastically, "Did anybody devise a plan for winning this war?"

One of the more unpleasant but necessary chores of war is digging: digging foxholes, digging protective emplacements for equipment and supplies, and digging latrine slit trenches. An army on the move must dig a latrine trench approximately one shovel wide (9"-10"), 12" deep, and long enough for number of men to use at the same time.

Everyone took a turn at digging latrine sites, including the Chillicothe Kid who, like a prowling cat, walked around the perimeter of our bivouac area looking for enemy snipers.

"Just can't trust them sneaky Japs!" he drawled.

As the Kid whistled a Bob Wills country tune and we dug the latrine trench, a Japanese light bomber appeared from nowhere, only a hundred feet or so above the treetops. Suddenly, a fat, dark bomb dropped out of the bay and tumbled straight at us.

"Cover!" screamed the Filipinos, who saw the three-hundred-pound bomb only seconds away from impact.

I looked over at my tall Texas buddy who couldn't see the bomb from his angle and yelled out, " Stick your head in the hole!"

Five Filipinos and I jumped behind a large tree just as the bomb struck the clearing where we had been standing only seconds ago. The ground quaked so violently I almost fell over. The deafening explosion blew shrapnel and debris in all directions. The blast's shock wave hit almost instantly following the bomb's eruption, immobilizing the body with a concussion that seems to come from inside, freezing the senses like an electrical shock.

"Mama! I've been hit! I'm dying!" wailed the Chillicothe Kid from the direction of the slit trench.

"Oh my God! The Kid's been hit!" I yelled. We dashed over to him through a cloud of bomb dust. His long, lanky body lay parallel in the foul-smelling latrine slit trench. He was covered in dirt and worst yet, brown, slimy globs of fetid excrement. A large clod of dirt from the explosion had struck his buttocks. "Mama, I'm dying," he moaned as we carefully rolled him over and off the slit trench. "Oh God. My butt hurts. Am I bleeding?" he asked?

I got down on one knee and looked him over for punctures or broken bones, but thankfully saw nothing that was life threatening.

I held my helmet over his face for shade and told him, "You're going to be okay, Buddy! Nothing's broken or bleeding."

"Frank, my butt's on fire," he moaned.

"Just lie here for a moment. It'll get better. I promise."

He wasn't seriously injured, but had a very sore bruise on his butt. Once we knew he was not mortally injured, our relief turned into playful teasing. One of the Filipinos started to laugh so hard that he rolled on the ground holding his belly. His howling incited the others who began to roar with laughter at the Texan's rather "crappy" predicament.

"Frank, tell them to lay off me," the Kid pleaded.

"Come on, guys. Give him a break," I said while holding back my own laughter. Thank God my best friend is still alive. Ironically, the slit trench probably saved his life. The Kid leaned painfully on one hip and elbow, sputtering and wiping filthy muck off his face. I knelt beside him and helped wipe the mess from his face.

"Hey, Buddy, you're going to be okay. A little soap and water and you'll be as good as new." I patted his back trying to encourage him to stand up and walk off the stiffness. The others were still snickering as they went back to digging. I forgave them for laughing. In this crazy war, how many things were there to laugh about? We fought with ammunition rounds that often didn't fire. We were hungry for decent food, and medical supplies were virtually non-existent at the front. And the rumors of reinforcements of men and supplies coming any day now were proving to be just that — rumors.

Captain Perrenot called me over and scribbled a note while he leaned on the front fender of his mud-splattered half-track. I thought back to the day ten weeks earlier when he had rumbled into our bivouac area in spanking-new half-tracks. According to the captain there were only fifty of the 75-mm self-propelled artillery half-tracks originally destined for Australia that had been "re-appropriated" for our use when the war started.

As I stood patiently waiting for the captain's message, I thought to myself how frightfully different everything was since that memorable day. The half-tracks were now encrusted with mud and scarred by mortar and tank shrapnel. We soldiers hadn't fared much better. The combined effects of dengue fever, malaria, shrapnel wounds, fatigue, and hunger had reduced us to thin shadows of ourselves.

The captain finished his communication, folded it and handed it to me and said in a frustrated tone of voice, "Lovato, I want you to deliver this message to the infantry command post. The damn phone line is dead again. Wait for their reply before you come back. Got it?"

"Yes, Sir. Wait until they reply. Got it," I repeated.

"Take this new guy with you and make it snappy, okay?"

The infantry command post was about a half-mile south through some heavy tree cover. These were ideal conditions for enemy snipers to crawl behind our lines under the cover of nightfall, climb the tall trees, cover themselves with leaves and branches, and then shoot at any one unfortunate enough to get in their sights.

*I wish the Chillicothe Kid was with me instead of this guy,* I thought as I departed with this new man at my side in the Jeep. Other than Brewster, the Kid was my one and only friend in the constantly changing flow of personnel that made up our battery. He made me laugh at his jokes and devil-be-damned attitude toward authority and when he was riding 'shotgun' on our missions, I never had to worry about Japanese snipers. He could shoot a handgun better than anyone I'd ever seen in the movies or in real-life.

The new Filipino soldier was quiet, older, and looked surprisingly better fed and cleaner than the rest of us. About a quarter-mile down the bumpy road he slapped my back and shouted, "Stop! Sniper in tree!" without identifying the sniper's location. As I stomped on the brakes and swerved into a clump of bushes that might give some frontal cover, he jumped out of his seat and scurried around to the rear of our braking vehicle.

"Damn! Where's the Chillicothe Kid when I need him?" I grumbled to myself as I brought the Jeep to a complete stop. I never had to bail out or hide with the Kid along.

With the engine still running, I rolled out the door-less Jeep and scrambled on my hands and toes around to the rear end, smack into the muzzle of my partner's .45-caliber, semi-automatic pistol. "What the Hell are you doing? The enemy is that way, man!" I burst out in anger. His tar black oriental eyes stared blankly at me down the barrel of his trembling pistol hand as though he was in a trance. *Oh, damn, damn, damn, what if this guy's a Jap infiltrator?* My mind tried to fathom what was going on. Before he could pull the trigger, I instinctively reached up and grabbed the barrel of the huge pistol and wrenched it out of his trembling hand in one downward twisting motion. I turned the gun on him and said, "There was no sniper, was there?"

He slowly bowed and shook his head no.

"Get back in. I should shoot you right here on the spot for what you did," I scowled at the whimpering would-be assassin. I knew I had to get Captain Perrenot's message to the infantry post before I dealt with this joker. Captain Perrenot always said to turn in any suspects because we can't get any intelligence out of a dead suspect. When we stopped at the command post I turned him over to the Philippine Scouts.

I delivered the answer to Captain Perrenot. As he finished reading the return message, I jokingly asked, "Captain Perry, could you give me a bodyguard who's not a Jap?"

He looked up surprised at my unexpected request. "What did you say, Lovato?"

"The guy you gave me this morning tried to kill me, Sir," I grinned, knowing that would get a rise out of our unflappable leader.

"Hold on, Lovato. Start from the top. I want to hear it all." As I related the story he shook his head in disbelief. When all was said and done he replied to my report with the statement that I had come to expect from him. Grinning, he said, "I don't know about you, Lovato!"

CHAPTER 10

# "...Carabao Fetch"

*March 1942 - Between Mount Natib and Mount Samat*

We were hungry, tired, and frustrated from the lack of supplies and support, but we managed to hold the front line and kept the Japanese at bay. If the Japanese had known how poorly supplied we were, they could have overrun us with their large numbers. We continued to inflict severe damage on their charging infantry and tanks. By this time we had no food other than what we scrounged off the land. If we were lucky we'd find an occasional can of chipped beef, sardines, or tomatoes. Wild onions, green bananas, and coconut milk were dinner when we could find them. The green bananas and coconuts often created a painfully sour stomach since they were too unripe to eat. Each day we picked through the jungle shrubs for edibles. Without the knowledge of the Filipinos, many of us would have died from eating poisonous berries and plants. Filipino patrols sometimes found rice in hidden caches of food, which had been prepared and left by Japanese supporters in anticipation of the invasion. Precious gas and oil were also found on those foraging missions. Unfortunately medicine, particularly quinine, was the rarest find of all. The intermittent finds were not enough to sustain our fighting forces. One of the rumors that everyone griped about came from a guy who returned to the front line from one of the medical stations. He claimed the food situation was better in the rear echelon and that MacArthur and his men had moved all of the food that was left on Bataan to Corregidor. Captain Perrenot said that this retreat had been planned for several years. Whoever came up with this "strategic withdrawal" had done a lousy job on food, medical supplies and ammunition. *What a hell of a way to fight a war! I'm starving, sick, and low on energy. Is this how I will die?*

But now we had been forced to move farther south where it would be more advantageous to make another stand. During the rapid retreat southward toward Orion we passed a small herd of carabao grazing in an abandoned rice field. The carabao looked fat and every bit as delectable as American beef cattle. Carabao were not raised for food, but were cherished by the Filipinos, as they provided the muscle for farming, carrying wood and bags of rice, and pulling carts. The carabao looked pretty good to our hungry eyes and growling stomachs. The only problem was they were north of us on the edge of enemy lines.

The word spread that a raiding party was being formed to go after some carabao meat. The organizing group was made up of several American Navy sailors who had been fighting with the regular army. They were part of the Battling Bastards of Bataan. We Bastards at the front consisted of Filipino civilians, Philippine Constabulary Army troops and Scouts, American Army, American Navy and even US Air Corps pilots and flight crews. There were even a few Aussies and Brits who were unlucky enough to be caught on Bataan. We were dedicated to defend the line at all costs and our differences didn't matter

A couple of the landlocked navy guys came over to our half-track and one hollered, "Anybody want to go and get some carabao steaks back there in Jap territory?"

"Heck yeah, I'll go" I volunteered. "I was thinking the same thing when we passed that herd earlier." My stomach growled at the mere thought of fresh meat.

Captain Perrenot conferred with another officer to arrange half-track support while we sneaked into the narrow strip of no-man's land rice paddies that separated us from the Japanese. The enemy had been relatively quiet since we had set up our new line of defense. Aside from a couple of minor skirmishes resulting in no major damage on either side, it seemed they were content not to advance on our coordinated line. Maybe our 110-mm Howitzers and the 155-mm big guns did more damage to them than we thought.

One thing we knew was that the enemy was not expecting us to venture into their territory for carabao. According to our intelligence, a unit of Japanese was bivouacked near the north side of the shallow paddy. The half moon was our only light for the mission into no-man's land. We made our way back to the carabao with mouths watering in anticipation of fresh meat. *If we don't get them, somebody else will. We can't eat the rumors about when and how we would be re-supplied with food. This is dangerous.* But so was everything else I did for the past four months of chaos and calamity. *I made it this far without catching a bullet, so why not take a chance to get something solid to eat? It will be exciting to penetrate into the enemy's territory without his knowledge.*

Led by Philippine Scouts, who knew the terrain better than anyone, we moved slowly and quietly through the tangled roots and thick foliage. The half-moon's stark white light cast a broken leafy pattern on the jungle trails that led to the rice paddy. The gentle carabao seemed to favor the abundant grass sprigs in the cool, shallow water. Perhaps the surrounding water provided them protection from the packs of wild dogs that roamed the night. What the docile carabao didn't know was that the most dangerous predators on earth hunted them in the dark. Our hungry hunting party was in search of life-sustaining food. This was different from hunting trips with my father and brothers. *This time, I could get killed as easily as the prey.*

Brewster put his hand on my shoulder and whispered, "Hey, Frank, this is fun out-sneaking those sneaky Japs!" I nodded and kept walking, thinking that there was not much fun in war. *Too bad we couldn't settle this whole mess with the Japanese with a game of baseball. Set it up like the World Series. The best of seven, winner takes all. Loser goes home and we forget about this crazy killing.*

I turned around and asked Brewster, "Do the Japs play baseball?"

"I think so, Frank," he whispered.

About fifteen minutes later, we saw the herd of about twenty carabao standing complacently in the shallow rice paddy. Fortunately, they were closer to our side of the paddy than the enemy side. A tough-looking sergeant from the 31st called us together to outline the best possible strategy. "My men and I will wade into the water to get the cows. The rest of you cover us while we're roping them and bringing them back." Everyone, including the Scouts, respected the men from the 31st Infantry because of their extensive jungle experience in the Philippines, their knowledge of military tactics, and mostly because they were the meanest, toughest, grittiest fighters on the face of the earth. If anybody could succeed in carrying out this zany mission, it would be the 31st. The rest of us set up positions at the edge of the trees on the south side of the large paddy as the sergeant and his squad quietly waded into the dark water. They moved like shadows in the dim moonlight, leaving only silent ripples in their wake. The soldiers used the huge carabao to shield them from the unsuspecting Japanese on the opposite side. Once they arrived at the tame animals, the men roped them in smaller groups and led them back toward us like a caravan. As the last group of men and animals exited the water, the graveyard stillness of the silent night was broken by the sharp report of a Japanese machine gun from the other side of the paddy. Someone shouted, "They spotted us!" Seconds later we fired back across the open paddy.

Enemy bullets ripped through leaves and ricocheted off gnarly roots and branches around us. We kept the pursuers at bay long enough to get the carabao: our mission's primary objective. I hoped they would stop shooting at us once we were in the jungle, but about thirty Japanese charged across the paddy, shooting blindly into the trees. Captain Perrenot met us at the half-tracks that were positioned midway between the rice paddy and our bivouac area. He fired a 75-mm into the ranks of the pursuing enemy soldiers before they made it into the trees on our side. The Japanese finally retreated to their side of the paddy.

The mission was completely successful. We stole all the carabao from the Japanese without losing a single man in the process. This was the first time since the war began over three months ago that we had full stomachs. It was, as one of the British soldiers so aptly stated, "A very successful carabao fetch!"

The remainder of March was relatively quiet, with the exception of a few long distance artillery exchanges and small patrol skirmishes. Every day seemed to get longer and hotter than the day before. When I had arrived in the Philippines in September, occasional tropical rains cooled the temperatures. Old timers from the 31st Infantry, who had spent over a year in the Philippines, commented with a grin, "If you think March is hot, you'll feel double this hot next month and the rest of the summer until the rains come again." During the day we had to wring the sweat out of our rotting khaki shirts. None of our clothes ever dried in the muggy, mosquito-plagued conditions. How I missed riding my bike along the Rio Grande on a warm early summer night with the sound of a million crickets singing. *When I got home from this ugly war, I'll buy a Chevy coupe and take the family up to Tijeres Canyon and Jemez Springs.* Dreaming and talking about better days in the future when this war was over was all we could do to keep up our spirits amidst the growing sentiment that we had been abandoned, with nowhere to go to but the tip of Bataan.

We're the Battling Bastards of Bataan:
No mama, no papa, no Uncle Sam,
No aunts, no uncles, no nephews, no nieces,
No rifles, no guns or artillery pieces,
And nobody gives a damn!
*Author unknown*

A rumor spread that the Japanese General Homma had committed suicide because he was unable to defeat our combined allied forces line of defense in Bataan. There was even a rumor that the Japanese were going to withdraw their forces because they lost so many men and could not afford to lose any more. Maybe the strategic withdrawal plan was working. I remember Dad telling me about the Apache Chief Geronimo and his small band of warriors who held off the huge US Cavalry by using hit and run tactics. His band always retreated to defensible positions in the high mountain canyons where the cavalry could easily be ambushed. We were the allied front, but we were unable to take the Japanese head on due to the lack of ammo and manpower. If the Japanese knew how low on ammo we were, they would try to overrun us. We were forced to take shots and then retreat and it did slow them down. Because the Filipinos knew the terrain so well, we were able to avoid the Japanese heavy artillery moving down the main roads.

Our biggest enemies were hunger, malaria, dysentery and dengue fever. Men were losing so much weight that their tattered uniforms hung around them loosely. After three months of war every man looked as though he had aged ten years. Deep wrinkles in our faces and our dark sunken eyes revealed the ravaging effects of malnutrition, disease and fatigue. Captain Perrenot, who was in his late twenties, looked older than my forty-year-old father. His deep blue eyes sunk deep into his ashen skin. I felt so bad for him. He was a good man who never cursed or complained, no matter how bad the situation. I had a feeling, regardless of the rumors that the Japanese were giving up, that Captain Perrenot was right: the war was just beginning.

I see no gleam of victory alluring,<br>
No chance of splendid booty or of gain.<br>
If I endure—I must go on enduring,<br>
And my reward for bearing pain – is pain.<br>
Yet, though the thrill, the zest, the hope is gone,<br>
Something within keeps me fighting on.<br>
*Lieutenant Henry G. Lee / Philippine Division*

CHAPTER 11

# Hell Breaks Loose

*April 3, 1942 — Good Friday*

It was almost Easter and I remembered how much I loved the beginning of spring and the ceremonies in church. Every year Mother made Easter dresses for my sisters, Polly and Annie. My bothers and I wore starched white shirts and navy blue slacks to Sunday Mass. After Benediction at Sacred Heart Church, we went home to feast on Mother's delicious baked ham, creamy mashed potatoes, garden grown green beans, fat ears of corn, and homemade apple pie and ice cream. During Lent I normally gave up something I considered a treat. Easter was the day I resumed chewing gum or going to the movies. *There was nothing good to give up this year in Bataan.* I never realized how fortunate I was growing up in America, until I was halfway around the world from it. The little things I remembered were important to me now: Saturday afternoon movies, a bicycle ride across town to see my Tio and Tia, clean clothes, a Coca Cola.

Dark clouds loomed heavy in the gray morning sky, looking as though a nasty storm might break the monotony of the quiet standoff. I woke the Kid and asked him, "Hey, Kid, how about riding shotgun with me this morning on a recon?"

He stretched out his long sinewy arms, yawned, and scratched his head before sitting up and putting on his sweaty ten-gallon hat. I remembered when we first met how spotless and creamy white his hat was. Its once perfectly curled brim and tall crown were like the rest of our clothes: dust covered, ragged on the edges, and in need of replacement.

"Okay dokey, Frank, but you've got to buy breakfast. You hear?"

"You got it, Buddy!" I smiled at the misplaced cowboy as he stood up still stretching. "But you're going to have to wait a couple of weeks until we get done with this little war. Then I'll buy you the biggest steak and eggs breakfast you ever saw. I promise."

"Okay, but don't forget, I want a pile of grits, biscuits and white gravy on the side. Big stack of flapjacks and butter with hot maple syrup, too." I could hear my stomach growl in response to each vivid description. That's what I liked so much about the Kid. He kept his sense of humor throughout the worst of times.

I replied, "You're on, Kid. All of the above and then some, and when we get home to the states, I want you to visit my family in Albuquerque. Wait till you taste my mother's enchiladas, tamales, and tacos."

"Can't wait. What would you do without me, Frank?" he joked again.

I prayed I wouldn't have to find out. The thought of losing the Kid scared me more than the thought of facing Japanese tanks. The Kid was a big brother to me and certainly was my best friend in this land. Since he was from Texas, we often spoke of the Southwest and our homes. All of my buddies in the 200th that I came over with were either assigned to anti-aircraft units in Mariveles, or had been reassigned to the infantry. We, the few Americans assigned to the provisional half-track units, were certainly the forgotten Battling Bastards of Bataan, orphans without a home.

Our objective was to scope out a small village about a mile northwest on a small oxcart road. We drove to the edge of the village and parked the Jeep in the trees. We walked down the dusty road, not expecting too much excitement. Hopefully we would meet some locals who could tell us something about the Japanese. As we approached the village it was dead quiet. Nothing was stirring, not even the wild dogs. It was so still it was scary.

"What do you think, Frank?" asked he Kid, his guns drawn and ready.

"They must all be gone," I retorted.

Suddenly, from out of nowhere an explosion rocked the ground behind us blowing us face first into the dirt.

"Damn! Where in the hell is that coming from, Frank?" yelled the Kid.

The big Japanese projectiles screamed down from the dark gray storm clouds, beginning as a barely noticeable high-pitched shrill, rapidly building in timbre and reverberation until right before impact when it thundered like a continuous crack of lightening that blocked out all other sounds.

We scrambled into one of the shallow holes made by one of the big shells. The Kid and I covered our heads from the showering rocks and clods of dirt that clobbered us. It rained projectiles without a second of silence between the salvos. Explosions rocked the ground in every direction.

I peeked out of the hole, looking for a direction for us to escape the intense barrage. We figured it was better to stay in one place than risk being hit running for cover, so we dug in frantically. I thought that lightening and artillery projectiles never hit the same place twice. Then again, the ones that did never left any witnesses.

"Frank! I don't want to die, Buddy. Do you know any prayers?" quivered the Kid. That was the first time I saw him break down and actually seem afraid.

"Can you teach me a prayer?" he asked, like a child afraid of the dark. His eyes, no longer confident and sharp, showed the fear and hopelessness of a wounded rabbit.

"Sure, Buddy," I consoled him. "Our Father, Who art in heaven, hallowed be thy name. Thy kingdom come, Thy will be done, on earth as it is in heaven."

I continued as dirt and rocks pelted us, "Hail Mary full of grace, the Lord is with thee. Blessed art thou amongst women. Blessed is the fruit of they womb, Jesus."

When I later heard the phrase: "There are no atheists in a foxhole," I understood what it meant. I never doubted that there is a God. I just questioned the meaning of this absolute craziness. But who was I to understand any of it? I was just doing my best to stay alive and left the rest to God.

"Dog gone it Frank, I've never been baptized." The Kid turned to me sheepishly. "I don't want to die un-baptized."

I remembered from my childhood catechism that anyone can baptize in an emergency, and being bombed by the Japanese surely qualified as an emergency.

"Don't worry Kid, I can do it," I assured him.

I took out my canteen of water and laid the Kid's head back on one arm and poured a stream of the canteen water over his forehead.

"I baptize you in the name of the Father, and of the Son, and of the Holy Ghost. Amen. That's it."

"That's all?" he asked, as he lay cradled in my arms.

"Yeah. You're baptized, Buddy." The shelling continued and rocks and clods rained down on our little ceremony in the backwoods of Bataan. Hugging each other tight, the Kid and I started to laugh uncontrollably. He seemed relieved to be baptized. I was glad I could give him something for his lifesaving sharp shooting, and most of all, for his friendship.

The shelling went on for what seemed like hours. We figuring the prayers were working and started singing under the gloomy sky. We sung "You Are My Sunshine," and "God Bless America," over and over again. Then, as quickly as it had started, the shelling stopped. The silence was eerie, but welcome.

"Thank you, God, Holy Mother and all the saints in heaven. We made it!" I cheered. So near, and yet we had been spared. It's another miracle.

"Amen," confirmed the Kid. He blew dust off his ten-gallon hat that was now several shades darker with a fine coating of Philippine brown dirt.

We crawled out of our foxhole and stretched our tired bodies. All around us were holes made by the exploding artillery fire. The only structure left standing in the abandoned village was a small shed-like building.

"In battle you will find no atheists in a foxhole."

*US Army Catholic Chaplain, in Bataan, William Cummings. Chaplain Cummings died in a POW camp.*

"Let's check it out, Frank," the Kid suggested. We opened the door. A large tub of foaming liquid that smelled like yeast was in the middle of the room.

"What the heck?" I exclaimed. I scraped back the stinky foam and dipped my canteen cup in the concoction, sniffed it, took a sip and handed it to the Kid. He took a quick sip and confirmed my suspicians instantly.

"By God, it's home brew!" cheered the Kid. "Yahoo! There'll be a good time in the old town tonight," he sang out.

The liquid was like green wine. Whoever had been brewing it had left in a hurry. There we were, dangerously near enemy lines, and wondering what to do with our find. After sampling a canteen or two, the Kid and I decided to take it back with us to the unit. We made a carrying device out of a rope and a pole, picked up the caldron of fermenting brew, and loaded it into our Dodge. What a sight we must have been as we sang and laughed while we drove toward the mission church at the next village where we were to meet Captain Perrenot and the rest of the battery.

There was no one to be seen as we pulled into the village and found the abandoned mission site. The magnificent Spanish Catholic structure was located on the main road heading north and south, about halfway between the entrance to the Bataan peninsula and the tip at Mariveles. It reminded me of the old mission churches back home in New Mexico. Like all of the other villages we came to, the inhabitants had fled the approaching Japanese whose reputation for cruelty preceded them. All that was left were the buildings and statues that were too heavy to move rapidly. I was in a ghost town created by war.

"Hey, we were supposed to meet here two hours ago. We're late and they're still not here," I wondered, slightly tipsy from the brew.

"So what?" replied the Kid. He had a strong dislike for military protocol and preferred to be with me, rather the captain or the other Philippine officers. The Kid respected Captain Perrenot and the Filipino lieutenants. He just didn't like taking orders.

I saw the telltale half-track tank tread marks leading up to the mission church's huge wooden doors. Silently we walked up to the doors and peered in. There in the cavernous interior was our entire half-track battery resting in the cool, dimly lit sanctuary. The mission had walls that were two and a half feet thick and provided excellent protection.

"Where the heck have you been and what's in the pot?" barked the captain.

By now the Kid and I were feeling no pain. The alcohol had hit hard on our empty stomachs, and we were relieved that we had made it back to our unit alive one more time. I related quickly "We got caught in an artillery barrage and had to lay low until it stopped. It was raining mortar and cannon fire. We got pinned down for several hours, Sir! Then we found the, ah, brew."

"Brew?" questioned the captain, showing no emotion.

The captain glared at us like a principal who had just caught a couple of boys playing hooky.

"You can't court marshal me," stubbornly muttered the Kid. "I'm not enlisted."

The kid and I stood there smiling, filthy dirty from all the exploding dirt clods and dust.

"Get rid of that crap!" snapped the captain.

"Yes, Sir," I replied.

He walked over to the caldron, peered in and whispered, "Save me a canteen of it before you dump it."

"Yes, Sir!" I answered, trying not to smile.

"I don't know about you, Lovato," grinned the captain.

I knew everything was okay when he said that.

The Kid and I managed to find a good home for the brew, and we filled the captain's request. Just as it had appeared, it soon disappeared. *It is like everything else in this war: now you have it, now you don't.* There was neither predictability nor certainty about anything in this crazy war. Everything was planned moment to moment.

The captain said something I couldn't quite hear because my ears were still ringing from the explosions back at the village.

"What did you two bootleggers find out at the village?" the captain asked again.

"Oh, pardon me, Sir. Everyone had already evacuated by the time we got there. Then almost immediately the shelling began. It was long-range stuff, possibly from the northeast. There was no one, no food, nothing for us or the Japs except the brew. That's all I can tell you, Sir."

Captain Perrenot said, "We got hit hard in that shelling, too. That's why we pulled into this mission church." Captain Perrenot started thinking and I could almost hear the wheels turning in his brain. The Japanese had been relatively quiet the past three weeks. Their infantry tried to infiltrate and break through our lines on several occasions, but was turned back after suffering heavy casualties. We had held the line and we were feeling as if we had a chance. We hoped the rumors were true that the Japanese were retreating. A man wants to believe the best.

While shaking his head and taking a deep breath he said the words that struck my heart like a cold knife, "This is the beginning of something big — real big!" Looking grim, Captain Perrenot continued, "It won't be long now before the Japs try to come through this village with their tanks. We have to stop them at all costs. Why they waited this long before using their tanks against our lines, I'll never know."

We were low on 75-mm and .30-caliber machine gun ammo for the half-tracks. Every shot had to count. The cannon barrel linings on the half-tracks were hopelessly worn out, resulting in poor accuracy beyond anything but point-blank range. There were no more replacement linings back at Mariveles. It meant we could only shoot when the enemy was almost on top of us. We had to fight with what we had.

Captain Perrenot, hollow-eyed from lack of sleep, laid out our defensive strategy for the expected tank attack.

Our orders were to defend the village. The local inhabitants had already abandoned their nipa huts. All the buildings were stripped of food and the mission church was nothing more than a shell. I had been through this village once before when I had brought the half-tracks down to Mariveles to replace the cannon barrel linings. Back then the local Filipinos still occupied the village because the Japanese were much farther from their doorsteps.

With a stick, the captain scratched the plan on the dirt like a coach during a football game. First, he drew the main road leading into and through the village. Next, he marked our tanks' locations and then our half-tracks' positions. Our tank battalions would be the first line of defense, and the remaining battalions of half-tracks were to set up in positions on the flanks to destroy any enemy tanks that broke through. Like a defensive play in a football game, Captain Perrenot marked the anticipated Japanese tanks. He didn't know how many or what type of tanks they had because our reconnaissance was unable to determine what was going on behind their lines. The Kid disappeared while the captain outlined his plans.

I thought back to the morning of December 22nd at Lingayen Gulf, when hundreds of enemy landing craft began their journey to the shore. I thought of our loaded cannons waiting, hidden beneath our camouflaged beach emplacements. Only four months ago we were like our half-tracks: fresh, strong and untested. For over one hundred days and nights we had fought this war, not only against the Japanese, but also against hunger, disease and the lack of ammunition and supplies. These battles had taken their toll on every single one of us as well as on all our equipment. Our cannons' barrel linings were soot black and had no visible spirals. Our half-tracks were covered with the scars of battle: bullet and shrapnel holes, scrapes and dents. We, the Battling Bastards of Bataan, looked even worse. Gaunt and emaciated, in dirty, sweat-stained uniforms, we waited for the Japanese to make their move.

At about 0900 hours artillery bursts shook the ground in the village. They were big shells shot from the northwest. Seconds later another shell whistled down and exploded, followed by other bursts that cut into our two and a half mile main line of defense the joint American and Filipino defenders' fragile positions across the Bagac/Orion line.

The continuous and unabated heavy artillery barrage rocked the earth like an earthquake. Japanese bombers rumbled overhead and dropped incendiary bombs that spread waves of fire and black smoke in every direction. Our men crouched in foxholes, under fallen trees, anywhere they could find to escape the constant barrage of falling rocks, shrapnel, and clods of dirt that stormed down from the bursting heavy ordinance. But there was nowhere safe to hide from the unending rain of destruction. This was the first time since the Japanese had landed at Lingayen Gulf that they had launched such a large multi-pronged, heavy attack. About noon the artillery shelling stopped briefly and low-flying planes dropped more incendiary bombs. Fires broke out everywhere burning virtually all of the grass, shrubs and trees to a blackened nightmare of leaping orange and yellow flames. Everything took on a hellish quality unparalleled in bizarreness and scope. Firestorm winds whipped the fire across the crumbling defensive line of infantrymen crouched deep in their shallow foxholes. Raging fires consumed any remaining caches of precious fuel, ammo and food. Frantic and disoriented soldiers abandoned their burnt out positions to flee the oxygen consuming flames. Enemy bombs and artillery shells exploded in an unabated and thunderous pounding for six continuous hours. Gray smoke from the burning cogan grass rose ghostly into the already dark storm cloud covered sky.

Barely audible over the incessant artillery pounding, the first wave of Japanese tanks rumbled into the entrance to the deserted village that G-Battery was assigned to defend. Simultaneous cannon fire roared from our tanks' semi-concealed positions. Plumes of gray smoke lingered for a moment in a straight line from their smoking barrels, revealing the point of origin of the projectile. Counter-fire from the medium-sized enemy tanks ripped back, almost in unison, at our tanks and half-tracks hidden behind village structures. The battle was on. In the vacant ghost town the battle that forever changed the course of G-Battery, 2nd Provisional Group, Self-Propelled Artillery was underway.

Standing tall, helmet strapped tight under his chin, Captain Perrenot waved his half-track battery into the thundering free-for-all of blazing cannons and machine guns and tanks jockeying for position in the dust-choked streets.

There was no time to think; there was only time to react.

From behind the slower Japanese tanks emerged their smaller tanks. Small, quick, and highly maneuverable, they accelerated, spun and changed directions so rapidly that it was impossible for us to get a line of sight on them.

The driver of one of our half-tracks yanked his front end around to line up the 75-mm, as our Filipino Scout officer cranked the adjusting wheel on the cannon barrel to the correct elevation. We were attempting to shoot at the enemy less than forty yards away. Each time we shot, Brewster twisted the breech mechanism counterclockwise, opening the breech of the single-shot cannon. The rear breech piece swung open, and ejected the spent brass shell casing in one motion. I slammed the twenty-four inch long 75-mm shell in the barrel, as Brewster cranked the breech shut. All this was done as the multi-ton half-track rotated in the loose dirt, jockeying for a good shot at the enemy tanks that were maneuvering to do the same. For a brief ear-shattering moment the thundering booms of firing cannons and exploding projectiles interrupted the mechanical sounds of big gas engines screaming in low gear and the metallic steel tank treads clanking on the hard earthen streets. To avoid being a sitting target our driver quickly maneuvered the half-track out of the line of fire of a charging enemy tank that had its turret barrel pointing straight at us. We were nearly hit. Like a bat out of hell the soldier drove back into the battle where we could get a better shot. The small Japanese tanks were armed with 37-mm cannons and they moved and fired so quickly that we had virtually no time to line up a decent shot. Meanwhile, their heavier tanks rumbled into the fray, firing at our M-3 Stuart Light Tanks on the front line. We were almost out of 75-mm shells so each shot had to count. Most of our shots missed the targets because our barrel liners were hopelessly worn out. What had begun as an organized defense in the village at our front line had turned into a free-for-all of roaring tank cannon fire and non-stop staccato machine gunfire. The village buildings were destroyed and the thatched grass roofs lay burning in the streets. With no time to think about anything but loading and firing at the charging enemy tanks, we used the last round of our 75-mm ammo. Brewster and I dug through the spent brass shells still hot from firing in search of one last live shell that we might have missed. We had not been re-supplied with 75-mm's from the Mariveles depot since late January.

"That's it, Captain. We're out! We're all out!" I shouted over the whine of our motor and the thundering shells bursting in every direction.

As we maneuvered through the smoke of burnt powder to avoid being a still target, I got a quick glimpse of a burning American tank. Leaping flames and black smoke poured from the open cabin, where the tank's turret had been mounted.

The Japanese tanks outnumbered us two to one. Without the 75-mm ammo capable of destroying their tanks, we were sitting ducks in the half-tracks. Captain Perrenot ordered us to retreat. All we had left was a few hundred rounds of machine gun ammo, our rifles, handguns, and a few bandoleers of rifle bullets, and they were completely ineffective against the armored tanks.

First we faced the unrelenting artillery barrage in the morning, followed by the aerial bombing and then the massive tank attack. All the rumors about their retreat were just that: rumors. It was clear to me that if we did not receive reinforcements, ammunition and supplies immediately, it would be a fight to the death.

I kept wondering where the Kid was. I hadn't seen him since we had "disposed" of the caldron of brew. I figured he had probably found a quiet place to sleep off a hangover. I knew he was capable of taking care of himself, and since he didn't have to follow orders and stay at the front like the regulars, he could retreat to a safer position at the rear anytime.

We saw one of our half-tracks, a mangled pile of twisted steel and burning tires. The front had been hit and the driver had been killed, but the box was intact. We sped to the unit to see if any of our crew was in it, but they were gone.

"Check out the box for ammo!" yelled the captain. Brewster and I leaned over the side of the box, and a quick inspection revealed that it, too, was out of 75-mm shells.

"Let's get out of here!" shouted the captain.

The other two half-tracks of G-Battery had already pulled to the rear. They were out of ammunition too and were unable to match the power of the rapid-firing Japanese tanks. We had thrown everything at the enemy, but it wasn't enough to stop them. We were down to nothing but tired, malaria-ridden bodies and handguns and rifles against tanks, bombers and a fully equipped army of foot soldiers.

It would take a miracle to save the day, like the cavalry in a Hollywood western swooping down to rescue a wagon train. Reinforcements were as non-existent as miracles.

Four months of malnutrition and disease had reduced the American-Filipino fighting force to a ragged collection of men fighting for their lives with nowhere to go except south toward the end of the Bataan peninsula. G-Battery had been reduced to two half-tracks and they were running on empty.

Captain Perrenot, a man of few words, gave his final order to disband G-Battery forever. It was his order to destroy the remaining half-tracks, rather than abandon them for the Japanese to use against us. In his direct, monotone voice he said that we were on our own to hook up with any infantry unit, because there was nothing more we could do as a self-propelled artillery unit. He said that he was proud to serve with each of us and we had done our best to take the fight to the enemy.

G-Battery, 2nd Provisional Group, Self-Propelled Artillery, that began December 8, 1941, was now history. We fought the Japanese from Lingayen Gulf to the tip of Bataan for almost four months and held back their superior power.

We ran to find shelter from the explosions that struck in front, behind, and all around us. There was no place to find protection, no place to take a stand in the burning inferno. We had no place to go but south toward the end of the peninsula. Thoughts of making it to Marivelles, evacuating the island and the return of MacArthur raced in my head. I was faced with the possibility of engaging the enemy on the last bit of Philippine ground with only pistols and rifles. *Would I die today?*

I grabbed bandoleers of bullets from the dead, knowing that they were the only ones available. By now, everyone I knew — Captain Perrenot, Brewster, the cadre of Filipinos, and my best friend and angel, the Chillicothe Kid — were nowhere to be seen. I prayed that the Kid got out of the village before the tanks arrived. At this point, I didn't know the names of any of the men who were fighting alongside me.

All sense of order and command was lost in the in the deafening roar of bombs and artillery concussions. Men, many unarmed, ran in mass confusion from the advancing enemy's frontal attack. Low flying bombers and strafing fighter planes roared overhead. Nothing we had could stop them from dropping their bombs and shooting the disorganized bands of fleeing soldiers. Screams of pain and fear pierced the air. Staying alive would require keeping my senses, moving at a steady rate southward, and killing the enemy before he killed me.

As I scrambled through the dense Bataan terrain in search of a command post (or even an organized unit) the jungle ground shook through the worn soles of my boots like a continual earthquake. Winds stoked the hundreds of bomb fires higher and hotter in the already stifling tropical heat.

Without warning, a deafening blast of crimson fire blew me off my feet and hurling through the smoke. I crumpled to the damp earth. "I've been hit! Oh, please God, not my legs," I prayed.

I felt a hot, stinging pain burning from my right shin and lower leg. Fresh blood oozed through the pant leg of my khaki pants. I quickly checked the extent of the damage and breathed a sigh of relief. My leg was intact except but had several irregularly shaped, bleeding punctures. An ugly piece of hot shrapnel protruded from one of the wounds in my calf. Without thinking, I reached down and yanked it out with a quick tug and a scream. The burning sensation must have been from other pieces of hot shrapnel that were so embedded that I couldn't reach them with my bloody fingers. I felt lucky to still have my leg in one piece. I patched the bleeding wounds and tied them off as best I could with a makeshift bandage made from my torn pant leg. Using my rifle as a crutch, I stood up on my good leg and slowly put more weight on the injured one. Although it was extremely painful, it was strong enough to walk on. The shrapnel didn't seem to do any serious damage to the muscles or nerves.

"Thank God," I prayed as I limped off slower than before, but still alive and mobile. Nothing had changed around me during those few moments. The shelling waited for no one. Dad's words of "never, never give up" echoed through my mind during that never-ending barrage.

We were surrounded on three sides. The Japanese Army and Air Corp were squeezing us into the tip of Bataan. Soon there would be no place to go but into the water and I couldn't swim. I swore to God right then and there that if I ever got out of this mess, I would learn how to swim.

There was virtually no communication between soldiers, officers and the command posts. The feeling that prevailed among the broken units of soldiers was beyond despair. We huddled and waited silently for the Japanese to make their next move. We had no illusion of the possibility of defeating the enemy because they had superior artillery and aerial firepower. We were depleted. All we could do was survive.

Ragged, frustrated and exhausted, our small group of mostly American soldiers dug in at Cabcaben Airfield to make our last stand. We had retreated through thick jungle with the Japanese at our heels, and now the open airfield gave us an advantage in which to make a stand and do the most damage. The advancing enemy would have to cross the open airfield landing strip to get to us, and when they tried crossing the clearing we had the best chance of killing as many of them as we had bullets. We were ready to make our last stand with our backs to the sea. I recalled childhood memories of newspaper pictures featuring Pancho Villa's band of Mexican fighters, outnumbered by US soldiers, standing defiantly. By now, the prevailing attitude among the men was: "Let's get it over with. Stop the shelling and bring on the infantry." We couldn't last much longer. *I would rather die fighting than by starvation.*

Captain Perrenot told us three months ago that the plan was to withdraw. Since we met at the mission church, we fought and retreated for six days and nights. We were through withdrawing. *There is no place to go. The ocean is at my back. Is this it?*

---

*December 8, 1941 (Dec.7 in U.S.)*
*Manila, Luzon, Philippines*

General Douglas MacArthur was notified at 3:30 am of the Pearl Harbor attack by his Chief of Staff, Brigadier General Richard Sutherland. For reasons still unknown, MacArthur repeatedly refused to give permission to Major General Lewis Brereton, the Commander of his Far East Air Force, to attack and bomb known Japanese airfields and a major harbor on Formosa only 600 miles to the north. The frustrated Brereton was instructed to only prepare his planes and wait.

Even after two reports came in at 9:25 am that two airfields on Luzon had been attacked, MacArthur continued to refused permission to Brereton.

During the same period of time Japanese pilots of the 11th Air Force waited anxiously for low hanging fog to clear before theywere able to take off, thereby postponing their planned dawn departure time to attack Clark Field and other targets on Luzon. Like Pearl Harbor, their primary mission was to surprise and destroy MacArthur's Boeing B-17 heavy bomber threat to the Japanese mainland before it had time to respond. Although the fog prevented the enemy planes from departing until after 10:00 am, MacArthur's hesitation allowed the enemy bombers and fighters precious. time to find the majority of his Air Force on the ground two hours later.

Shortly after 12:35 pm, 54 Japanese bombers and 36 fighters arrived at Clark Field and were surprised to find no protective air cover and all of the B-17's parked neatly in the open. Determined, but mostly ineffective antiaircraft fire from units of the 200 Coast Artillery fired on the high flying bombers and shot at the swarming Zero's with machine-gun and rifle fire. Five enemy planes were shot down with the loss of only two men from the 200th.

*Strategic Outcome*

Although MacArthur's Command was forewarned, Japan was able to make another devastating first strike on U.S. forces, effectively wiping out any bomber threat to Japan's mainland and inner circle bases of defense. Of the planes parked on the runway, only three B-17, survived, none of the P-40's, or any of the 30 B-26's. The Japanese had lost only 7 fighters and no bombers. Without an adequate air force deterrent, joint U.S., and Filipino ground and naval forces would be even more vulnerable from enemy air attacks in the future.

*December 8, 1941 (U.S.)*

President Roosevelt addressed Congress and the Supreme Court, asking Congress to declare war on Japan. 'Yesterday, December 7, 1941- a date that will live in infamy, the United States of America was suddenly and deliberately attacked by naval and air forces of the Empire of Japan...' With only one descending vote, Congress declared war on Japan. Great Britain had done the same hours earlier. Within three days Germany and Italy, honoring treaty obligations with Japan, declared war on the United States bringing about a full scale World War.

Japanese forces land on Malaya's east coast to begin an over six hundred mile march down the Malay peninsula to attack the British occupied capitol city of Singapore. Other Japanese battalions prepare on the mainland to attack Hong Kong following a bomber attack on the weakly defended city.

Admiral Isoruku Yamamoto, one of the principal designers of the Pearl Harbor attack plan, was inspired by an 11/20/1940 incident when obsolete British aircraft carrier based biplanes torpedoed and destroyed three unsuspecting Italian battleships moored in Taranto harbor.

A Harvard University student and naval attaché in Washington, Yamamoto knew that the U.S. processed vast resources of raw materials and young men. He concluded that in order for Japan to achieve dominance in the western pacific, they must first neutralize the U.S. Navy based in Pearl Harbor, destroy MacArthur's B-17 bomber threat in the Philippines, and quickly destroy all other runways, bases and airplanes that threatened Japan. The swift attack model he initiated was modeled after the blitzkrieg-style offensive used by the Nazi Germans.

He also realized that the U.S. would soon recover from the attacks – but not before Japanese forces would have built an impenetrable defensive circle within the central and southwestern Pacific Rim. Based on past congressional military support and the apparent lack of support by the U.S. public regarding entering into another foreign war, Japan's war planners errantly predicted that President Roosevelt and the majority, pro-isolationist, anti-war factions in Congress would vote for a quick peace settlement. This would leave Japan alone to dominate their newly acquired British and Dutch processions, their conquered territories in China, and would open the door to natural resource rich countries like Burma, and Java. Prime Minister Hidecki Tojo's implementation of the "Tanaka" grand plan to dominate the "eight corners of the globe" had begun. The first part of the plan for a Japanese controlled Asian economy was called the 'Far East Asia Co-Prosperity Sphere.'

*Strategic Outcomes*
*Pearl Harbor*

Although over 2400 Americans were killed and many of the U.S. warships were sunk or severely damaged by the Pearl Harbor Attack Force, the strategic outcome of failing to destroy their primary targets, the American aircraft carriers, proved to be the Japanese fleet's undoing six months later at the battle of Midway. The U.S. carrier U.S.S Hornet later became the sea-based launching pad for Colonel James Doolittle's B-25 bomber attack on Tokyo.

After discovering that the U.S. aircraft carriers, airplanes and pilots escaped destruction, Admiral Yamamoto, an astute student of America economy, industry and human spirit gravely pronounced to his fellow officers, "We have only awakened a sleeping giant ...and have given him a terrible resolve."

*Philippines*

MacArthur's nine hour hesitation to launch an aerial attack on the known Japanese stronghold on Formosa resulted in a Pearl Harbor-like obliteration of his own Far East Air Force. Unable to adequately defend his bases and supply depots in the air he allowed Japanese aircraft to unabatedly bomb, strafe and destroy their targets. Material losses of ammunition, fuel, and medical supplies needed to wage a successful defense of the Philippines were destroyed by repeated aerial attacks. In less than an hour, Japan had gained aerial superiority in a war in which the airplane, either launched from an aircraft carrier or from a land base, would prove to be the dominant weapon.

*December 10, 1941*
*Cavite Naval Base, Manila Harbor*

Japanese light bombers attack and destroy the entire inventory of over 600 torpedoes stored in a single warehouse. This tremendous. loss neutralized the battle effectiveness of the 29 U.S. submarines based in Manila. This action cleared the way for the enemy's major troop invasion and the delivery of mechanized tanks, artillery, trucks and supplies planned for later in December.

Japan now controlled both the air and the sea above and around the Philippines.

Approximately 150 miles from Singapore, Japanese naval aircraft attack and sink HMS Prince of Wales and HMS Repulse, England's only two battleships in the Pacific Ocean.

*Guam*

400 U.S. marines and Navy personnel along with approximately 180 Guam Insular Guards, armed with nothing larger than .30 caliber weapons were overrun by over 5,000 Japanese Marines. The survivors became the first American Prisoners of War (POW) to discover that their Japanese captors were not going to abide by the rules of the Geneva Convention that provided guidelines to assure that POW's would be treated humanely.

*December 10,11,12, 1941*
*Luzon, Philippines*

Despite aerial attacks by three U.S. bombers and a group of P-40's and outdated P-35's, several small detachments of Japanese Army forces landed near northern Luzon coastal towns at Vigan, Aparri and at Legaspi in the south. The attack was actually the first U.S. bomber attack of World War II. They sunk several landing barges, three transport ships, and set some other ships ablaze before departing. Unknown to the defenders, the enemy troops were the first pre-invasion landing parties assigned to scout and prepare for the major invasion planned later in the month.

*December 15th*

Japanese troops invade Burma

*December 20,1941*
*Manila*

MacArthur's headquarters received a report that a U.S. submarine patrolling in the Lingayen Gulf area had sighted a large convoy of Japanese ships. MacArthur's staff pondered the question specifically where along the vast shoreline the Japanese would land their main invasion force. The planners mistakenly decided to place the majority of the beach defenses of tanks and field artillery at the mouth of the Agno River. They based their decision on an earlier incident when, on December 10th a single enemy reconnaissance boat had been spotted at that location and was fired upon. This decision left the Northern end of the gulf coast undefended except for two provisional half-track batteries (G-Battery and A-Battery) commanded by American artillery officers, their American troops, Philippine Scouts, and minimally trained Filipino recruits.

*Davao, Mindanao, South of Luzon, Philippines*

Japanese transports land 5,000 troops on shore in the early dawn opposed by only a single machinegun squad that was knocked out quickly by shellfire.

*December 22, 1941*
*Lingayen Gulf, Northern Luzon, Philippines*

Slightly past midnight, the first of 85 military transports carrying 45,000 of General Masaharu Homma's 14th Army, dropped anchor offshore in preparation for landing on the Northern Luzon beaches. Their goal was to take control of the Philippines within six weeks from the joint force of U.S./Philippine defenders. The landing site of gentle sloping beaches extended approximately 15 miles from Damortis and Agoo in the south to Bauang in the north. Everything, including tanks, field artillery, ammo, food and supplies, that they needed to accomplish this objective was aboard and ready for disembarking. Battleships, cruisers and destroyers would first bombard the beachheads in preparation for the massive landing of troops and equipment.

*Northern shore of Lingayen Gulf*
*December 22, 1941*

A single U.S. submarine had spotted the invasion fleet and fired several torpedoes. One struck a transport and sunk. More might have struck their intended targets but a mechanical flaw in the Mark 10 torpedoes caused them to run consistently four feet deeper than set. A few P-40's strafed the transports but were turned back quickly by an overwhelming flight of Zero's providing protective cover. By late morning, Homma had successfully landed his 44,000 strong invasion Army sustaining only approximately 30 landing boat losses that were later attributed to rough seas. Homma and his commanders had been out of contact with the landing force because Japanese communication radios had all failed due to saltwater corrosion. By early evening most of his tanks and artillery had also landed and were moving south along with troops down Route 3, the main road that connected north and south Luzon.

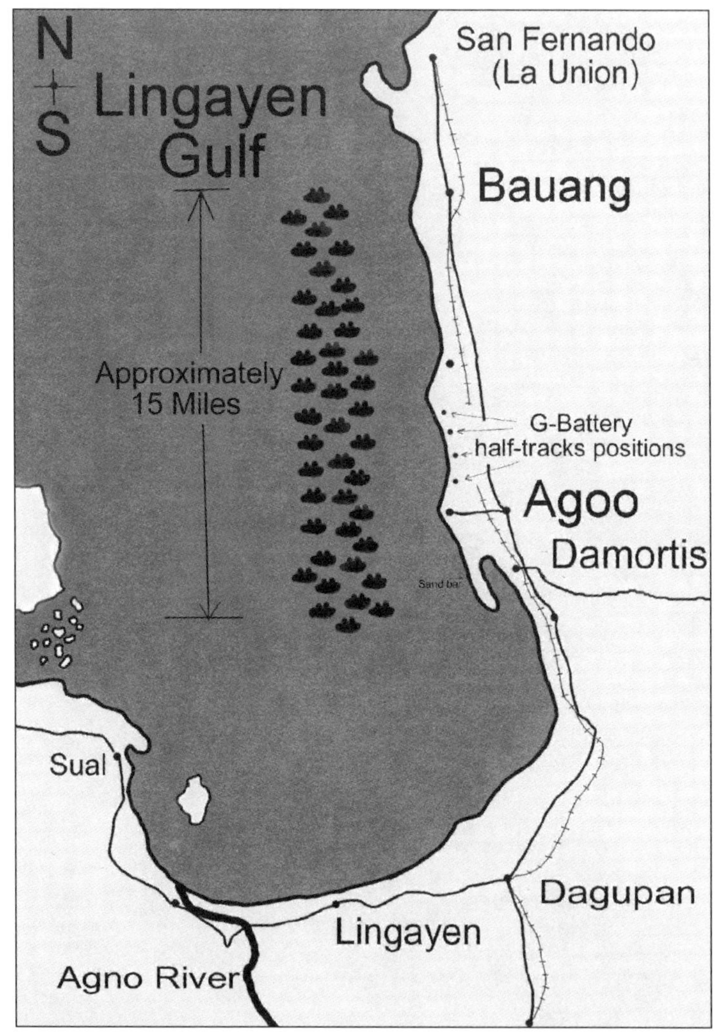


*December 23, 24, 1941*
*Manila, Philippines*

As numerous. reports of Japanese successes poured into MacArthur's office, he realized that his plan to stop the Japanese on the beaches had failed miserably. Without adequate aerial and virtually no naval support, his land army would be unable to stop the massive enemy invasion. WPO3 (War Plan Orange3) that outlined the strategic withdrawal of his forces to the Bataan peninsula would have to be put in to effect immediately. WPO3 had been designed years earlier as a last measure plan placing the defenders in a natural-barrier-protected terrain until reinforcement troops and materials arrived from Pearl Harbor or other Allied bases. What the retreating defenders did not know was that no help was coming in time to save them. Every Allied base in the Pacific was under attack or had already been taken. American troops and supplies originally destined to the Philippines were diverted to Australia to shore up defenses in Malaya.

*Wake Island*

Following several hours of unabated aerial bombardment and a continuous. barrage of aircraft strafing runs, the small contingent of U.S. Wake island Marines were finally overrun by a large detachment of Japanese forces. 1500 service men and civilians were taken captive and made POW's. Over 800 Japanese were killed at a loss of 120 Americans.

*December 25,1941*

*Hong Kong*

Hong Kong falls after three weeks of fighting by British forces made up of units from Canada, Scotland, India, and volunteers known as the Hong Kong Defence Corps.

*Bataan Peninsula, Luzon, Philippines*

Thousands of Filipino civilians fleeing the advancing Japanese invasion force flood the narrow roads entering into the Bataan peninsula in vehicles, oxcarts, and on foot. The vicious. reputation of the Japanese Army's 'Rape of Nanking' struck fear into the hearts and minds of the peaceful agrarian farmers and country people.

*December 29, 1941*

Japanese troops capture Clark Field, Fort Stotsenberg, Luzon, Philippines

*Bataan Peninsula, Luzon, Philippines*

By the first week in January 15,000 American and 65,000 Filipino troops had evacuated into Bataan and had set up the first line of defense against the advancing Japanese forces. Although the defenders' total number of troops was greater than the enemy's, only about 10,000 of the Philippine Army's troops were trained professional soldiers. The rest were a conglomerate of mostly poorly trained conscripts. Troop morale was high and now that everyone was clear there was nowhere to go, they were ready to make a stand and stop the Japanese Army for good. Unfortunately, there were not sufficient food, gas and medical supplies to support such a large influx of soldiers and civilians. A plan that looked good on paper fell hopelessly short in reality.

*January 2, 1942*

*Manila, Philippines*

Japanese forces enter Manila unopposed because all of MacArthur's forces had been withdrawn to the Bataan Peninsula.

*January 9-24, 1942*

*Bataan Peninsula, Philippines*

Bataan Peninsula All of MacArthur's forces had successfully withdrawn into the 30 mile long and 15 mile wide peninsula to make a stand against Homma's rapidly advancing forces. There was no escape for the over 100,000 troops and refugees corralled in the narrow spit of mostly impenetrable jungle and steep terrain. On the flatter eastside a single road cut through the thin strip of rice paddys and cane fields. This narrow passageway connected the north entrance of Bataan to Mariveles Point at the southernmost tip. It was determined earlier by military planners that the predominantly flat side of the peninsula and rugged westside made for a strong defensible position between the two. About midway, a small trail traversed between the two large volcanoes, Mount Natib and Mount Samat. This lone cobblestone trail was the only road that connected the east and west sides of Bataan.

MacArthur split the command of his eastside and westside to Major General George Parker and Major General Jonathan "Skinny" Wainright respectively. This first heavily defended line was known as the Abucay line. Rolls of barbed wire, field artillery, tank and half-track batteries backed up the rows of dug-in infantry troops along the east/central line. Thick, tangled roots and trees prevented any mechanized artillery and tanks from supporting the westside.

Although General Homma was aware that he could starve out the trapped defenders, he was under pressure from his superiors in Tokyo to take the Philippines within six weeks. Assuming that the defenders were weak and of smaller numbers, Homma's generals deduced that if they mounted a heavy bombardment and then charged the line on all fronts, the line would probably break and the defenders would retreat to Mariveles and concede defeat.

After several unsuccessful attempts to break through Parker's eastside defenders positions, Homma's general in charge withdrew his defeated troops under heavy fire from Parker's tanks, half-tracks, and artillery units. Unfortunately on the rugged westside, Japanese troops broke through the dense jungle and General Jones's defense line inflicting serious. losses and weakening Wainright's hold on the Abucay line. Realizing the whole line was going to get flanked from the west, MacArthur decided to pull back his troops to the next defensive line between Bagac and Pilar. Its boundaries were loosely defined by the cobblestone road that traversed between the east and west sides between the two volcanoes.

*January 24-26 1942*
*Bataan Peninsula, Philippines*

As the Japanese mounted a new frontal attack on the central and eastside of the crumbling Abucay line, tanks and half-tracks provided protective cover holding them back long enough for the infantry troops and refugees to withdraw about 20 miles to the new defensive line. By the 26th all of the battle weary, hungry, and malaria-ridden defenders had set up positions and were ready to fight.

Surrounded by the sea on all sides except the north made it painfully clear that unless MacArthur's forces received reinforcements and supplies, this might be their last stand.

*February 3, 1942*
*Port Moresby, New Guinea*

Japanese bomb Port Moresby, New Guinea making first steps to invade Australia and control shipping lanes to the Indian Ocean and beyond.

*February 8/9 1942*
*Singapore. Southern tip of Malay Peninsula*

Considered an impenetrable fortress because of its reinforced concrete embattlements and huge cannons facing seaward, Singapore was quickly overrun by 50,000 Japanese troops attacking, not from the sea as anticipated by the garrison of 88,000 British defenders, but from land-ward surrounding jungles from where they had marched over 600 miles down the Malay peninsula.

General Arthur E. Percival, General Officer Commanding Malaya, surrenders British forces on February 15, 1941 to Lt. General Tomoyuki Yamashita "Tiger of Malaya" in the largest capitulation of British Army troops in history. Reminiscent of the 1937 "Rape of Nanking," Japanese troops were allowed to torture, rape and kill tens of thousands of civilian inhabitants including those in hospitals and schools. Most of the British and Allied men became POW/industrial slaves to the Japanese war machine by being forced to work in mines, smelters, factories and construction sites including the infamous. Siam/Burma Railroad. Approximately 13,000 POW's died while building the ill-fated railroad line. After the war, Hollywood produced a sanitized version of the building of a bridge on the railroad line called "Bridge on the River Kwai." Over 200,000 Asian women, including some American, British and Dutch nurses, throughout the Japanese realm of conquest were forced to become "comfort women" or sex slaves for the Imperial Japanese Army.

*February 1-9, 1942*

*Bataan-westside of Bagac/Pilar line*
*Battle of the Points and Pockets*

Japanese troops that had broken through the Abucay line, together with reinforcements ferried in on barges from the north, attempted to break through in the saddle between the two volcanoes. Although U.S. torpedo boats, patched up P-40's and field artillery units fired upon and sank several barges in the bright moonlit night, the Japanese landed about half their men. Casualties mounted on both sides at an alarming rate as the battle progressed. Thick jungle conditions made this a close-in rifle and hand to hand combat fight. Philippine Scout losses numbered as many as fifty per cent in the grueling battle of attrition that was won by the intrepid defenders. Japanese troops were eventually pushed back into the sea or battled to their death rather than surrender.

*Strategic Outcome*

Following their hard fought victories, the troops' morale remained high since withdrawing to the Bagac/Pilar line.

The stalemate that followed throughout the remainder of February allowed the weary and hungry defenders an opportunity to strengthen their fragile line. Their main problems during this respite remained unconfirmed rumors, lack of food and supplies: especially quinine for malaria.

*February 19, 1942*
*On the Home Front*

Growing fear and anti-Japanese sentiment fueled the passing of Executive Order # 9066 that ordered all Japanese American citizens to leave their homes and be placed in one of ten "relocation centers." Even American born Nisei were forced to abandon their homes, jobs, and businesses under suspicion that they might be a threat to national security. Over 110,000 Japanese Americans lost their homes, businesses, jobs and freedom because of the growing paranoia that gripped the public. Young, draft-age Nisei men were allowed to enter the military service but were predominantly assigned to an all Japanese-American unit and sent to Europe. Some were utilized as interpreters in the Pacific theater. Ironically, by the end of the war, the most decorated unit recognized for heroism, combat-related casualties and outstanding duty was the Japanese-American regiment stationed in Italy.

*February 27, 1942*
*Battle of the Java Sea*

The Allied B D A fleet under he command of Dutch Admiral Karel Doorman battled Japanese Rear Admiral Takeo Tagaki without air support for several hours before The Japanese Admiral broke off and retreated.

Doorman pursued the Japanese fleet, fired upon them until enemy torpedoes eventually sank his ship and shellfire. Doorman went down with his ship the De Ruyter after ordering cruisers HMAS Perth and the U.S.S. Houston to break off. A total of five allied ships were eventually sunk.

"The fruits of war are falling into our mouths too quickly." Emperor Hirohito

*March 8,1942*
*Rangoon, Burma*

British abandon the strategically important capital city the same day as Java falls to the Japanese. These strategic victories gave the Japanese control of the major supply line road to China. The over 400 million citizens of China were cut off from the rest of the world now that Japan controlled its sea ports and land access.

*Bataan Peninsula, Philippines*

By the middle of March, the only holdouts in the Pacific against the Japanese were the stalwart American/Filipino forces on Bataan and Corregidor. Every edible food source was almost completely exhausted. indigenous. monkeys, iguanas, snakes and wild onions had been consumed by the foraging troops and refugees to augment an occasional can of old rations. The only remaining source of food were the 250 prized horses and pack mules of the 26th Cavalry. After they were slaughtered and consumed it was only a matter of time before complete starvation would eventually defeat the malaria-plagued defenders. What the Japanese soldiers couldn't do, nature accomplished rapidly as the temperature and humidity became unbearable.

*March 11,12, 1942*

Under orders from President Roosevelt, General Douglas MacArthur, his wife and young son, depart the Philippines under the cover of darkness in a small PT boat. They slipped through the enemy blockade to Mindanao then were flown by a B-17 to Australia. Upon his arrival at Adelaide Station he made his famous. vow: "I came through and I shall return." Two weeks later he was appointed Commander in Chief, South -West Pacific Area.

*March 28, 1942*
*Paris, France*

The first groups of Parisian Jews are sent to Auschwitz concentration camps for "relocation."

"In battle you will find no atheists in a foxhole"

U.S. Army Chaplain, William Cummings. Catholic Chaplain Cummings died in a POW camp.

*April 8, 1942*
*Bataan Peninsula, Philippines*

As all organized lines of defense broke down and his soldiers retreated in a disorganized frenzy amid a rain of aerial bombardment on a scale heretofore not seen by any of his troops before, Commanding General of Bataan, Edward P. King fatefully announced "We have no further means of organized resistance." He called his commanding officers together and made the decision to have his troops put up the white flag of truce at 6:00 am the next day.

PART II

# Prisoners of War

*April 9, 1942 — August 16, 1945*

CHAPTER 12

# Surrendered

*April 9, 1942*
*Bataan, Philippines*

I was prepared to fight the final battle with about twenty brave, exhausted American and Filipino soldiers I had never met before. We were in this together, ready to fight to the end, and I didn't even know their names. *Where is the Chillicothe Kid, Captain Perrenot and Brewster?*

As we waited in our foxholes with our rifles pointed across the airfield, I heard the familiar sound of tank engines as they approached our position. Once again the odds were stacked in their favor — all we had were rifles and pistols.

Our eyes and guns were fixed on the line of trees that bordered the north side of the airfield. Tension rose among the men as they listened to the tanks getting louder and closer. *We might have a chance to make it difficult for the infantry, but against their tanks?*

A cold chill ran down my spine as the first Japanese tank nosed its turret through the brush directly across the field from of us. The brownish-green camouflaged tank stopped at the edge, and revolved its turret back and forth slowly as though sizing up the distance to our feeble line of defense. This was it. Since the Japs had begun their massive offensive six days ago on Good Friday, they had pushed us to the southernmost end of the Bataan Peninsula. Between the twenty or so American and Filipino soldiers, we had no weapon larger than a 30 caliber rifle. None of our machine guns, grenades, mortars, or anything else had the firepower to inflict any damage on enemy tanks.

*God I wish we had a half-track and its powerful 75-mm cannon right now.*

Through the noise of the idling engine of the Japanese tank across the airstrip, we heard the sound of two other enemy tanks getting closer. No one said a word as we waited for the tanks to emerge from the trees.

Moments before the other tanks appeared there was a commotion and arguing about an order from General King that was being passed down the line.

"What the hell's going on?" I asked the guy beside me. He just shrugged his shoulders.

"We're ordered to surrender! Open your breech and tie a rag to the end of your muzzle," yelled one of the men who might have been an officer.

"What the hell? Is this for real?" I asked the soldier again.

"Is this some kind of Jap trick?" he retorted incredulously.

"Everybody is beginning to do it," I replied. "What do you think?"

The sudden turn of events was hard to comprehend. I was prepared to die at that lonely airstrip. In a flash everything had changed. I was not prepared to surrender to this enemy. I had fought at the front day and night. I even hoped that eventually MacArthur and reinforcements would arrive. But this was the reality. The Japanese had us backed against the sea and, according to the communication from General King, we were ordered to surrender our weapons immediately. *So this is it? What happened to all those strategic withdrawal plans? Damn, I'm mad.*

From the cover on the other side of the airfield, a Japanese officer walked out and shouted, "Surrender your weapons!" His perfect pronunciation surprised me and his words struck home. Our military forces had been defeated in Bataan.

All I had left was a handful of bullets, my rifle, mess kit, canteen, and my harmonica. I vowed they would not get my harmonica so I quickly stuffed it in my boot before they had a chance to inspect us.

The Japanese officer pointed with his long sword to a large rock on the side of the dirt airfield and barked out the order, "Place your weapons here! Now!"

Slowly, our small group rose and stood with our weapons breeches open, above our heads. Across the airstrip were four tanks and about a hundred Japanese infantry soldiers with rifles and machine guns that pointed ominously at us. Covered with dirt, sweat, and blood, we walked toward the boulder. Our troops were finally advancing, but only to surrender our weapons.

The closer I walked toward the rock, the angrier I became. I never could stand to give up on anything. When I started something, I finished it. *This didn't feel right.*

One at a time, the men leaned their weapons against the rock and walked in the direction another Japanese officer was pointing for us to go. It was now my turn to place my weapon down. I was so angry that it had come to this that I felt I could burst. Rifle above my head, left hand on end of the barrel, right hand on the stock, I stared at that big boulder with all our rifles leaning against it. Rage screamed inside my head as I swung my rifle down as hard as I could on the top of the rock. The stock on the rifle snapped in two at the grip and I dropped the barrel to the ground. *Oh God, they're definitely going to shoot me now!* Lost in the moment's silence, I stared at my broken Springfield lying in the dirt. It had been my faithful friend from the beginning. It never failed me once in four months of fighting the enemy. Now its steel barrel lay bent and useless on Cabcaben Field.

I lifted my head and saw the neat even row of Japanese infantry soldiers in khaki uniforms glaring at me down the barrels of their Arisaka rifles, ready to pull the triggers to end all this madness. Those few seconds seemed like an eternity, as I waited for my fate at the command of the Japanese officer.

*By Ex-POW Ben Steele*

The Japanese officer broke the nervous silence when he screamed in perfect diction, "Over there!" He motioned me to join the other captured soldiers.

We were a sad and pathetic sight to see: warriors worn out and hungry, ready to collapse from exhaustion, malnutrition, and dysentery. General MacArthur had said, "I shall return!" Well, he didn't return in time, and we fought with what we had, but it wasn't enough.

Corralled like cattle, we were moved to the beach end of the runway facing

Manila Bay and told to sit on the hot sand. Suddenly a US gunboat roared into sight from around the westernmost point of the peninsula and stopped about two hundred yards offshore. The enemy officer had placed us strategically between his troops and the gunboat. If the sailors on board the gunboat were going to fire at the Japanese positioned behind us, we would be in harm's way. The Japanese officer screamed into his radio and within twenty seconds Japanese soldiers wheeled a field artillery cannon behind us to fire on the gunboat, aiming its cannon in our direction. The unscrupulous Japanese commander was going to use prisoners of war as living shields. Not taking any chances, we sprawled as flat as we could on the hot sand with only our heads high enough to see the action about to take place on both sides of us. There was no doubt in my mind that the Japanese were going to fire as soon as they could get a bead on the idling gunboat. As the Japanese scrambled to prepare their cannon, my eyes were glued on the boat's big gun and I waited to see the telltale puff of smoke from its muzzle that signaled an incoming projectile. We were caught between a rock and a hard place. The gunboat fired a round that slammed into the beach with a loud thud about twenty yards to our right without exploding and slid along the beach burning the dry grass on the embankment. Since I knew firsthand what kind of damage an exploding artillery shell could do, I didn't know whether to get up and make a run for it, or lay there hoping the gunboat's artillery man got a good fix after that last shot.

Before I had time to make up my mind, the next shell arrived, but this time it was not a dud. It was dead on target, shaking the beach violently. The artillery piece behind us exploded into fragments that rained down in big chunks. One Japanese soldier's body flew by like a man shot out of a cannon at the circus. Another soldier was running around in hysterics with his face resembling a plate of spaghetti. *Man, those guys could shoot — maybe it was Captain Perrenot at the helm.* The US gunboat sped off as quickly as it arrived, because if they had stayed any longer the Japanese tanks would have had a fix on them.

Surrendered *U.S. Archives*

**The Voice of Bataan**

Bataan has fallen.
With heads bloody but unbowed, we yield to the enemy.
Besieged by land and blockaded by sea,
We have done all that human endurance could bear.
What sustained us was a force more than merely physical.
It was a force of unconquerable faith:
Something in the soul that is immortal!
It is the thought of native land.
All the world will testify.
Men fighting with an unshakeable faith
are made of something more than flesh;
But we are not made of impervious steel.
The flesh must yield at last,
and the rest of the battle must come.
Bataan has fallen.
But the spirit that made it stand
— a beacon to all the world —
Cannot fall…
Our defeat is our victory.

*Defender of Bataan and Corrigidor Salvador P. Lopez*

CHAPTER 13

# The Death March

*April 10 – 14, 1942*

With bayonets pointed at us, they prodded us into a line and marched us north up the main road to a fenced corral filled with other prisoners. Stripped of everything but our clothes, boots and mess kits, I managed to keep hidden a small bottle of iodine and my harmonica.

Corregidor Island Before the Pacific War *Courtesy of Loback Family*

Thunderous Japanese heavy artillery fire directed at Corregidor Island made sleeping difficult for most of us. The night sky lit up fiery red and orange with each explosion that struck less than five miles across the dark water of Manila Bay. The continual onslaught of firepower directed at Corregidor must have struck every square inch of the lone island fortress.

Throughout the bleak night, I woke up several times and saw my fellow soldiers laying like infants — their elbows, knees and heads curled up into fetal positions. Moans and muffled cries, mixed with the gurgling of empty bellies, broke the silence between the explosions on Corregidor. Some malaria-plagued soldiers mumbled incoherently in fever-induced delirium. I knew if I didn't get quinine soon, I too would have to endure the miserable effects of the infection when it flared up again.

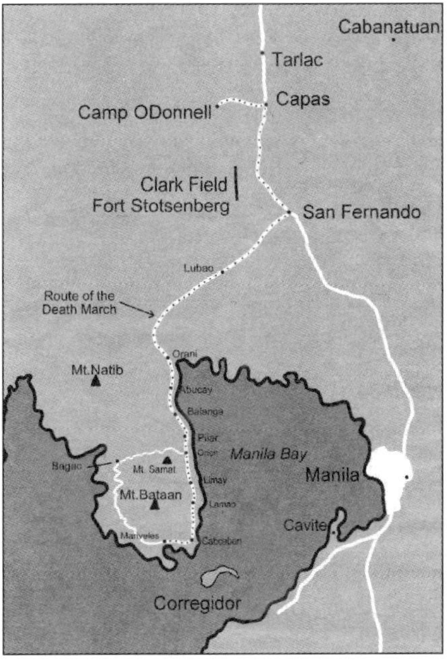


Route of the Death March
*By Francisco Lovato*

It was hard to accept that after all that had happened in the past four months we had come to this. In all the possible scenarios that I had considered, including death, I never imagined I would become a prisoner of war. At that moment, I felt abandoned by whoever allowed us to fight a war without the means to win. What hurt the most was the abject frustration of fighting for four months without communication or enough food, medicine, and ammo. Every time we took the fight towards the enemy, and were able to shove them back, we'd have to retreat because we ran low on ammunition and supplies. Until the day before, I believed Captain Perrenot and his superiors had a plan for us to fight and eventually defeat the Japanese invaders. No matter how bad it looked, we always felt we had a fighting chance.

I remembered what I'd seen on the newsreels following China's defeat in Nanking and I sensed that our nightmare was only beginning at the hands of our Japanese captors. Watching the explosions light up the night, I kept hearing Dad's words running through my brain, "Never, ever give up! Never! Pay attention to what is going on. Do the right thing. Do your best with what you have. Trust in God."

Early the next morning the guards screamed, *"Hyacco! Hyacco! Hyacco!"* (Pronounced HIGH ah coo, meaning "Hurry up!") With long sticks and bamboo poles, the Japanese forced us to form a line, two abreast, back onto the main road to begin the march north again. Through the hounding commands of the guards, I heard what sounded like the sharp crack of a baseball bat splintering into pieces directly behind me. I turned around and saw a Japanese soldier standing menacingly over a poor fellow on the ground. He had hit the soldier so viciously his thick wooden pole had broken. The Japanese soldier screeched, "Up! *Hyacco! Hyacco!*" as he jumped up and down, beating the bleeding soldier with the broken end of his pole.

We were quickly pushed forward by the other guards who themselves were worked into a frenzy and starting to beat the rest of us with their poles. It was obvious that we were going to be treated with little dignity, since our captors had already broken the rules of the Geneva Convention, which outline the fair and humane treatment of prisoners. First they had used us as human shields on the beach, and now they chose to beat us mercilessly for no reason.

More groups of marchers filled the long and dusty road in front and behind us. I recognized a few men from the "200th" whom I hadn't seen since we'd been separated in December. By the looks on everyone faces, it was vividly obvious that the effects and deprivation of the last four months of war had taken a toll on everyone's health. Back in December, before war was declared, we were the happy-go-lucky, cocky, devil-be-damned tough guys of the "Fighting 200th." We had earned this reputation by winning bar-room battles in Juarez, Mexico, El Paso, Texas, and on the training field at Fort Bliss.

The Japanese soldiers were cleanly shaven and their uniforms were in good shape. On the other hand, we looked like a hobo army. Our khaki's were tattered and torn, and we had dirty bodies and unshaven faces. Forced to walk three or four abreast down the middle of the road, we tried not to stumble over each other, which would waste precious energy or provoke a whipping. Local Filipino villagers along the dusty road waved and shouted words of encouragement to us as we trudged along. Their faces revealed sympathy for our plight. Japanese trucks passed us heading south, filled with troops and supplies, then returned empty, and choked us with more dust and gas fumes.

*"Hyacco! Hyacco!"* All morning we walked in the blazing sun without a rest break or a stop for water from the many artesian wells. One of the guards taunted us to join him as he drank large swallows of the crystal clear water, while the other guards prodded us onward. He purposely spilled the precious liquid into the dirt and laughed. If anyone had accepted his treacherous offer, I'm certain he would have paid with his life. The guard made it clear by his theatrical actions that his offer was merely to give himself the opportunity to have fun at our expense.

Japanese guard threatens to kill fallen POW *By Ex-POW Ben Steele*

Japanese trucks brought a group of fresh guards about every four hours. Each group made a point of establishing their authority by first yelling, jeering, and beating on us with their poles then making us walk faster while they constantly screamed. The brutal whippings were as humiliating as they were painful. They shamed us for losing the battle and surrendering.

With each painful mile of nonstop marching, the blazing sun's heat, former battle injuries, malaria, dysentery, and constant whippings began to take their toll on the weakest marchers. Slowing down or stopping brought on savage beatings and worse — a bayonet. We heard the blood-curdling wails of a man bayoneted in his abdomen, curled up in a fetal position and left to die a slow and excruciating death beside the road. The Japanese gave us horrific reminders of what our fate would be if we stopped or opposed their orders. There was no doubt we were dispensable and they would kill us if we resisted.

We carried the weak on our shoulders as far as we could and encouraged them to keep walking. We kept repeating, "Hold on. Don't give up." Those who said, "I can't" usually could not maintain the pace. It was as though the declaration of "I can't," was always a self-fulfilling prophecy. With my father's admonition that, "If you say you can't, you won't. If you say you can, you will," reeling in my mind, I resolved that I could. *I can go on. I can make it. I will make it.* I kept repeating silently to myself when the thirst and the pain made me want to drop.

All that first day we marched toward an unknown destination up the dusty road. We were on the main road along the eastern coast that connected southern and northern Bataan Peninsula. I wondered where we were marching and how long it would take, because I knew that if the pace or starvation didn't kill us, the sun surely would.

Into the night we staggered like winos, heads drooped, arms hanging limply, exhausted into semi-consciousness. "When are we going to stop?" mumbled a marcher. "I can't go on much more," said another voice from the humid darkness. "I'm going to drop." We had been marching continuously for almost fifteen hours with only one short ten-minute break.

Somewhere outside a small village, we were herded into a wire-fenced cattle yard, ripe with the smell of animal feces and urine. Realizing these were our accommodations for the night, I collapsed onto the ground, curled into a fetal ball, and slept like a dead man.

Death Marchers eat before a full day of marching in hottest weather of the year
*By Ex-POW Ben Steele*

*April 11 1942*

Daybreak and frenzied shouts of Japanese orders came without warning. It seemed that we had no sooner arrived at the cattle yard to rest, when the screaming began again announcing it was time to begin marching. During the short night, two of the men in our group had died. Their bodies were left in the corral as we filed out and were given a dirty, gelatinous cup of rice gruel to eat. It was pasty and smelled of fouled water. Because our stomachs ached for sustenance, we slurped it down anyway not knowing when we would eat again. Some of the men regurgitated the foul substance into the dirt. Needless to say, no one received second servings. The guards shrieked, *"Hyacco! Hyacco!"* as they prodded us out onto the road to begin the day's northward march. We were forced to march double time for the first few hours of the morning. I tried not to think of the horrors that befell my buddies at the hands of these sadists. Moans of pain from the injured accompanied us as we pushed our bodies beyond their limits of physical recovery. All I could do was put my head down and beg my aching, throbbing legs to keep moving one more step on the dusty road. Fresh blood oozed from our broken wounds that had neither medicine nor time to heal. If we slowed the guards struck our backs to keep us almost running. I knew that if I fell no one would have the energy to help pick me up. It was do or die and I wasn't ready to die, so I forced myself to keep moving with the group of men at the front of the column. Behind us where the slower, more injured and weakened marchers struggled, the cries of the beaten and bayoneted men pierced the air. Even though I was physically able to keep up with the faster group, my mind kept drifting in and out of consciousness. Sometimes I saw my own feet stepping in front of me and I thought they were somebody else's. My mind kept saying, "Keep moving!" And somehow my burning legs obeyed.

A small signpost marked the entrance into the village of Pilar where a large mission church stood in the center. By now, the noonday sun baked the hard-packed road like an iron skillet that scorched my haggard feet and sun-burned flesh. It was here, in front of the church, that I witnessed a vicious murder of one of our boys by a Japanese officer. The officer screamed at a fallen GI, who was on his hands and knees and couldn't stand up. He pulled out his razor sharp saber and with a sweeping blow, chopped off the soldier's head. For a second, the GI's body quivered, then dropped to the ground and blood gushed from his neck. My stomach wretched as the poor boy's severed head fell with a thud on the hard-packed dirt and rolled on its side with the eyes still open. The Japanese officer had a crazed expression and stood triumphantly over the decapitated soldier. He swung his sword back above his head as if he was going to strike a second blow.

Australian War Archives

Instead, he kicked the soldier's bloody head off the road in a show of absolute power, wiped the blood off the saber, and ceremoniously slid the glistening, long handled sword back into its scabbard.

"Damn that son of a bitch," I mumbled. Never had I hated someone so much. *He didn't have to kill that poor boy. What is wrong with these crazy people? I wasn't expecting anything decent, but this?*

"Hyacco! Hyacco!" Blows from our guards thundered down on the rest of us. They wanted us to keep moving without interruption. Now there was no doubt what our fate would be if we didn't move forward.

Since the Japanese had conquered the Philippines, death and suffering would be our immediate fate. The number of bodies of our dead or dying buddies continued to grow with each gruesome mile. My mind poisoned with malaria, still pushed me forward, one painful step at a time. I had to keep moving or they would pave this road with my body, too. I had a plan to fulfill. I needed to get home, gain the rank I was promised, meet and marry the most wonderful woman in the world, raise two boys and two girls, then retire and live the rest of my life in my beautiful New Mexico. My dream would keep me alive, God willing.

The malaria drained my energy causing me to lag behind the faster group. I knew from the previous day's experiences that getting water was next to impossible if I was not near the front. The guards only allowed water to the first half of the prisoners at each stop. I didn't understand what was on their minds, and all they said was *hyacco. If we were all killed, would anyone besides these sadistic monsters, ever know the pain and suffering we endured?* We were the Battling Bastards of Bataan. Would our poem live on after we died? In my head it echoed

We're the Battling Bastards of Bataan
No mama, no papa, no Uncle Sam,
No aunts, no uncles, no nephews, no nieces,
No rifles, no guns, no artillery pieces,
And nobody gives a damn.

Whoever had written it before the surrender epitomized our condition and plight, then and now. Would our countries and our families ever hear the stories of the brave men who fought the Japanese invaders and our own individual battles just to keep alive? Above all, would they ever know just how much we loved them? I thought, Whatever happens to me here in the jungles of the Philippines, God bless my dear family and God bless America.

We kept walking, stumbling over the bodies of those who died before us. All the while we fought the aching desire to quit and end all our pain. I prayed to God, the Holy Mother, and all the blessed saints that our suffering would end.

I was weary, fever burned my brain, and it took a mental effort to make my feet walk. My ankles were swollen as big as grapefruits and the first day's blisters were raw, cherry red sores that burned like salt was in the open wounds. The dribbles of sweat running off my face stung my eyes, and wet my parched lips. I was afraid that if my tongue swelled any larger it would be impossible to breathe. With a borrowed penknife, I cut holes in my boots where the raw spots of skin bled. Every muscle ached for rest; there was no part of me that didn't hurt.

My head swam with questions, while I tried to keep my body moving. I was becoming delirious from the heat, the malaria and from the death and suffering all around me. The searing heat of the tropical sun beat down on our dehydrated bodies. *Why are the Japanese being so cruel to us? Without water how will we be able to go on? The body can't exist without water. I've seen caged animals die after three days in the heat. Would this ever end? Where were they taking us?*

A man in front of me dropped to his knees, while crying out in pitiful moans, "I can't go on. Please, water." Whimpering incoherently, his back and head were bowed, his spirit was broken. I knew the guards would kill him when they saw him. Though hardly able to keep our own weary bodies vertical and moving, we attempted to lift him to his feet before a guard saw him.

"Come on Buddy, get up. We'll help you," we muttered. Stumbling to pick up his crumpled body, we all fell down on the hard-parched road. More pain shot through my muscles, as I tried to spit out the choking dirt, but there was no saliva in my mouth. Other guys started to lift us up by our arms. "Get up, Buddy! Get up!" The words seemed to come from far way. God, I felt like lying there for just a minute more. I was down and didn't want to get up. Then I could hear my mother and father talking to me: "Get up Frank! Keep walking! Don't give up!"

"Come on, buddy, get up! Let's go! "Hurry, the Japs are coming! The Japs are coming!"

The Japs were always coming. They came out of the air at Clark Field, they came in droves in landing boats from the sea at Lingayen, they came through the night in tanks, and they came through the trees, screaming like banshees. "Snap to it! Don't give up!" With a helping hand from my fellow marchers, I got back on my feet and continued. I took one step, then another, and another

"What about the guy that was down?" I asked the fellow trudging along beside me. Without looking up, he just shook his head slowly. *Poor suffering Bastard of Bataan. God rest his soul. His hell on earth is over. He's out of the nightmare. Oh God, when will this end?*

*"Hyacco!"* From out of nowhere came the sharp crack and the pain of a pole slamming across my back. I had become a target in the open road as I staggered toward a group of marchers, trying to muster my strength from the last fall. The guards didn't permit us to stray from our little groups.

Barely walking, I dreamed of when I would return home. *Only those of us who would survive this march of death would believe the hell we were going through.* One more step. One more excruciating step. *Do or die! "Hail Mary full of grace the Lord is with thee"* One more step. *"Blessed art thou amongst women, and blessed is the fruit of thy womb Jesus"* Another step. *God bless my parents and family.* They gave me my faith in God. If I did not have my faith, I knew I would have lost my mind by now. *Pray. Keep the faith. Keep walking. "Holy Mary Mother of God. Pray for us soldiers, now and at the hour of our death. Amen."*

Hour after endless hour, we marched toward uncertainty. The thoughts of my family and my faith supported me in staying alive, one more step. The grotesque, bloated bodies alongside the road increased with each passing mile, and served as vivid reminders. A foolish stumble or a twisted ankle would result in a bayonet in the groin. The burning sun beat on my back and brain, hotter than I remembered high noon on the desert in New Mexico. We had so little water and rest. I had only eaten my golf-ball size portion of dirty brown rice on this day. Some of the slower guys hadn't received any. *Did they expect us to walk in this sun all day and into the night with no food or water?*

To my right, there was a rustle in the thick vegetation as a green mango rolled from the bushes into the column of marchers. Someone must have been hiding in the brush trying to get food to us. If the guards saw them, the local

Filipinos would be murdered. Oh, please God, let one of those fruits make it to me. I walked by looking out of the corner of my eye at the source of the fruit, but no luck this time. My stomach growled at the mere thought of the possibility of food. I was hungrier now, thinking that I might have tasted a bite of the wet, sweet mango from heaven. Maybe next time I would be the lucky one.

As we were crossing over a small river, an American colonel walked to the edge of the bridge, stopped and stared blankly at the deep crevice below. "Come along, Sir. You've got to keep walking. Don't let them see you. They'll clobber you, Sir," I said. He was in a dreamlike state, oblivious to me and everyone around him. His head hung limply, chin on chest, as he gazed at the river and rocks about twenty feet below. I felt as though he was thinking of jumping down to a more certain fate.

"Let's go, Sir," I pleaded along with a couple of the other soldiers.

"I can't go on," he said with a resigned sigh. His eyes had a far away look — maybe he saw a farmhouse in Kansas or a river in Ohio. I didn't know. Maybe he was in a dream or deep in memories of better times back home with family and friends. Maybe he was thinking of fishing at his favorite river when he was a kid, but he was not thinking of marching — not anymore.

"We must keep moving, Sir," I said as I fell back alongside the others. Suddenly a baby-faced guard came running up to the colonel, roaring commands in Japanese at the top of his lungs. The colonel didn't flinch or even blink at the guard's antics. He just stood there silently and oblivious to his frenetic commands.

"Come on, Colonel. Come on," I whispered. "Something bad is going to happen if you don't."

Looking back over my shoulder I saw the Japanese guard pull out his pistol and shoot the colonel in the back of the head. Oh No! Oh God! A crimson spray of blood burst from the colonel's head. His body crumpled forward over the edge of the bridge and tumbled down the rocks into the dark water. Watching him die, I screamed inside my skull, "Damn you to hell, you merciless bastard!"

They used any opportunity to kill us. These soldiers had gone mad in a blood lust. I remembered reading the newspaper reports about the "Rape of Nanking," and about the atrocities the Japanese committed against the Chinese. It was almost too horrible to believe at the time, but now I was seeing their cruelty firsthand. "God bless you, Colonel, whoever you are," I whispered. "You're free now."

Mile after mile we walked northward through the choking powder of the dirt road. The memory of the colonel was fresh in my mind. I would never forget that distant look in his eyes as he stood, feet perched on the edge of the railless bridge. He knew his time had come. They say that at the moment of death our entire life passes before us, like a motion picture. It seemed as though he were watching that movie. I prayed he had a full life up to that moment. Thank God, no one in his family will ever know about the grief and misery that had brought him to that bridge across eternity. *Is this the end of freedom and now will the Japanese rule the world? Did MacArthur understand their mentality when he left us behind? Will anyone ever know?*

Finally, we had a break for water and a change of the guards. A Japanese jeep pulled up to the group of guards going off duty. There was a commotion and yelling. The officer in the jeep singled out the guard who had shot the colonel, and they both walked to the opposite side of the road. The officer began ranting and raving at the top of his lungs at the guard, who cringed in terror, almost in tears. The guard's worried comrades huddled together like schoolboys and watched nervously as the baby-faced guard got his butt chewed out by the raging officer. *Good! Finally the little Jap bastard has his sorry ass on the grill. Does this have anything to do with the colonel?*

The guard's face turned pale. He stood with his head bowed toward the officer. "Good, he is in deep trouble," I smirked to the fellow beside me. Suddenly, the officer drew his pistol and fired point blank into the forehead of the guard. The guard's head jerked back as his body crumpled to the ground. Shocked by the demonstration of command, my mind reeled over our chances for survival. I shook my head in disgust and hoped their civilian people had a higher respect for human life.

I remembered that Captain Perrenot said the Japanese soldiers had a code of honor that made dying for their emperor and Japan the greatest honor a soldier can achieve, while surrendering was considered a disgrace. Americans, on the other hand, were fighting for human ideals and values, not personal honor. I only thought of survival on this road littered with the bodies of my fellow soldiers.

*"Hyacco! Hyacco!"* shouted the guards. Stride after painful stride, we marched and died on the endless road north. The endless beatings pushed us faster. The group changed faces, as those who were ahead fell to the back. Faces were missing, faces of those who marched no more. It was close to nightfall, and we kept on marching. The guards were changed again to keep them fresh and alert. They were young men like us, kids no older than twenty, who had other lives before the war. They must have had families, maybe like mine. I wondered if I would have liked them as friends or neighbors if we weren't at war.

What was it like in Japan? Did they have deserts and mountains? History told us about wars and battles and conquests, but what did it teach us about the people who lived and died? The history books teach us about generals, kings, and queens, but no one ever tells us about the people who are chosen to die. I wondered what history would say about "I shall return" MacArthur? Well, one thing was for certain. He didn't return in time to give us half a chance against the Japanese army. I prayed that someday I would have the chance to tell everyone how brave and courageous we were. There were no newsreels, no photographers; only those who made it home would remember this war. I prayed to God that I would be one that did.

All day long we marched in the burning sun with only one fifteen-minute break. They pushed us beyond limits of the human body. My malaria was getting worse with each passing hour. I felt burning hot on the inside, as my skin shivered cold at the same time. Weaker and weaker, I trudged on in a semi-conscious daze. My mind was foggy, and it was hard to comprehend anything but the wrenching agony of the disease eating my body.

Don't give up! Never give up! Keep walking! I repeated to myself when my body wanted to drop. It would be a miracle if I made it. Quinine was a luxury of the past; we had run out over six weeks ago. I had heard that the Japanese didn't have any either — not that it mattered, because they wouldn't have shared it. If they were trying to kill us by marching, then malaria was their quiet ally.

Finally, we stopped for the night. I was beyond exhaustion. My body kept moving in my mind, even though I was lying flat and still. The words, hyacco, hyacco rang in my ears and mixed with the painful cries of those bayoneted or beaten to death and left along the road to rot. I know that my father's words sustained my spirit throughout this death march. This night I wanted to dream of home, dream of my dear mother and father, dream of my sisters Polly and Annie, and my brothers A.T., Joe and Abel. I prayed I would hold them again and feel their loving arms around me. *Dear Lord, please save me.*

At first light the yells of Japanese guards awoke us from our dead sleep. *"Hyacco!" God, don't they know any other words?* The guards were scurrying around counting us in Japanese as though something was wrong. Apparently, some Filipino prisoners had escaped into the jungle during the night. The Filipinos knew their way around the jungle and would hopefully join up with other guerrilla fighters. They prodded us to form a line for food. A Japanese guard dispensed the globs of dirty rice onto our mess kit plates for breakfast. How can we live on this? I was so sick with the malaria I could hardly eat. Knowing I would die if I didn't, I forced myself to swallow the pasty, dirty food just to stay alive. The dejected faces of those around me revealed their suffering and pain. The gooey rice tasted more like glue than food. We had no water other than what was carried in our canteens from yesterday's fill. The sun seemed hotter on this day as they whipped us into the marching line on the road. Every step forward stung like fire, and my wounds throbbed with each heartbeat. I had rubbed iodine on them to keep them from getting infected, but it didn't seem to be doing much good. Finally we came upon some water at a dirty stream. One at a time, they allowed us to fill our canteens with the foul-looking water. Desperate, we took our chances on the only water they allowed us to drink.

Ex-POW Ben Steele

Suddenly, after only about half of us had filled our canteens, screaming guards and warning gunshots were followed by the cries of the men who didn't get any water. Again more than half of the men were turned away. "Oh God, please," begged the injured, the weak, and the dehydrated. I wished I could help them in some way, but I wasn't moving very fast myself, because the fever was coming back. This was a hell of a place to lose physical strength. I had just barely made the waterline cutoff. I pulled out the tiny bottle of iodine and put a few drops into the muddy water. I hoped that the iodine might kill the bacteria in my canteen. Dad's words rang again in my mind. Pay attention to what the drill instructors teach you in boot camp. It might seem unimportant today, but it may save your life someday. The instructors had told us to use the iodine to purify any foul water or infected injuries.

We had marched over forty miles in two days. I looked ahead and saw three guards laughing and yelling, while kicking someone on the ground. As I got closer I saw that they were kicking a fallen man's mouth to knock out his teeth for his gold fillings. I was fading back into semi-consciousness because of the effects of the malaria. I felt like a boxer knocked out on his feet, automatically moving in the direction of his brain's last message to his body. *Keep going. Keep moving. Don't stop.* Thank God I loved sports and ate plenty of nutritious food growing up to keep myself in good physical shape. I needed every ounce of strength I could muster to keep my legs from collapsing and signing my death warrant. I hardly remember anything else the rest of that day, other than being hit by the guards until I collapsed on the ground when it was dark. When the malaria flared up, it was hard to remember my own name.

*April 13, 1942*

Once again, the morning light and the high-pitched screaming voices of Japanese guards came too soon. My head felt clearer than it had the day before as I stood up to get in the food line. It was so hard to remember anything anymore. My life's purpose was to put one foot in front of the other, and to guard my head from the blows of the bamboo poles. During the night, wild animals had fed on the dead bodies along the road, which left them mutilated, adding to the grotesque landscape and giving us a cruel reminder to keep up with the group.

Everyone staggered about at first until the guard whipped us into a line. The excruciating pain of being struck on the back with a bamboo pole takes my breath away. It was hard to imagine that we would be able to march another day in the intense heat. Men stayed alive by walking. Falling and not getting up guaranteed that they would never get up again. Men fell because they were too weak from battle injuries which had not been treated, too weak from the malaria that ravaged minds and bodies, too weak from being beaten on the head and body, and too weak from little food. Some fell because their minds gave up the will to live.

I remembered coming down this road in better days with G-Battery. During this march I had not seen anyone from our half-track unit. The few guys I did recognize were from New Mexico and the 200th. I had come over to the Philippines with them in September. I hadn't seen my best friends from Albuquerque, Herman Tafoya or Arthur Garde, since I was transferred to G-Battery on the day the war started. I prayed they were doing better, since I was on the edge of complete collapse with every step.

The guards spit on us and prodded and taunted us. Seeing a marcher bend over and painfully defecate a stream of blood from the effects of an attack of dysentery elicited peals of laughter from our guards, as they pointed their bayonets at the suffering soldier's bare buttocks and screeched some ridiculing epithet. I thought that if I had had any strength left, I would have snatched one of their poles and crammed it down one of their throats. According to my catechism teachings, Jesus felt as though he had been abandoned. "Father, why have you forsaken me?" he asked while hanging on the cross. It seemed as though we too, had been forsaken and left to die by MacArthur.

Dad had always said in Spanish, "Cava cavesa es un mundo." Every head is a world. Every man's thoughts exist in a world of his own. We don't see the world as it is; we see it as we are." I couldn't imagine Americans treating anyone the way we were being treated by those young Japanese soldiers.

During brief water stop at a carabao wallow I heard a rumor that we were heading to a train at San Fernando. At least we might be able to sit down on a flatbed or an open boxcar. Anything would be better than this infernal marching. The predominant questions among the men were where were we going and what are they going to do with us? We finally arrived at the train. A sea of exhausted men who preceded us on the march were waiting to be loaded into the boxcars. A few of the luckier men huddled under the sparse spots of shade. The rest of them sat back to back in the blinding sun. Getting a chance to rest our feet, even if it was in the sun, was better than walking. I thought this would be an opportunity to see if I could find some of my friends from the 200th or G-Battery. This was the first time in the four days of marching I had a chance to look.

I stepped slowly through the field of the fatigued and near dead. The men looked up at me; their sweaty faces revealed their abject despair and pain. Dark, sunken eyes had witnessed their worst nightmare, an experience so horrible, it couldn't have been imagined. Suddenly in the field of unfamiliar faces, I spotted Lieutenant Shamblin of the 200th; his head lay limp on the leg of another collapsed marcher. Shamblin had always been one officer to avoid. He seemed to enjoy belittling Spanish-Americans with his superior attitude and officer status. He was part of the reason I asked Captain Grimmer for a transfer, and although his prejudiced behavior was a thorn in my side, he wasn't my enemy. He was about to die.

I knelt down on one knee beside him and tried to encourage him. "Lieutenant, it's me, Lovato. Hang in there, Lieutenant."

Everyone stood up around us. The cry of *"Hyacco, hyacco"* signaled time to begin loading onto the train. The lieutenant looked at me with the eyes of a man breathing his last breath. I had seen this look too many times before on the battlefield.

I said, "God bless you, Lieutenant." Even though his eyes stared at me, I don't think he heard me. His breaths were short and shallow through his open mouth. He was in a death stupor, the place somewhere between life and death only those who die will ever know. I cradled him in my arms like a mother holds her baby, as he lay there looking at me, helpless and dying. He said nothing. His eyes stared peacefully into mine before closing forever. I prayed, "God bless you, Lieutenant, and may God take your soul from this hell." As I laid his head down on the hard Philippine soil, I thought how ironic it was that I, a Spanish-American, would be there with him at the time of his death. He acted like he had hated Americans of a different color. Maybe he would find eternal peace and understanding where he was going now.

Herded again, we lined up in front of the row of closed boxcars. As the guards swung open the wooden doors of the stinking cattle cars they commanded us to crawl into the dark, hot bench-less dungeons on wheels. With bayonets pointed at our backs they crammed us into the cars. The guards forced us in, stuffing us like sardines into a can. The doors slammed shut, squeezing us so tightly we could hardly breathe the hot stifling air. Agonizing moans and cries called out for more air in the hot wood and metal boxcars.

"I can't breathe," whimpered someone fading in the darkness. We begged for the doors to be opened. Small cracks in the wooden walls allowed only a sliver of sunlight and hardly any fresh air to enter. Men fortunate enough to be squeezed against the exterior walls pressed their noses against cracks to inhale any amount of air. Our hot sweaty bodies were sandwiched in so tightly I thought we would surely die of asphyxiation or heat stroke if we had to stay in the oven very long.

"Oh God please end this," groaned a soldier.

With a heavy jerk the train lurched forward, probably taking us inland away from the coast where our rescue would be more difficult. If MacArthur has any plans for returning now, it would be most appreciated! The tugging motion of the locomotive jerked the boxcars backward and forward, and because the rolling coffins were overloaded, they began rocking sideways as well. The putrid stench of our own filthy bodies mixed with acrid smells of cattle feces and the dizzying motion in the claustrophobic darkness caused many of the men to vomit uncontrollably. *How much worse can this get?*

"He's dead on his feet. Let him drop," shouted someone in the suffocating darkness.

A dying man's whimpering last cry of "Mama" faded across the borderline of life, as he sank to the floor and died unceremoniously. It would break his mother's heart to know her son died in so much pain. Perhaps in that final brief moment, he would find comfort in her loving, smiling face one last time before his heart surrendered the gift of life she had given him.

The floor was wet and slippery from blood, urine, vomit, and the uncontrolled defecation of those with amoebic dysentery. Anyone who dropped to the floor, if not dead already, would surely die in the disease-ridden sewage of the boxcar. Praying I wouldn't pass out and fall, I locked my knees and stood staring upward gasping for air. Every muscle burned the raw blisters on my feet and the open wounds on my legs stung from the vile excrement that sloshed on the floor.

My mind floated in a fog of rancid hot air, and I clung to a thread of life wrought with indescribable pain. Somehow this can't last forever! Dad's words repeating in my mind, and kept me going with each labored breath. *Keep the faith. Keep the dream. I'm going to return home to my beloved New Mexico, get the rank I was promised, marry, have children, and eventually retire in the land of enchantment, and see my children and grand babies grow up in a world of peace. So help me God. This can't last forever. I prayed.*

After several hours of what seemed like eternity, the train slowed down and stopped abruptly. Almost at once, the wooden door opened, letting in sunlight, fresh air, and the cries of "hyacco!" Almost in unison, we all gasped for the fresh air while trying to make our way over the dead bodies and out of the stifling boxcar into the Capas Station near Tarlac.

Stumbling and falling out the boxcar onto the hard-packed ground, we were immediately lined up by the new guards. The dead were left hideously sprawled on the foul floor of the death train. Guards wielding sticks counted the disembarking "lucky ones" then allowed us to sit and rest. Dazed and staggering to stay upright long enough to find a patch of shade from the blazing sun, I first emptied my boots of scum so I could walk again without falling. I was exhausted and even weaker than when I boarded the train. I saw that most of the men around me didn't have the energy to stand, much less talk. To escape the intense rays of the sun, scores of men huddled tight under the sheltering shadows of the few trees that bordered the loading area. For those of us who couldn't fit under the shade, a torn piece of shirt fabric from one of the dead provided a minute sun block. Before the guards ordered us to the next stage of our march, many of the men tried to recover by bending over and taking deep breaths, laying down, or sitting with their heads bent between their knees. By now, we each knew that conditions were not going to get any better. So every man did whatever he could to muster his remaining strength and move on when the screaming and beatings began again.

After about a thirty-minute rest, the guards roared that contemptible

Japanese word, "Hyacco." The sharp cracking sound of bamboo poles striking sweaty wet backs and legs signaled it was time to get up and move again. Prodded into lines of two abreast, a group of guards quickly counted and inspected us head to toe and took whatever personal possessions we had.

"Get rid of any Jap money or souvenirs," whispered the guy beside me. His warning was clear. The guards would assume that I must have robbed one of their dead soldiers to get it. I had nothing but my mess kit, and the little bottle of iodine and my harmonica stuffed into the side of my boot.

"Please, not my wedding ring," loudly begged a fellow up ahead.

His plea was answered with a pole strike across his face and a vicious yanking at his treasured ring by a second guard. The married soldier was on his knees from the savage blow. The short Japanese guard held the little band of gold high for everyone to see. There were muffled curses from the rest of us, as we witnessed yet again another humiliating episode. It had been obvious from the beginning of the march that everything we possessed, including our lives, belonged to our captors. If we wanted to live we had to give them what they wanted or conceal it and take our chances. School class rings, belt buckles, watches, pocketknives, neck chains, Philippine money, and sadly, more wedding rings were thrown in a bucket.

I quickly hid the small bottle of iodine firmly between my buttocks. I didn't think they would be willing to inspect all parts of our filthy bodies closely, and if they did, they could pick it out themselves. I passed through the inspection uneventfully, showing them the empty contents of my mess kit and ring-less fingers. I silently whooped a victory cheer. I kept what I had started with on this infernal death march.

Relieved not to be stuffed back into those suffocating train cars again, we marched another seven miles in the burning sun across the treeless rolling hills, to the prisoner of war facility, Camp O'Donnell.

## CHAPTER 14

# Camp O'Donnell

The unrelenting sun beat down on us, as hard and heavy as the flailing sticks of the camp guards. At Camp O'Donnell they prodded and pushed us into the barbed wire compound surrounded by wooden guard towers. The guards lined our group in front of the wooden, nipa-thatched roof headquarters to stand and wait in the blazing afternoon sun as others marched in lines behind us. All of the Filipinos had been separated from the Americans, English, Dutch and Australian prisoners and were put in a camp nearby.

Thousands of us Battling Bastards of Bataan stood in the sweltering heat for hours in tight rows awaiting the first announcement by an authority of the Japanese government. In boot camp, we were taught that prisoners of war were afforded certain human rights under the accords of the Geneva Convention. At that time, we never thought that it would be we who would need them. After the inhumane treatment we had received following our capitulation and the ensuing death march, I hoped that now we would be treated fairly.

The camp commander emerged from out of the wooden, grass-roofed headquarters. He was short and comical looking and he strutted pompously. He was so short he had to hold his sword so it wouldn't drag on the ground behind him when he went to the wooden table that became a platform to deliver his "welcome" speech. Machine gun barrels poked out at us ominously from tall wooden lookout towers. Nobody dared to giggle at the arrogant little runt as he stepped up and stood on the tabletop leaving his entourage of subordinate officers in a row facing us at ground level.

Camp O'Donnell POW Camp Commander Tsuneyoshi lectures POWs
*Ex-POW Ben Steele*

Through his interpreter, Captain Tsuneyoshi began by declaring that we were "guests" of Emperor Hirohito of Japan since the Japanese military did not have regulations for the care and treatment of prisoners of war. He told us Japan had never signed the Geneva Convention. Listening to the squeaky-voiced camp commander rave on would have been funny if I weren't so sick from another attack of malaria. On and on he ranted in the blazing sun about how Americans were all dogs and would be treated as such. My mind screamed, Okay, I get it. We're "guest dogs" of the Emperor Hirohito. Now, can we go back to our kennels and rest?

The longer he ranted the more he worked himself into a frenzy. He jumped up and down telling us that the lucky ones were the ones who had already died. It was clear that we were on death row and every Japanese soldier could be our executioner. The "welcome message" was clear — it was going to get tougher.

Scalding hot flashes burned inside me more than the blistering sun above me. I was alternating between hot fevers and icy waves of bone-chilling shivers. I closed my eyes to concentrate as I started to shake, remembering from past episodes of malaria attacks that I sometimes passed out. I thought if I passed out in front of the camp commander I surely would be shot like a sick dog. I kept repeating Dad's advice: *Hold on, keep standing, hold on.* I felt death's wet and clammy hands clutching me, like a cold, stinking sweat, trying to penetrate into my heart and brain, and steal that faint breath of life to which I was clinging on to.

I cocked my head back and stared at the hazy blue-gray sky. I thought of the crystal blue skies of New Mexico. *I will survive. I will get home. I will hold on.* In a daze, I imagined my mother's sweet loving face smiling down on Dad and me next to her offering me words of encouragement. The pain in my legs and feet began to fade into a numb tingling as though they were about to fall asleep. My weak knees started to wobble uncontrollably. *Oh God, what am I going to do? I'm about to collapse. I'm so weak! They'll shoot me if I do. Do whatever the Japs say. God, if I could only think clearly enough to figure a way out of this place.* "Hold on," echoed the voice in my head.

Tsuneyoshi raved on and on about how the Americans, British and other allies had no right to do business in the South Pacific and that our predicament was completely our own fault and the fault of our superiors. "America for Americans. Asia for Asians. England for English. Asia for Asians. Asia for Asians!" he repeated incessantly through his interpreter. Americans no right to meddle in affairs of countries like Philippines! Philippines rightfully under jurisdiction of Imperial Japanese Emperor. Philippines for Filipinos. Filipinos are Asians. Not Japanese army's fault you here! It's you own fault! It you general's fault! It you President Roosevelt's fault!"

I heard the thud of someone behind me collapse on the sun-baked ground. I kept telling myself to hold on as the squealing voice droned on through the loud speaker. My fevered brain was burning from the inside and my body was burning from the sun. I felt like my whole skull was melting off my shoulders like a flaming marshmallow falling off a campfire stick. *Please, God, give me the strength to hold on.* As I closed my eyes the Commander's voice began to fade, as if someone were slowly turning down the volume on the radio.

When I opened my eyes again, I was laying down trying to focus my eyes on a bare, dim-yellow light bulb hanging by a wire from a rafter. *Where am I? How did I get here?* I was barely able to keep both eyelids open simultaneously. A sour whiff of ambient ammonia vapor woke me to an even grimmer reality than what I had left. Lying there beside me were men more dead than alive, their mouths agape waiting to die.

I panicked. *Oh God! This is not a hospital! It's a morgue!* I tried to sit up and clear my head, but my muscles lay dormant and unresponsive, as if a sack of potatoes replaced them. I thought maybe I was paralyzed but gradually my muscles began to respond and the painful awakening of my tired and wracked body began.

"Ugh, now I remember," I moaned.

All the shrapnel wounds in my legs and raw blisters on my feet stung sharply, and my emaciated muscles ached to the bone. I was confused, because I couldn't remember how I got there. *Where in the hell was I?* Quite certain that I hadn't died and gone to heaven because it looked too much like hell. I lifted my head enough to see the full spectacle of horror that surrounded me. In the narrow, thatch-roofed shed, I saw unconscious men lying in the filth of their own excrement. Some were bandaged with torn bits of soiled khaki or had makeshift splints of bamboo. Others groaned pitifully in pain as they lay sprawled side by side on thin, dried grass mats on the hard dirt floor. *How in hell did I end up here?* The last thing I remembered was standing in the scorching sun listening to one of Tojo's henchmen scream at us.

*Hey! Somebody get me out of here!* I thought, but couldn't utter a single word. The dark, dried grass rafters seem to be closing in on me like a tropical coffin lid. "Help me, help me," I whispered repeatedly, with barely enough strength to push the air out from my quivering lips. My brain said I was alive, but my body was so weak it felt as though it was filled with sand. *Oh God! Did I get shot?* I moved my hands across my torso feeling for holes or bandages, but felt nothing new. *Did I get hit on the head?* I examined my head with both hands, like it was a melon. "Cavesa okay," I confirmed.

I had played football for Albuquerque High School and our biggest rivals were from the Indian Academy across town. During a game on their field, I took the handoff from the quarterback, broke through a hole in the line, and ran full speed down the field. Suddenly, I was tackled simultaneously by three defenders. One hit me high in the chest, another hit me low in the knees, and the third Indian hit me in the stomach. I regained consciousness flat on my back staring at puffy clouds in the pale blue sky. I could hear the roar of the opponent's home crowd cheering the gang tackle. It was as if I was waking up from a dream. I wondered when I had fallen asleep, why I was wearing my football helmet, and why I was outside.

*Okay, okay, get it together. What do I need to do to get out of here alive? Who should I talk to? Somebody has to know what is going on.* I rolled my head over to the side and whispered to the guy lying next to me, "Psst! Hey, Buddy, can you hear me?"

He opened his eyes slowly and stared at me blankly.

"Hey, Buddy, do you know when they brought me in here?" I asked.

His lips quivered and mumbled something I couldn't quite make out.

"Say again, Buddy?" I asked again. "Can you tell me when they brought me here?"

He blinked his eyes as if to clear his mind and mumbled a little louder. "Japs brought you. Doctors, one of ours, theirs too, gave you big shot, something.

Passed out, maybe two days." He closed his eyes and was quiet again.

I lay there and thought about what that fellow had told me. *A big shot? A big shot of what? Well, whatever they gave me it didn't kill me.*

I was thirsty and hungry and realized quickly I had to get out. I always hated hospitals — not that this shack resembled a hospital. When I rolled over I saw that the guy on my other side was sitting up, his head and shoulders propped against the rough board wall.

"Hey, Buddy? Who's in charge here?" I asked him. The poor guy's white skin hung loosely from his protruding bones. His eyes stared blankly forward, and his chin rested on his chest. He didn't say a word. I rattled on trying to get him to talk. He just kept staring and didn't move.

"Come on, Buddy. Tell me about yourself." He still said nothing. Why didn't he say something, anything? "Come on man, talk to me." I thought maybe he was Dutch and couldn't speak English. I then watched in horror as a fly landed on his lower lip and disappeared into his half-opened mouth. I realized then why he wasn't answering. I bowed my head and closed my eyes. I said a little prayer for another lost soldier. "God bless you, Buddy. May your soul rest in heavenly peace far away from this hell hole."

I've got to get out of this place and soon!

I laid back and stared at the thatched-roof ceiling and thought of ways to escape. Although I was feeling weak, my mind was no longer foggy from the malaria. Whatever the doctors had given me in that shot seemed to be working. There didn't appear to be any guards in the building. They obviously were not concerned with any threat possible by a few dying POW's.

Unarmed Japanese medics checked the dying and carted off the dead on a makeshift stretcher. I lay still with my eyes closed to not draw attention to myself because I planned to be out of that building by daylight. After dark, when all was quiet and the medics were gone, I rolled quietly off my mat and crawled along the wall looking for a weak spot. The walls were made of bark-like planks loosely nailed to flimsy boards. I pushed on a few planks and they gave way and I slipped out into the yard. Without making any noise, I crawled under the wire fence that separated the building from the prisoners' huts, joined others lying on the ground and fell asleep.

"What the hell you doing coming back here? You crazy bastard!" said one of the guys from the 200th. "Man, I thought you were a goner when you stepped out of line and headed for the camp commander."

"I what?" I gasped.

Another fellow remarked, "Headed right at him. All the guards whipped up their rifles and took aim, but you kept going like a sleepwalker. I thought you'd be hit by thirty bullets, plus. Man, don't you remember?"

"No! I had no an idea. I don't remember anything," I answered. "Then what happened?"

"Tsuneyoshi stopped his whooping and hollering for a moment, stared directly at you, then said something to his assistant who yelled out a command to the guards. Two of them grabbed you under the arms and dragged you off."

"The rest of them still had their guns on you though," interjected another prisoner.

"Whew! Why didn't they shoot me?"

"I guess you're a lucky guy, Lovato."

"Yeah! Real lucky. Ending up here," I joked.

"Where the hell did they take you?"

"To a hut where everyone is dying. You don't want to end up there. That's all. Period! If you want to stay alive, stay out of that hellhole!" I described the filthy conditions that existed in what was supposed to be a medical ward. They shook their heads in disbelief.

Within days that wretched excuse for a medical facility became known as Zero Ward. Its name referred to the probability of survival of those who ended up there. The most seriously injured, those mortally sick from dysentery, malaria, gangrene, infections, or beriberi, and those who had given up on living came to their end in a Zero Ward. The door out of that place led straight to the burial pit. It was the last stop for the living dead.

Water line *By Ex-POW Ben Steele*

The first month at Camp O'Donnell was disorganized and the Japanese were ill prepared to accommodate over nine thousand prisoners. Waiting in line to fill a canteen from one of the trickling spigots could take several hours. Slit trench latrines checkered the open area. Many prisoners had to sleep in the open because there was not enough barrack space. There was no medical facility other than Zero Ward. Every day more and more men died and had to be buried immediately to prevent further epidemics. Our own officers organized food, latrine, and burial work crews to facilitate an operational camp within the camp. Makeshift kitchens were constructed so our cooks could boil and serve lugao, and rice. Our cooks put thistle weeds in the bug-infested rice when they could find some growing along the fence. All the water we drank from the near-by creek had to be boiled first to kill parasites and bacteria. If we had any chance of surviving the horrendous conditions, it would take unselfish cooper-ation from all who could work. The poor sanitary conditions for almost nine thousand men crammed into such a small area created an epidemic that killed more men per day than their battlefield wounds. Most of us were weak and delirious from dehydration, loss of blood, lack of food and nutrients, and malar-ia. The ground we walked on was dotted with puddles of contagious, diseased excrement left by contaminated prisoners who, unable to reach a latrine trench, spewed blood, mucus, and feces. Dead bodies were stacked in piles out-side the camp fence to prevent disease from spreading among the living. With daily temperatures over 90 degrees, the fly-covered bodies had to be disposed of quickly.

I was assigned to the burial detail and each morning before dawn, after a paltry serving of watered down lugao, we began the grisly duty of finding, car-rying and burying the dead prisoners. We hauled bodies from Zero Ward or found them sprawled where they had fallen during the night by the latrine trenches. With a makeshift pole and canvas stretcher we carried them to shal-low grave pits located outside the camp's barbed wire fence. Grave holes were shallow because the water table was only about four to five feet below the hard packed surface. Even at four feet deep, water seeped into the pit and caused the bloated bodies to float upward. One person grabbed all the dog tags or wrote down a name if anyone knew it. Those without dog tags or who couldn't be identified were marked UNKNOWN on the burial roster. After we laid the naked bodies head to toe, ten on the bottom and ten on the top, we placed heavy rocks on their bellies to keep them from floating up. Their clothes and boots were stacked into piles and later boiled in water to disinfect them before they were distributed to the living. An occasional groan emanated from a body as trapped air from their bloated stomachs or lungs exhaled over the vocal chords for the last time. This bizarre phenomenon prompted us to take a sec-ond look to be certain that he was dead. Sometimes a buddy of the deceased said a brief prayer. The continuous disposal of human flesh and bones outside the compound of Camp O'Donnell held little if any ceremonial dignity. A brief whispered prayer and a sign of the cross was all we were allowed for our fallen fellow Battling Bastards of Bataan.

"God bless you, Buddy. I'll never forget you."

When a pit was full, a thin layer of dry dirt was thrown over the bodies to cover them from the ever-increasing swarms of black and blue flies that fed on the rotting flesh. The dirt also helped to smother the foul smell of the decaying corpses. That same wretched smell lingered on our bodies long after the burying crew ceased its duties for the night. Without soap or running water, it was difficult to remove small pieces of thin, sticky flesh that stuck to our skin or beards. I used dirt to scrub it off my arms and face whenever I noticed the tissue clinging to me because once it dried it stuck like wallpaper.

As we carried the dead out on a stretcher, my mind often shifted to the past when I worked occasionally for my Godfather, Frank Salazar, at his mortuary when business was good. Grinning a mischievous little smile, as he rubbed his hands together, he joked with me and said, "They all have to come to me eventually, Mehito." But most of the people in his preparation area were older or victims of accidents, not young men my age.

The youth we carried to the mass graves were victims of the Japanese emperor's policies of neglect and cruelty. These men didn't die from bullets or bombs. Camp commander Captain Tsuneyoshi made it clear that the Japanese were not going to abide by the rules of the Geneva Convention. We were only "guests" of the Emperor. These men died because of his 'house rules'.

For the first two months, the sick and injured died on the average of fifty to seventy-five a day. Sadly, many of the men who worked on the burial assignment ended up being buried by their replacements. There was no escape, only survival. At night we heard wild dogs snarl and bark at each other as they fought over pieces of the most recently buried they had dug up. On moonlit nights, it was a living nightmare to watch those mangy dogs drag off a head or an arm and hand away from the laughing guards high in their guard towers. The next day we gathered what the dogs had left behind and reburied them. Men were dying faster than the survivors could dig burial pits. Sometimes, as many as forty bodies would lay stacked in the blazing sun waiting for additional burial trenches.

Two or three times a week we were forced to stand at attention in the blazing sun to listen to Commander Tsuneyoshi's boring and arrogant lectures. He ranted for hours about Japan's two thousand-year history of never being defeated and repeatedly made the reference to the superiority of the Japanese race and that all other races would eventually bow to the rising sun. Tsuneyoshi claimed that the Gods decreed the Japanese people's right to rule the eight corners of the world because they were direct descendants of Gods. Again, he reiterated that our miserable conditions were not his or the Emperor's fault, but our own leaders who put us here. Tsuneyoshi's sun torture sessions were almost as hard to bear as the burial detail.

By the end of April none of us had any fat left on our bodies. Our bodies were consuming our muscles to survive, making it continually more difficult to accomplish anything physical. It was hard work to muster the motivation to just stay alive. Some of the men looked like walking skeletons; their pale-white skin stretched over their protruding bones and their shoulder blades stuck out from their backs like flat bony, feather-less wings. I struggled to look into their sad eyes, sunk deep in dark hollow sockets. Their eyes showed that the men knew they were only a few days away from the piles awaiting burial. It was only a matter of time.

We all ate the same miserable worm-infested rice and got about the same quantity of dirty water, yet some men, including myself, fared better than others.

Chow Line *By Ex-POW Ben Steele*

The human mind is perhaps even more fragile than flesh and bones. The human will is a powerful ally or deadly foe. I had to believe that I was going to survive or else the inevitable death would win out. It hurt watching proud men crumble emotionally under the mounting weight of the Emperor's cruel, inhumane neglect. Every one of us crossed that fine line between crazy and sane at different times. Some who crossed over never came back. One POW filled his canteen with small rocks, then under cover of darkness, smashed the skulls of sleeping neighbors. When he was apprehended, the guards stripped and bound the deranged fellow, tied a rope around his neck and tethered him to a large stake like a rabid dog. Sadly, we watched our countryman and soldier, who had made it this far, finally succumb to madness. The once normal "all American boy" thrashed and dug in the dirt with his bloody fingers like a wild beast. All the while, Japanese officers taunted and jeered him on with their swords or whipping poles. It was Tsuneyoshi who said all Americans were all dogs. His pronouncement now had living proof. We looked at the crazed, broken man as an example of what could happen to any of us. They bombarded us with sticks and poles, starved and dehydrated us, gave us no medicine or medical supplies, and made us listen to demeaning speeches. They used anything at their disposal in an attempt to break us down. Gathering whatever mental power I could muster in the form of good thoughts, I proclaimed to myself, *My mind is my own and these Japs will not take it from me before I die. My body is their only prisoner. My mind is still free, and it will stay that way, so help me God.*

Every day during the first few weeks in O'Donnell I asked everyone I met if they had ever seen Captain Perrenot, Brewster or a tall cowboy in their sector of the camp. I hoped Captain Perry was as good a survivor as he was a leader. Even during the most dangerous moments at Lingayen Gulf, I never heard him use foul language or take God's name in vain. Although I never had a chance to find out, I thought he must have had a good family and a religious upbringing. I missed my captain, his get it done attitude, and his trust. I couldn't remember the Kid's given name or if I'd ever heard it. I called him the Chillicothe Kid from the first moment I met him all decked out with pearl-handled six-shooters and a large white cowboy hat atop his a six-foot-seven frame. I did find my old high school buddies, Herman Tafoya and Arthur Garde, who were in the 200th Coast Artillery with me.

Herman was near death when I found him with Arthur. Arthur was desperate. "Frank, you've got to get Herman to eat something. He doesn't listen to any of us. Maybe he'll listen to you," begged Arthur.

I knelt on one knee in front of Herman and looked at him. His eyes stared right through me as though I weren't there. I tried to reason with him. "Wolf, it's me, Snake (our nicknames in high school)! I'm really glad to see you alive. You need to eat buddy. You really need to eat something, anything." I tried over and over, but to no avail. Our friend had given up his will to live and be a part of that which was too horrible to endure. I had seen this behavior too many times before by those stacked up like cordwood waiting to be buried.

"Come on, Wolf. Snap out of it," shouted Arthur almost in tears.

Herman didn't bat an eyelash. He just sat there in a trance oblivious to everything we did, as though he didn't know us. Arthur's tormented face revealed his fear of losing one of his best friends. He looked at me and moaned, "Damn it, Frank. What's happening to us? Are we all going to die? Look at Wolf. He's going to die today or tomorrow if we don't do something."

I didn't want to hear those words even though I knew it was true so I snapped back, "Hell, no, he's not going to die, and neither are you and I — not here in this stink-hole!"

I apologized to Herman for what I was about to do, then slapped him sharply on one cheek and then the another. "Wake up, Wolf. Snap out of it." I slapped him again and again but he continued to sit in a stupor. "All right. Then we'll stuff the rice down your throat if that's what it takes to make you eat."

Arthur had saved a couple of rations of Herman's rice. Together, Arthur and I pulled opened Herman's jaw with our fingers, and pushed a glob of the sticky rice into his mouth, then held his jaw shut until he swallowed it. Herman neither resisted nor cooperated with our force-feeding, but we did get two meals' worth of food into him. Another prisoner offered to buy Herman's ration stating, "Don't waste that on him. He's going to die." He wasn't joking. Food was no joking matter. We ate every single rice grain, every single white worm or black weevil because they too were life-bearing sustenance.

Herman was our best friend from home, and we weren't going to let him die without trying everything possible. For about a week, Arthur (Gopher) and I force-fed Herman every morning and night, until he finally came out of his trance and started to feed himself. It was good to have our dear buddy, Herman, back among the living.

I didn't worry about Arthur as he watched after Herman like a mother hen. He looked and behaved as though he was in reasonably decent health. Although he had lost a great deal of weight, his muscle tone looked fairly good. Maybe I should have looked more closely. It broke my heart to find Arthur two weeks later dead on top of the burial pile. That was the way of life in the camp. I never knew what was going to happen next, except that it probably wouldn't be good.

*May 5–6, 1942*

*Japanese Army launch attack on Corregidor*

Following an artillery bombardment that left the once tree-covered island completely leveled; Japanese soldiers invade the minimally defended island by small boats. After overwhelming a small group of defender's they enter the underground passageways of the Malinta Tunnel and capture mostly bedridden injured, nurses and refugees from Bataan.

" With broken heart and head bowed in sadness but not in shame I report to your excellency that today I must arrange terms for the surrender of the fortified islands of Manila Bay…" Major General Jonathan Wainright wrote his final communiqué to President Roosevelt prior to his capitulation to the Imperial Japanese forces. He later surrendered the remainder of the American/Philippine forces on Corregidor to Japanese General Masaharu Homma. Most of POW's were convoyed by boats to shore then sent by truck to POW camp Cabanatuan north of Manila.

Note: Captain Travis E. Perrenot was captured on Corregidor and sent to Cabanatuan.

## CHAPTER 15

# God Bless America

*Late May, 1942*

So far I had experienced almost two months of indescribable horrors watching helplessly as more of my fellow prisoners died from malnutrition, beatings, poorly treated injuries, malaria, and despair. All day long, we dug more trenches and buried even more poor souls. Even in my worst nightmares, I never imagined how horrible an abusive death could be. Together the monsters in the movies "Frankenstein," "Dracula," and "The Werewolf" could not have created a more ugly death for a human being to endure than the conditions we had to face in the Japanese prisoner of war camp.

No one was immune from contracting malaria. What we needed to combat the mosquito-borne disease was quinine and there had not been any since the last part of December. The first symptom of malaria was the relentless chills followed by a high fever and uncontrollable sweating. The intermittent chills and fever would go on for hours or days and the soldier would become delirious and sometimes unconscious. The convulsive attacks left the body weak and exhausted or dead.

What we called 'wet' beriberi was maybe worse than malaria. The infected were unable to walk because their swollen testicles were the size of a football. Anyone within earshot cringed in sympathetic pain as the medics, without anesthesia, cut a hole in the infected's scrotum to drain the fluid.

I once saw one of our officers beg for quinine and medical supplies that clearly were available in the Red Cross boxes and crates stacked up outside of the camp fence. The Japanese officers replied by making him dig his own grave then shot him in the head.

The most difficult thing to bear was seeing men so depressed that they gave up the will to live. They would stop eating and within days they would drift into a coma-like state and die. *Was it crazier to live this way or crazier to die?* When my mind struggled to keep going, I closed my weary eyes and thought of my beloved Mother and Dad, my sisters and my brothers, and our home in the beautiful Rio Grande Valley. I recalled the beautiful ember-red New Mexican sunsets. How the rich, velvety orange and reds deepened as the sun set behind the black volcano dotted horizon or when the big sky above melted from blue-green to deep purple as the fiery pools of starlight magically appeared. I remembered simple things like getting up before sunrise with Dad and my brothers to go hunting at the Rio Puerco in his 1927 Chevy, or Mother making red chili enchiladas topped with an egg, sunny-side up. These memories made me happy inside and reminded me of what was really important. My thoughts of returning to my loving family and beautiful homeland helped me keep my mind focused and strengthened my will to survive.

*God Bless America*

I had kept my harmonica hidden during the death march and had yet to play it at Camp O'Donnell. Its soothing notes and melodies always lifted my spirits and helped me to forget the trials and tribulations of life. I had felt it in my pocket, familiar and comforting against my thigh, as I trudged every step on the march. It was my constant companion when I felt alone, my only personal possession I had left before being surrendered. Even the clothes and boots I wore came from one of the dead we had buried. Getting this far with my Hohner Marine Band harmonica was my secret little victory. Late at night when darkness fell over the camp and we took the only respite from the day's toil, I took "Little Victory" out from my hiding place under a loose board beneath my dried grass mat. Just touching it to my lips reminded me of times with my family singing, laughing, and playing alongside Mother on her piano songs like *"La Paloma,"* (The Dove) and *"La Golindrina"* (The Swallow).

It was late one warm tropical night in June when I felt I needed to actually play and hear its beautiful notes. Up until this point in time I feared I might get shot or beheaded if I dared play it out loud. Undaunted or maybe out of defiance, I walked to a spot along the fence, farthest away from the nearest guard tower, sat down and took out "Little Victory." Bright lights from the guard towers illuminated the barbed wire fences around the perimeter and cast a cold, stark glow over the thousands of sleeping bodies.

At first, I didn't know what song I was going to do when I pressed the harmonica to my lips and closed my eyes to play. But in that quiet moment I thought how a person never really knows how much they love someone, a place, or a thing until it is completely gone and the chance of ever seeing, touching, feeling, or holding them again is only a dream and a prayer. Everything I had ever loved, and now so dearly missed called out to me in the one song that reminded every single one of us of our home and land we loved. In my mind I saw and heard my mother's sweet voice singing and her piano playing "God Bless America."

I blew softly through the harmonica so as not to wake the fellows around me or alert the guards. As the notes softly cut through the tropical night silence, the words rang out in my head "God bless America, land that I love, Stand beside her and guide her, through the night with the light from above."

"Please, play a little louder, buddy," the fellows who awoke around me whispered.

Without thinking of the consequences, I blew those sweet notes a little louder. More men began to wake and sit up to sing along just above a whisper with my harmonica. Like a tidal wave, the voices in the night quickly spread throughout the camp. Within a few seconds, over eight thousand prisoners were singing at the top of their lungs with fearless passion. Men with bodies more skeletal than human, bodies ravaged by tropical diseases and injuries, all of them starving, sang out with pride and longing for our homeland.

Guards screamed, *"Ni, Ni, Ni!"* (No!), but were quickly drowned out by the choir of our voices. Their machineguns shot into the night sky as a warning. But nothing they did could stop our rally of heartfelt pride and prayer to God to bless and save our home. Noble men again stood together, arm in arm, and as tears streamed from their eyes they sang our national prayer "God Bless America." After three months of degradation and humiliation at the savage hands of the Japanese military, we stood proud and reclaimed our dignity, while asking God through the lyrics to stand beside us and guide us. With each passing minute the voices grew louder. Thirty thousand or so Filipinos imprisoned nearby in a separate compound heard the song and joined the concert of freedom.

As long as I live I will never forget the emaciated faces of some men, more skeleton than flesh, as they sang out with their hearts, and some with their last breaths. No choir in the world could have sung with more feeling, passion, and glory than the POWs on that hot tropical night halfway across the world.

It was hopeless to try to stop the singing, short of killing every last one of us. And sing we did, for at least an hour. When it was over and the whispering had subsided I laid my head down on my tattered grass mat and reaffirmed my will to stay alive and to get back home to the land that I loved. I realized then that many of us weren't going to make it. But that night, eight thousand miles from home, I finally realized why my dad ritually played "Taps" on his army bugle each time he took me and my brothers hunting to the high desert plains of the Rio Puerco. In the twilight, just before the sun rose over the hazy, purple Manzano Mountains, Dad would ask us to wait while he took his traditional walk alone. He always said the same thing, "Wait here, mehitos. I'll be right back." He left his 16 gauge shotgun with us, took the brass bugle out of its canvas bag and made his solitary walk to the same spot on a small knoll, about a quarter mile away. Dad never said much about the "Great War," other than that he hoped it would never happen again. As he marched up the sloping grade to the knoll, my brothers and I always retold the story about when dad was playing his bugle during a battle charge. An enemy bullet ricocheted off his bugle, interrupting his playing for only a couple of seconds. A bullet-sized dent on the front of the brass instrument was its battle scar.

From where we waited we could see Dad, a solitary sentinel, raise his bugle to his lips. Slowly the haunting notes of "Taps" broke the quiet, autumn morning. As the returning echoes bounced off the nearby canyon walls, Dad accompanied the echoes with additional notes, making it sound as though there were two players. It was like Archangel Gabriel in heaven playing "Taps," the "Good Night-Good Bye Buddy song" with God. Although he never said it, I realized that night in Camp O'Donnell that he must have played his noble tribute for his fallen buddies in The Great War.

I thanked God for my parents and for the skills they had given me to survive. I prayed for the prisoners who were still alive. *God bless us all and God bless America.*

CHAPTER 16

# Transfer to POW Camp Cabanatuan

*June, 1942*

We had been in the Camp O'Donnell death hole for almost two months when we heard from our officers that some of us were going to be transferred to another camp. The scuttlebutt was that the Japanese military had not figured on such large numbers of prisoners. They had no idea what to do with us. By June, over three thousand American bodies had been buried in the shallow graves and maybe three to four times as many Filipinos.

The first of us to be transferred were the healthiest and those able to walk the seven miles back to the train depot at Capas. Groans and cries of despair emanated from even the most emotionally hardened when we arrived at the waiting cattle cars. Vivid memories of my last horrific train ride flashed into my mind. My body began to shake and my empty stomach retched uncontrollably. Actually seeing the hot, airless rolling coffins again was scary enough to tell the guards to shoot me and get it over with. Again, the will to survive outweighed the will to die, so I crawled into the hot box for the journey east to Camp Cabanatuan. Fortunately, this time we were given enough room to sit on the floor, back to back, with our legs drawn to our chests. Though the suffocating air made us all dizzy and faint, no one died.

By July the Japanese must have known the exact number of prisoners of war they had in the Philippines. Even though they stated unequivocally that they did not recognize the terms of the Geneva Convention, we hoped conditions would be better at Cabanatuan. O'Donnell was a hopelessly inadequate sewer of death and disease.

Prisoner of War Camp Cabanatuan
*Courtesy of Loback family*

Most of the prisoners we encountered when we arrived at Cabanatuan appeared much healthier and heavier than our group. They were the soldiers brought directly to Cabanatuan following their capitulation on Corregidor on May 5. They had avoided the traumatic effects of the death march and the epidemic dysentery that ran throughout the cramped quarters of O'Donnell. They were shocked to see us dragging into the camp. I overheard one of their officers quarreling with one of ours. The officer suggested we be separated from them, citing disease prevention. They must have feared our condition was a preview to their own fate as "guests" of the Emperor. They were correct, but nothing could be done to separate us. There simply was not enough room in the compound for effective segregation. There were prisoners from England, Holland, Australia, New Zealand, and Canada who had been captured when the Philippines fell to Japan. Trainloads of prisoners arrived daily for the first few months. Grass-roofed barracks originally designed to sleep forty men now were stuffed with over one hundred and twenty.

Prisoner of War Camp Cabanatuan
*Courtesy of the Loback family*

At first, the existing latrine trenches filled up faster than the work crews were able to dig new ones. The result was reeking pigsty puddles. Even though Cabanatuan was larger and had more covered barracks, it was still inadequate to provide safe and sanitary conditions for all of the prisoners destined to arrive from O'Donnell. It was clear that more men were going to die from disease and infections. We still had to wait for hours in the hot sun for a canteen of water that dripped from the spigots.

Our prison at Cabanatuan was, at first, no better than at O'Donnell. The original Corregidor prisoners had not prepared the facilities for this influx. From the discussions I overheard in the yard, the Japanese had not warned them of our numbers or physical condition. Food quality and quantity decreased when we arrived. The Imperial Japanese Command did not care enough to prepare for our survival.

Every chance I had I asked the Corregidor group if any of them knew Brewster, Captain Perrenot or the Kid. None of the Filipinos who had been segregated earlier at Camp O'Donnell came to Cabanatuan. Most of the remaining officers and enlisted men of General MacArthur's American forces in the Philippines were held captive in Camp Cabanatuan.

Captain Travis Perrenot was captured on Corregidor and was assigned to a different section of Cabanatuan than Frank Lovato. Burl A. Brewster had also been assigned to Captain Perrenot's section.

Shortly after our group arrived there was an outbreak of diphtheria. Before the month was over the epidemic had wiped out another six hundred men. Herman was always too sick to do much work and was on the verge of being placed into Cabanatuan's Zero Ward. The Japanese authorities decreed the non-working sick would receive a reduced rice ration, which made no sense. Fewer nutrients compounded their already weakened condition. It was a miracle that Herman held on each day because he kept slipping in and out of consciousness. Every morning before I left for work detail I checked in on him to make sure that he ate his lugao to prevent someone from stealing it.

The first thing the Japanese demanded is that we learn *"tenko,"* to fall in formation and count off roll call in Japanese. *Tenko* followed an early morning reveille of Japanese guards stomping through the barracks, kicking and hitting sleeping prisoners with bamboo sticks or rifles, while cursing and yelling at the top of their lungs, *"Ichi, ni, san, shi, go, roku, shichi, hachi, ku, ju."* The number eleven was *ju-ichi,* twelve was *ju- ni,* and so on. Each of us had a number; mine was *San be yaku ju hachi* — 318.

If the last man counted was an even number, the final sound-off was supposed to be *"bango."* We often answered with an enthusiastic "bingo" in defiance. If a man was missing from the work detail, the squad leader reported the cause saying, *"Ichi may batai* (One man dead)," *"Ichi may benjo* (One man latrine)," or *"Ichi may bioki* (One man sick)." The guards chastised any sick man with a disdainful remark like *"atama bioki* (sick in head)." The prisoners began making up nicknames for the guards. We called one "Four Eyes" because he wore glasses. Another one was called B17 because he was continually beating us and could really unload on us.

No one was allowed to eat until tenko was successfully completed to the guards' satisfaction. Sometimes tenko took an hour if the pronunciation was not to their approval, or because of death the count could not be reconciled. When a man died, another would be added to the squad to keep the number even. The Japanese kept us in groups of ten. So many men died that the Japanese had to disband groups to keep the numbers even. If a man was missing or unaccounted for, such as an escapee, the camp commander implemented a punitive and barbaric retribution to punish innocent POWs who neither conspired nor assisted the escapees.

## CHAPTER 17

# Blood Brothers

What began as work detail to repair a bridge outside of camp turned into another horror of Japanese Army savagery. We worked all day on the bridge and bunked in a movie theater for the night, sleeping on benches, seats and on the dirt floor. During the night a Philippine guerilla group infiltrated the town, shot Japanese soldiers and took a POW with them. The next morning the guards smacked and prodded us into long rows on the street. We marched double time to a schoolhouse where the Japanese officers had set up their command post. Machine guns pointed directly at our contingent of 150 men. "What the hell's going on with these crazy bastards?" asked the man on my left.

"I don't know but they are really pissed off about something," I replied.

Without any explanations guards began yanking men out of the line who were wearing green armbands. Apparently the man who had escaped was wearing a green armband. The guards picked out ten men. Two brothers and three others allegedly assisted the escapee. The ten men were forced at gunpoint to line up in front of the rest of us as the Japanese colonel ordered ten guards to be the firing squad.

"Why in the hell is he punishing innocent men?" I asked under my breath. I closed my eyes and prayed for my brother soldiers and their families. Knowing they were facing their death, the condemned men shouted passionately, "God Bless America!" and "Tell the President about this!"

Hoping for a miracle, I opened my eyes in time to see them bravely face their captors. I heard, "God Bless America!" as the shots rang out in unison. I began shaking when I saw that the first volley of shots only wounded or completely missed some of the condemned. It seemed like an eternity of screams and agonizing moans while the firing squad reloaded and took aim again at the poor Bastards of Bataan. One of the brothers who was not hit shrieked, "Oh God, please!" as he witnessed his brother dying from a stomach wound.

Curses and prayers from our group rumbled in the wake of each volley. After the second volley, one of the bloody innocents uttered a garbled, but understandable, "God Bless America." It took several more volleys to finish the massacre. We stood shaking, and trembling, not from fear but from helplessness and despair. I saw death take my fellow soldiers in the battlefield from disease and starvation. But when they shot those ten innocent men my heart ached more than I knew was possible. One of our own officers tore off a patch of his scalp during the grisly execution.

Strutting out to acknowledge his vile deed, the pompous Japanese colonel stated the new rule concerning escapees: "Everyone responsible for escapees!" he shouted. "One escape, nine will be executed!"

Following the burial of our buddies we began to refer to ourselves as blood brothers and our anonymous groups of ten as blood squads. All POWs in the camp were divided into random groups of ten. The Japanese commander kept the group lists secret, so no one knew who was in which group. If an individual escaped from an anonymous group, the other nine members would be shot. The guards must have thought that since we had no idea who was in our group, we had to keep a watch on everyone who might consider escaping.

About a week later I was awaken by guards screaming *"Hyacco, Hyacco!"* as they whacked and prodded me from my sleeping mat. *What the hell is going on? They're not taking everyone in my barracks, only certain individuals.* "Why in the world are they waking us in the middle of the night? What kind of work detail is there to do now?" I asked the soldier next to me.

"You! *San be yaku ju hachi!* (318) *Hyacco!* Go!"

Outside the barracks, heavily armed guards lined up the nine of us, marched us to the Imperial Japanese commander's headquarters, and ordered us to sit down. Soon another group of nine men joined us.

"Why did they pick us out from the rest?" we asked each other. "Why are we so special?" Twenty guards surrounded us and I figured whatever was happening: they were making sure that we were not going anywhere. The guards were fully armed and their bayonets pointed at us, as if we were going to rebel or attack.

I didn't know any of the guys in the eighteen-man group although a few knew each other. We all came from different sections of the prison camp.

One of the guys shouted "Hey, Tojo! Are you going to set our little group free?" Nervous chuckles came from the group, a comic relief from fear of the unknown. This was not going to be picnic. I was sure that whatever the camp commander had in store for us was not going to be fun.

After two hours passed, which felt like an eternity, the officer in charge of the soldiers casually announced that two men had escaped and we were in their blood squads. Apparently two guys named Stobal and Kelly had escaped and had not been captured. This explained why we had been corralled and heavily guarded. We were sentenced to die when the sun broke first light as examples for the rest of the prisoners. The next few hours before dawn would be the shortest and perhaps the most soul searching in our young lives.

Up until the notification of our blood squad status, there was always the possibility that things might change for the better. When my back was to the sea and the enemy was advancing in huge numbers, I hoped that MacArthur would arrive at the last moment to save the day. Hope, faith, and dogged determination to survive was all I had. The men who had lost hope during the death march or at Camp O'Donnell did eventually wilt away and die. It was as though their spirits had left their bodies behind.

At first, our group was dead silent as the cold, ugly truth sunk in. We were going to die by a firing squad at sunrise! Eighteen men, boys mostly, all waited to die. None of us had been given a chance to live like adults before we volunteered for the army or navy. Like many of my classmates, I was still in high school when I joined the National Guard. We were condemned to die before most of us had the chance to know the love of a woman or the smile of our firstborn.

An occasional sniffle cut through the thick silence of disbelief and denial. *Maybe this was only another bad dream in the continuing series of nightmares we faced, both awake and asleep?* We fought courageously until we were ordered to surrender. We were promised reinforcements and supplies, but they never came. Over three thousand of us who made it through the death march into Camp O'Donnell were buried in shallow graves. We hoped the move to Cabanatuan would be an improvement, until we realized it could not accommodate the mass influx of the sick and weak from O'Donnell. And now, Emperor Hirohito's officer decreed that eighteen innocent men would die because two of our blood brothers escaped.

The harsh, bright light from the guard tower illuminated our group in a ghostly mixture of dark shadows and light. The silent guards nervously shuffled their feet or checked their weapons as though they knew they were guarding condemned, maybe desperate men. Everyone seemed lost in his own thoughts. Every breath was closer to our last. I thought of my dear beloved mother, my dad, and my sisters and brothers and the good times we had shared. They were the treasures of my life. I thought of Captain Perrenot, Brewster, the Kid, and all courageous American and Filipino men who had fought beside me. I whispered, "Where are you now with your blazing mother-of-pearl six shooters? I could use your humor and dead aim right now." *God bless you all who have enriched my life, and may your lives be free to live far from this tyranny and madness.* It was at that point that I decided to do something I loved that stood for everything and everyone that meant anything to me. I took out Little Victory, pressed it to my lips and played "God Bless America."

As glistening tears of sadness streamed down gaunt, dusty faces we repeatedly sang the anthem of our home with love and pride. The sadness was not only from knowing we were going to die, but mostly from the heartfelt pain of absolutely knowing we never would see our beloved families, friends and homeland again.

Somebody shouted out "Hey Buddy, can you play 'The Battle Hymn of the Republic'?" I did, and followed it with "America the Beautiful," and even "God save the Queen" for an English fellow. We sang like proud and valiant soldiers, taking it to the enemy with whatever weapon we could muster. The enemy could take our lives but not our heart and souls. Our guards stared in amazement at what they must have thought as peculiar behavior for condemned men, but didn't try to stop us.

"Oh I wish I had wings of an angel
Over these prison walls I would fly
I would fly to the arms of my darling
And there I'd be willing to die."

To the east, the night sky began to change color to the deep turquoise of dawn. The rising sun was now our Grim Reaper. During the night a few of the men had curled up and fallen asleep. It was sad to see the shocked look on their faces when they realized that their bad dreams were still there. For a moment we watched the first rays of the rising sun without uttering a word. I remembered happier mornings at home. I always loved getting up with Dad before sunrise to feed my chickens, rabbits and ducks. He taught us the importance of taking care of our responsibilities before doing anything else. An early start was the best guarantee that I would have time for schoolwork, football, and my job after school. Dad said he always loved the early morning since he was a child and he and his father got up to feed the animals. I imagined I could smell Dad's coffee brewing and bacon and eggs frying on the wood stove while I fed my animals. When I finished my chores, Dad and I ate a quiet breakfast as the sun crested the Sandia Mountains. I realized how lucky I had been, and I was grateful to have had those beautiful mornings.

The officer in charge barked a short order that prompted the guards to open and inspect their rifles' breeches. We heard the metallic snaps of their bolt-action rifles sliding open, followed by the dull ring of the bolt sliding forward to install a new live round in the breech. My heart pounded. I wondered which bullet had my name on it. With each passing minute, the tension mounted between the condemned and the guards. I needed to stop thinking about what was going to happen, so I began to play my harmonica again. I considered the urgency of the moment and didn't know if this would be my last song before the Japanese officer gave the orders for our execution, so I chose a religious song my mother had taught me. I closed my eyes and started to play Little Victory. I could see the sad scene on Mount Calvary on a dark day, a long time ago as I began to play "The Old Rugged Cross."

The words from that song gave me hope that it was not my day to die. I was ready to die if I must, but I was ready to live if I had the chance. My fear increased with every gradual ray of the emerging blue light glowing from below the eastern horizon.

From out of the silence someone started to pray out loud. Others did the same. We prayed the Lord's prayer together then everyone prayed their own private prayer. I prayed that God protect my family and my country from the Japanese Empire

From among the whispered prayers an angry voice shouted to the guards, "What the hell you waiting for? The wild dogs are waiting for their feast!"

Another answered, "Shut up, you idiot. What do you care what happens to you after you're dead?"

The sun began to peek over the horizon but there was no movement from the guards.

Someone asked, "What's going on? I thought they were going to shoot us at dawn?"

"Shut up, you fool. Don't give them any ideas." someone snapped back.

I think most of us were in complete agreement with the last reply. Then a Japanese soldier with round glasses, who looked more like a Western Union messenger than a soldier, rode his bicycle up to the guards. The POW's and guards waited in anticipation as he dismounted and delivered a brown envelope to the officer in charge. As the officer read the letter, the messenger turned, looked at us with a half-smile, and announced in awkward English: "You lucky people." We looked at each other quizzically, wondering what he meant. Some of the prisoners didn't hear his message and whispered, "What did he say?" One of the guys answered, "He said we're rocky people? "What the hell does that mean?"

"No, not rocky! He said lucky."

The word "lucky" was one word the prisoners didn't often use when referring to ourselves.

So we waited. *What did the messenger mean? Lucky we get to wait a few more minutes? Are we lucky that we will die before the other prisoners? Lucky the camp commander slept late? What did he mean?*

About an hour passed, and daylight was near. Suddenly guards began assembling rapidly in front of the camp commander's quarters. Prisoners and guards alike stared at his headquarters. The camp commander stepped out of the door dressed in a white shirt, riding britches, and knee-high shiny brown boots. He stood overlooking the yard from the high porch as if he ruled the world.

"*Ki o tsuke!* (Attention!)" Screamed the captain of the guards. We stood up in formation. The commander strutted down the steps and marched arrogantly ahead of his entourage toward us. One guard brought his stepstool and placed it in front of our group. Neither the Japanese guard nor the prisoners spoke a word. The only sounds were those of shuffling feet and the clinking of metal parts of their gun belts as the guards snapped to full attention.

All eyes remained fixed on the short, pompous man as he marched to the stool and stepped up to his perch. He overlooked all but the tallest of the POWs. He pursed his lips and slowly looked each one of us up and down. Then he took a deep breath and burst out in broken English, "No one must escape from this camp! Everyone responsible for each other's life! One try to escape — nine die!" Clutching his fists and shaking as though he was going to burst, he screamed, "This is law of camp! You responsible for lives of nine other men! If you escape, you will be caught and killed anyway!"

I remembered during our last "sun-treatment" that he ranted and raved for hours about how much all oriental people hated the Americans and British, and that prisoners were considered less than animals: The same message Camp Commander Tsuneyoshi relayed on our arrival to Camp O'Donnell.

The fellow beside me mumbled, "Oh God, he's going to torture us with words first."

"Just shoot us," murmured another.

He paused for a moment as if he heard the disgruntled comments. His expression changed from a scowl into a grin. Then he said the words that stunned us, "The great General Masaharu Homma, Chief Commander of the Imperial Japanese Army, has given order to spare your lives!"

I took a deep breath, closed my eyes, and whispered, "Thank you God." I almost fell over as my knees buckled. I wanted to scream, cry, and be silent all at once. The emotional preparation to die by firing squad had been debilitating.

"Return to quarters. Dismissed," he concluded.

My nerves were so shot I shook like crazy as I stood staring at the sun cresting the horizon. One man fainted and dropped to the ground. Some cursed the Japanese, while a few cheered. A few dropped to their knees and prayed out loud. Most of us wept, quietly.

Exhausted from the mental anguish and lack of sleep I walked back to the barracks for a couple of minutes of rest before joining my work detail. *Holy Jesus Christ! A miracle in this crazy nightmare at the hands of the Japanese.* I was prepared for death. *What a nightmare! We had been shaken from a deep sleep and told we were going to be shot at sunrise. Is this a Japanese ruse to break us down one more time, to bust our inner resolve and our comradeship? Or is this some horrible lesson to prove they would kill us if any one else tried to escape?* They could do anything to us they wanted because they had no respect for us as human beings.

Shortly after the shooting squad miracle, I was selected by a Japanese officer to be on the woodcutting work detail. He picked about fifty men who appeared to be strong enough to cut and carry heavy logs a long distance from the camp. The monsoon season would soon be upon us, so we needed to build more covered shelters for cooking, sleeping, and sick wards.

Following my breakfast of a cup of watered down *lugao,* guards armed with rifles and fixed bayonets marched fifty of us double time across the dry, straw colored rolling hills toward a grove of trees about thee miles from Cabanatuan.

About a mile and a half from camp, I thought that so far the excursion was uneventful and it felt good to be out of the miserably crowded conditions and constant stench of the prison camp compound.

Suddenly the guards shouted, *"To-Mare!"* (Halt) Without warning, the guard in charge ran screaming down our two-by-two line, apparently upset at something we had done. He worked himself into frenzy, and screamed so fast that I couldn't translate any of his words. Ever since the death march we had learned the standard Japanese commands, or were beaten until we did. We also listened carefully to guards' conversations on work details, and learned a few other words. When a guard wanted to learn a word or phrase in English, we usually learned the Japanese counterpart. I could not understand complex sentences when spoken rapidly or when the speaker was screaming.

"What the hell's going on with that crazy bastard?" the man on my left whispered.

"I don't know. Can't make out what he's screaming." I answered without moving my lips.

Something was terribly wrong. Beads of sweat streamed down the guard's chubby red face as he stormed up and down the line screaming, *"Yoroshii-nee* (not good)".

"You!" he screamed as he pointed his bayonet in the face of one of the POW's. He motioned for the terrified young man to put down the long tree saw he was carrying.

"What the hell? I didn't do anything," he stammered, appearing confused.

"Run!" the guard screamed as he pointed his rifle and bayonet up the steep hill.

Before he could start to move, the trembling fellow got a sharp bayonet jabbed into his buttocks.

The other guards screamed hysterically, "Run! Run! Run!" as they jumped up and down.

The young man's face turned ghostly white with fear. He looked quickly at the rest of us in stunned disbelief, then bolted up the hill.

"My God, what are those wacko Japs going to do to that poor boy?" whispered the fellow next to me.

"What the hell did he do to piss them off?" I asked in reply.

When he had scrambled about thirty feet up the steep rocky hill, the guards raised their rifles and began to shoot at the poor fellow. Rifle bullets ricocheted off rocks only inches away from him. The terrified young man wailed like a wounded animal as he struggled on his hands and knees to get up the hill. When he reached the top, the guards stopped shooting and yelled *"To-Mare!"* Trembling and exhausted, he stood bent over with his hands on his knees and cried. The guards laughed and howled hysterically as they mimicked the poor fellow's terrified actions.

"What the hell did he do to deserve that?" I asked again. *Probably nothing at all except be unfortunate enough to be surrendered by our generals to the Imperial Japanese Army.*

Then it was our turn!

"You! You! Run!" demanded the guards as they turned to the rest of us and pointed their bayonets in our faces.

What started out that morning as a chance to get some fresh air and scenery had turned into a deadly game of cat and mouse with real bullets. From the time of our capitulation, the Imperial Japanese Army had done its best to degrade us and make our lives as miserable as possible.

With no other choice but to run and leave the rest to God, we clambered up the hill as fast as we could. Within seconds, the guards began to shoot. Loud blasts from their large caliber rifle muzzles exploded like a string of firecrackers behind us. A rain of bullets whizzed past my ears and ricocheted with a zing off the rocks. I remembered what Captain Perrenot said back at Lingayen, "Don't be afraid of the ones you can hear, Lovato. They're already past you. It's the ones you can't hear that'll get you." *So far I've heard them all, thank God.* Near misses struck the ground and sprayed dirt and rock so close to me that I felt the sharp sting of fragments hit my legs and arms.

When we reached the top of the hill they ordered us to halt as they squealed with laughter at their little game. We gasped for air and attempted to regain our sanity from the mental torture that was more painful than a physical whipping. It was that kind of heinous torment, along with the sun treatment, near starvation rice rations and beatings on the heads with poles that was killing us. Most of the Imperial Japanese soldiers were brutal, sadistic, and devoid of values that respected anyone who surrendered. We were not only their prisoners; we were also their source of sadistic pleasure.

I looked back down the hill and saw one of the guards lying on his back holding his stomach, and laughing uncontrollably. As my anger built up inside me, I thought that those idiots didn't realize that this kind of treatment only made us stronger in our resistance. I may be a New Mexican-American with roots that go back to Spain, but I was born an American on American soil of American parents, and that is exactly how I will live and die. *I will see these guards and their officers defeated by their own cruelty someday, so help me God.*

## CHAPTER 18

# Nature Strikes

I hated being dirty all the time. Without soap or access to baths or showers we could only wipe our sweat-soaked and dirt-covered bodies with pieces from torn uniforms that we moistened in the irrigation ditch. Something as simple as toilet paper, soap, or hot water might have prevented the outbreaks of amoebic dysentery that swept through the camp. Through no fault of our own, I am sure that a great deal of illness was spread through the less than sanitary conditions that prevailed in the food preparation area.

The hazy blue skies and wispy high clouds of the dry period gave way to gray, towering thunderheads of the monsoon season. The once dry, hard-packed soil could not absorb the continuous rainfall or drain it off fast enough to prevent flooding. Our latrine trenches overflowed and mixed with the thick mud to crate a soupy, stinking slop that we had to walk through. When it rained, the cool fresh water poured off the eaves of our thatched-roofed barracks in sufficient quantity to rinse off the outer layer of sweat and dirt. But, without soap it was impossible to scrub off the months of oily grime and the foul smell of death and disease.

One day during a torrential downpour, while I waited in line to get under the cascading water, I told the fellow behind me, "Man, when I get home, I'm taking two hot showers every blessed day for the rest of my life."

He sniffed me like a hound dog and responded, "Hell Buddy, it's going to take a lifetime to get that smell off you."

I nodded in agreement and laughed at the humorous statement. He was probably right if we didn't get out of here soon. Suddenly a blinding white flash and thunderous explosion knocked several us off the deck into the muddy yard. It sounded and felt like the mortar round that hit me back in Bataan.

While men on the deck scattered for cover indoors, those of us knocked into the yard scrambled in the ankle deep mud to do the same. Although I felt I needed to run I truly didn't know where to go get away from the next possible incoming bomb or artillery round.

Someone yelled, "Lightning!"

The smell of burnt flesh that lingered in the air emanated from the poor fellow who was in front of me. A bolt of lightning had struck him dead. His burnt, naked body had crumpled face down into the soupy dark mud. The guy behind me was screaming "My finger! My finger! I lost my finger!" He had also been struck by the lightening and it burnt off one of his fingertips. He fumbled through the ankle-deep mud, and searched for the top digit of his smoking finger. I felt sorry for him and helped him look for it in the soupy mire, but to no avail. Several other prisoners ran aimlessly around the barracks also in shock from the blast. Perhaps the lightening strike reminded them of the horrific bombing and shelling during the last days of the fall of Bataan. Some POW's wept openly, others laughed, but everyone was shaken up from the blast. I thought to myself, thank you, God. It is another miracle. I somehow am not even scratched

We carried the dead fellow to a burial pit and I remarked to the other pallbearers "Every day in this miserable camp there is always something or someone trying to kill us."

"Yeah. If it's not the disease, infection, starvation or stinking Japs, it's the damn weather," another replied

In the past six months of war and imprisonment, I had seen men die in many ways by the hands of the Japanese, but this was the first time Mother Nature had taken one of us.

The radical change of weather gnawed on our nerves as much as the unpredictable behavior of the Japanese. Maybe it was the booming thunder that was reminiscent of the continuous artillery and bombing we endured that triggered the uncontrollable shakes and diarrhea in some prisoners. A few prisoners sat staring into empty space in their private worlds, miles away from the present terror. They were unresponsive to friends. I had witnessed that behavior whenever someone reached his limit to cope with the horrible reality we faced. I preferred to go out of camp on the woodcutting detail, rather than to stay penned up in that quagmire of physical and mental sickness. The wood cutting detail offered an opportunity to get fresh air and see something other than barbed wire and caged men.

One morning it was heavily overcast when our detail left the camp to cut poles for building posts. Battleship gray skies, drizzling rain, and foul weather didn't stop any work detail during our fourteen-hour work shifts. We spent most of the morning sawing down six and eight-inch trees. Dark, ominous clouds moved slowly in our direction from the east. The sky seemed to be disappearing behind a black curtain that would soon reach us.

About noon the guards ordered us to load up; since there were no trucks, we were the mules. At first, two of us doubled up on each log, but that was changed because the guards figured they could get twice as much done if they made each of us carry one pole. The only one that dared to complain was beaten to his knees by two guards. Ahead of me in the dim light, the staggered row of POW's looked like crucified men against the gray horizon. An overhead curtain of black clouds made the gloomy scene even darker. Strong gusts of howling wind and rain stung my skin like tiny needle pricks, whipping the logs around like a sail and constantly blew us down into the slippery mud. I imagined how Jesus must have felt carrying his cross up the hill to Mount Calvary.

The guards' heinous laughter cut through the raging wind as we slipped and fell in the mud. Their orders to make us do the impossible seemed to amuse them. But no one stopped because they poked and prodded us in the buttocks with their sticks and bayonets.

*"Hyacco! Hyacco!"*

Finally the guards allowed us to double up on a log, not out of kindness, but out of practicality. No man could possibly carry his log alone in the fierce wind. Dark clouds had smothered the midday sun transforming day to night and reminded me of the typhoon we had encountered last September at sea that had nearly sunk our transport ship. In this war everything existed at the extreme level: extreme weather, extreme pain, extreme fear, extreme horror, extreme hunger and thirst, extreme everything.

Eventually the wind raged at such intensity that it blew everyone down, including the guards, forcing them to give the orders and leave the logs and return to camp. As we leaned into the howling wind, it occurred to me that both the Japanese and POWs were powerless in the hands of God's natural fury.

Almost everyone was indoors when we sloshed and stumbled up the wooden steps of our barracks. We took turns washing off the mud under the eaves of the deck. A poor guy, who had fallen into the latrine trench while relieving himself, was covered from head to toe in excrement. We held him up and helped wash him in the water cascading off the roof.

Still shaking from his frightening experience, he related his grisly story to us. "When I squatted over the latrine trench, a gust of wind blew me backwards headfirst into the shit. I thought I was going to die when my shoulders wedged in the narrow trench and I couldn't get my head up to breathe."

We huddled around the openings in the barracks walls and watched in awe as the muddy brown water rose like a lake before our eyes. Fortunately for us, the barracks were constructed on posts that elevated the floor about five feet above the ground. Uprooted fence posts, wood planks, shack roofs, and trash floated past us in a sea of rising dark water. Because of the storm, no one could cook our evening ration of rice.

One of the guys joked, "If we had known that the rains would be this bad, we could have built an ark and sailed out of this camp."

The storm howled throughout the night and blew pieces of wooden siding off our barracks, leaving large open gaps for wind and rain to come in. I lay curled up like a snail in my GI rain jacket that I had inherited from one of the men who died. Everything was wet inside the barracks, including our sleeping mats. All the warmth of the months of hot sun washed away in the torrents of water and left our weary bodies numb and aching. Not only were the Japanese making our life a living hell, the weather was also trying to break us down. We were soaked to the bone and we looked like drowning rats. I kept reminding myself that I was still alive and better off than many of the others. I prayed, "Please God, Holy Mother, and all the saints in heaven, see me through this wretched night and get me home alive."

We were awakened the following morning before dawn by the barking pack of wild dogs that frequently robbed our burial grounds. It was still too early to see the destruction the wind and torrential rains had left behind. As the sun rose in the cloudy sky, the dawn's light revealed a macabre image of naked, decaying corpses, hanging on the camps barbed wire fences. Other bodies bobbed limply in the shallow brown swamp that was our prison yard. The scene of our old friends and buddies desecrated one more time made some of the most hardened men vomit. The storm left Cabanatuan a mess of sewage and mud up to our ankles that added to the grisly task of recovering the dead and reburying them.

The wild dogs were having a field day on the higher ground, barking and fighting over the body parts scattered over the countryside. We watched them slosh in the slick brown mud, tugging and pulling each other back and forth with a leg or an arm in their gnashing jaws. While some men curled up and buried their faces in their knees and cried, other men laughed at another bizarre day in hell. One fellow said, "I don't know why they're fighting over bones — there's no meat on them anyway." Another group of men where laughing hysterically about a bizarre occurrence that happened during the night. A grass roof from one of the barracks had been lifted completely off its walls and had miraculously landed on the roof of the barracks alongside it. Whatever it took to survive, each man did his best. Being a prisoner of the Japanese Army or "guest" of Emperor Hirohito, was surely hell.

"Oh, I wish I had wings of an angel.
Over these prison walls I would fly.
I would fly to the arms of my loved ones,
and I'd leave these prison walls far behind."

CHAPTER 19

# Angels of Bataan

War is the domain of men. The older men start it, the middle-aged men lead it, and the young men fight it. The majority of women and children I had seen so far were Filipino refugees fleeing to the tip of Bataan trying to avoid the fighting. Hordes of women and children had fled in cars, carabao-pulled carts, or on foot. They had heard of the savagery of the Japanese during their occupation of China and the massacre of thousands of innocent civilians in Nanking struck fear in the minds of these gentlepeople. They had run to escape General Homma's advancing army.

One afternoon I was surprised to hear the sound of men actually cheering. Usually a large group noise was the sound of disappointment that followed an announcement by the camp commander that more work was expected of us or that our food rations were going to be reduced yet again. There weren't many opportunities for cheering by a POW. This time it was different. It was elation!

"What is going on over there?" I asked. No one in our sector had any idea, but whatever it was it had to be very good to make the men shout and whistle like that.

"The Japs are going to start beating people up if this keeps up," a prisoner commented grimly.

"Let's check it out. It's got to be good," another shouted as we all ran in the direction of the cheering. Men were waving their arms in the air as they whooped and whistled.

"What's going on? Who is it?" I asked a guy in the back of the horde.

"It's our nurses. The Angels of Bataan," he proudly answered. "The Japs captured them and are transporting them somewhere else."

These brave women stayed on Bataan to treat the injured and dying throughout the final siege. They could have escaped to Corregidor but they remained in the heat of battle, as they patched up the wounded, ministered medicine and hope, and risked their lives for the Battling Bastards. They were our blood sisters. They fought their healing battles with limited supplies of quinine, sulfa, iodine, tape, and pure guts.

All the prisoners wanted to get a glimpse of the angels, to give them a cheer and an acknowledgment of our appreciation for their devoted and heroic contributions, and to wish them good luck and Godspeed in their journey. As prisoners of the Japanese we knew that they were going to be physically abused; we could only hope that they were not going to also be sexually abused. The sight of them in their tattered nurse's uniforms, holding their heads high for us brought tears even to the most stoic of us. Above the clamor we shouted encouraging tributes and supportive prayers.

"God bless you."

"Thank you. Thank You. God bless you and keep you safe."

"Hang in there. Don't give up."

"We love you. Our thoughts and prayers are with you."

"You're the best."

We were tough guys, the survivors of disease, battles, the death march, beatings, torture, and starvation, yet in the presence of these women many men cried at the mere sight of their courageous faces. We knew that they had probably already suffered painfully as guests of the Emperors' Imperial Japanese soldiers.

"We will win! We'll beat these damn Japs. Keep the faith," bellowed another soldier.

Words alone can't describe the camaraderie we felt for those nurses who had the same hellish experiences of Japanese brutality.

The Japanese convoy carrying the Angels stayed a few hours longer before it departed for some unknown destination. When they loaded the nurses onto the trucks and drove them out the camp, we cheered them on again. I thought of my mother and sisters when I saw the Angels of Bataan trucks disappear over the hill. Although we had become hardened by the continuous horror of the Japanese brutality, the sheer sight of our courageous women sparked a flame of compassion among us all. True to form, the Angels of Bataan saved lives by their mere presence.

CHAPTER 20

# The Farm

*Late 1942*

It had been a long year since the first Japanese bombs started the war and destroyed most of our air force back at Clark Field. I was unable to locate Captain Perrenot, Brewster, or the Chillicothe Kid at either O'Donnell or Cabanatuan. I assumed that by now they had either joined the guerrilla fighters or were dead. I missed Brewster's calm and gentle company. He never complained, no matter how hard the job was during the fighting. Herman Tafoya's physical condition improved, but he always seemed to be on the verge of a breakdown. Often he didn't know who I was. The stress of the prison camp pushed him over the edge of sanity. He did not lose all control, but stayed in a perpetual daze, oblivious to everything going on around him. I made sure he got at least one meal a day, and others from his unit saw that he ate a bit more.

When I heard the Japanese wanted to create a farm in the rocky field next to the camp, I couldn't believe they were serious. I had a lot of experience digging burial pits in the hard soil and wondered what kind of plant would grow in those conditions. But I wasn't a farmer, and I didn't have a choice in the decision. A Japanese sergeant volunteered me for the job.

"Looks like some heavy labor to me," said one of the guys.

"We'll find out if we can grow vegetables in this rocky ground," I said.

Except for a few patchy clumps of wild grass, nothing grew in that soil. But it was not ours to decide, only to do. The guards took a few hundred of us and gave us heavy hand tools. Once we had our tools, they lined us up and gave instructions on how they wanted us to work. I was on the pick detail, the first to attack the hard ground. Each man on the pick detail was responsible for a 36"X 36" workspace. I prayed the pick would sink a couple of inches into the rocky ground, or else the shock vibration returned through the handle rattled my brain. After the one square yard space was broken up, I moved forward to the next piece of ground, and so on. If anyone lagged behind the advancing pickers it resulted in a beating for the slow guy. If anyone raised their head or tried to straighten their back, another whacking would ensue. Periodically all of us were beaten as a group with bamboo poles the size of fire hoses to encourage us to stay in line and move faster.

*"Hyacco! Hyacco!"* screamed the guards.

Behind our pick line was a row of men with hoes who broke up the big clods we had unearthed. Then there was a line of prisoners with rakes who smoothed the soil for planting. Behind each row of workers were the Japanese slave masters providing their brand of painful encouragement.

Vicious beating of a POW on a work detail *Ex-POW Ben Steele*

One peculiarity I observed about the Japanese guards was that when they were one-on-one with a prisoner they weren't as cruel. Sometimes a guard attempted to converse in English or wanted to learn the songs that we sang at night. Others related proudly that they knew something about American baseball or movie stars. But when they were in a group, each attempted to outdo the others' cruelty.

"This reminds me of a Hollywood movie about slaves," I grumbled to the guy on my right.

"What movie?" he asked with a puzzled look.

"The Ten Commandments. Remember the pyramids, the slaves, the guards, and the whips?" I reminded him of the scene where thousands of slaves trudged along, dragging huge solid blocks on carts. While the slaves groaned in the blazing sun, the guards whipped them non-stop.

"God, that's what happening to us," he whispered back.

I said, "Hell, it isn't any wonder they could build those pyramids with thousands of slaves doing all the work."

"Yeah, we might even turn this into a farm and get some decent food for a change," he remarked.

"What? Are you getting tired of rice soup in the morning and rice and bugs at night?" I asked jokingly, referring to the mealy worms and black weevils that we ate.

"I just can't get enough of it," he answered seriously. It was true.

Within a few days the hard-packed ground had been broken up, the rocks removed, and it was raked neatly for the next phase of the farming operation. I had never planted anything back home but I did know that fertilizer was necessary for the plants to grow. The farmers in the farm communities of the Rio Grande Valley used cattle manure. *What are the Japs going to use for fertilizer? There aren't any carabao left.* Along the rows of planted seeds we dug a trench for irrigation water and human manure we affectionately called "honey" scooped from the camp latrines. The "honey dipper" detail was armed with buckets and ladles for scooping out the thick, soupy liquid to feed the fast growing plants. We also diverted a slow moving stream that ran by the farm into a large trench we called the Panama Canal. Each man on the water detail was given a square five-gallon bucket to fill and carry to each plant. Long lines of prisoners marched to and from the rows, in a non-stop, continuous circle. The return cycle with an empty bucket was the most dangerous because the guards beat the prisoners to speed up the line. When our buckets were full we were relatively safe. We quickly discovered that trying to get away with less than full bucket resulted in a severe beating. Each day was the same — first the honey bucket platoon, then the water brigade made an endless circle of scoop, carry, and pour.

At first I thought we might be receiving some of the bounty of our hard labor, after all, we did all the work. The farm was the idea of one of the POWs we called "Farmer Jones." The camp gamblers had bets on when the various crops would be ripe, and how much we would receive. The answer to the second question became evident when the first radishes were ready. They disappeared into camp headquarters and never showed up in our mess kits. And so it went throughout the harvest season. Only the Japanese guards got the crops. We were merely their farm animals.

"Well, at least I have the satisfaction of knowing that they're eating my shit," smirked Herman.

"I thought we were the guests of the Emperor," snickered another soldier. "Hell of a way to treat a guest!"

"I can hardly wait to have the Emperor as a guest at my place back home. I'd teach him a few manners on how to treat a guest," joked a medic called Doc.

"I've got a few jobs around my place that I could use a hand with," I heard someone remark sarcastically down the line.

"Shhhh! Here comes B-17." B-17 was the guard who hit us from above. When he whipped me, I felt as if the entire load from a bomb bay had fallen on me.

After hearing us sing American songs while we were working, Four-Eyes demanded, "You show me song." So we taught him "I'm a dirty, yellow, stinking, slant-eyed, son of a bitch" sung to the melody of the "Battle Hymn of the Republic." We got a few laughs before an English-speaking Japanese officer who didn't think the lyrics were funny chastised him. Four-Eyes gave us all a whipping after his embarrassing reprimand. The beating hurt, but I sure did enjoy watching him proudly march around singing his new song.

CHAPTER 21

# Unsung Hero

*Late Spring — 1943*

"Farmer Jones" had our farm productive in no time. Rumor had it that the original plan was that the prisoners would raise their own food, including rice, to reduce the responsibility of the Japanese. We had the land, climate, know-how and, of course, the slave labor. As a young boy I didn't have much of a green thumb. Although I raised rabbits and chickens, and once Dad made me a small pond to raise some ducklings, growing vegetables was a new experience for me.

In reality, after all our work, we were never given any of the vegetables. Instead, we were fed dirty rice every day, every week, and every month, but never enough to fill us. Once in a blue moon we would get a slice of pickle or some other weed thrown in. The closest thing to meat protein were the bugs that were tossed in the pot along with anything else that was on the floor at the time the rice was bagged. Our own cooks apologized for the rice we had to eat and stated it was probably the sweepings off the packaging floor. Often they found cigarette butts, paper wrappings, metal nails, or splinters of wood mixed in with the rice. Dirty or not, I ate every last grain of rice, the bugs, and even the wood chips if they were reasonably soft. We survivors were eating a diet deficient in vitamins, fat and protein. Everyone had become skin and bone, mere shadows of our former bodies. After losing all our fat, our calorie-starved bodies began to eat our muscle own mass. It hurt me to look at my fellow prisoners — American, British, Australian and Dutch — standing in line like beggars, waiting for the paltry rice ration and whistle weed.

"You Americans don't look so big any more," laughed a tiny guard nicknamed Rat Face. I suspected then that maybe the Japanese military was trying to reduce our larger bodies down to their relatively small stature.

My stomach growled and my mouth watered as I marched to and from the farm, past the perfect rows of green plants at various stages of growth. I thought about how bountiful we had made the barren field. I recalled a conversation in the mess hall over something suspicious in a soldier's mess kit plate.

"Hey look! There's something black and green in my rice."

"Does it have legs?" asked the next fellow.

"Fat ones?" questioned another as he peered into the plate.

"Give it to me! I'll eat it! Juicy legs and all," grunted a voice from the back of the line.

"It's a vegetable," proclaimed the owner of the prize.

"I never saw a vegetable that looked like that," said his friend.

"Those are the weeds we pulled out of the tomato patch," announced another in line, which was probably the truth.

"I guess they must think we need a salad every once in awhile," I remarked.

One day, as we approached the farm there was a commotion. Our guards made us stop to witness a gruesome scene taking place beside the road. A group of guards were kicking and beating a POW mercilessly, as he lay helpless on the ground.

*"Wa do ie, Wa do ie!"* they yelled as they struck him repeatedly.

"Bad boy! Bad boy!" clamored the guard nicknamed Air Raid, who was known for his severe attacks. Apparently the kid had taken a tomato and had been caught with it.

"This what happens to bad boys," mocked the guards as they kicked his face and beat his frail body with poles. There were no boundaries or limitations to what the guards could do to us. They were going to beat the poor boy to death.

Suddenly, Marine Major John Mamerow from our group broke rank, stepped out in front and shouted, "Stop hitting him!"

*"Wa do ie!* He steal tomato and must be punished!" blurted out one of the guards.

The Major stepped forward and placed himself between the young POW and the guards. "Hit me instead," he demanded, offering his own body for punishment. So they did. He stood erect and rigid, like a statue. His face grimaced with every blow, but the Major stood steadfast with each punch and kick. We heard the sound of either his ribs or their poles cracking. I wondered how he could take it, and if they would stop before beating him to death. They had killed a POW officer last week when he asked for more food and quinine. The guards forced him to dig his own grave, then shot him in the head, and kicked him into it.

Almost in unison the guards stopped, dropped their weary arms and stared, mouths agape, in amazement at the major. "Take bad boy," commanded the head guard.

The major bent over and knelt beside the beaten young man and gently cradled him in his arms like a baby. Slowly, he picked up the frail boy and stood erect again facing the guards. The boy was bloody from head to toe and in no shape to walk. We had witnessed an incredible example of bravery and self-sacrifice. For at least a half-minute none of the guards moved a muscle or said a thing. Major Mamerow stood there holding the boy, and waited for the next command.

"*Take wa do ie* to quarters," announced the guard in charge.

I'll never forget the Major's bravery. His strong silent stand demonstrated to the Japanese guards what guts and glory were all about. He could have been shot for merely breaking rank. He knew his own life was in danger. I had witnessed many other prisoners killed for less. He did what he thought needed to be done in spite of the danger. Why the guards didn't kill him, I'll never know. Perhaps they were curious to see if he would continue to take the beating. Perhaps they respected his courage enough to spare his life. I'm certain they'll never forget him.

---

*April 18, 1942 (U.S.)*
*Tokyo, Japan*

Twelve U.S. Army Air Force B-25 Mitchell medium bombers under the command of Lt. Colonel James Doolittle dropped their bombs on Tokyo, Yokohama, Kobe, and Nagoya, Japan. The daring raid was launched in high winds from the aircraft carrier U.S.S. Hornet approximately seven hundred miles from Tokyo. Although they bombed mostly insignificant targets it alerted the Japanese that they were not invulnerable to air attack as their military leaders had assured them. Eight pilots that were shot down were tortured, publicly humiliated and tried as war criminals for 'inhuman acts' Three of the Doolittle pilots were executed while the remaining five were made prisoner of war.

*Strategic Outcomes*

The Japanese General Staff were so embarrassed at their failure to protect the Japanese mainland that they embarked in a series of complex and grandiose war plans that became their undoing three months later at Midway.

More than a military victory, the raid was a major boost to the American public following the devastating disasters of Pearl Harbor and the fall of the Philippines. Realizing Japan was not invincible, U.S. industry and the public rallied by every means possible to contribute materials and manpower to defeat the enemy.

Because the Japanese high command had assumed the strike force had originated and returned to Chinese National airbases, the China Expeditionary Force commenced a punitive, retaliatory attack on the Chinese civilian population killing over 250,000 men, women and children.

*April 29, 1942*
*Lashio, Burma*

Japanese forces 'Banzai' through Burma and capture Lashio, the southern end of the 'Burma Road' thus. closing off the fuel, food and supply pipeline to ally China.

*May 4-8, 1942*
*Battle of the Coral Sea*

In an attempt to thwart a suspected Japanese strike force against Port Moresby, New Guinea, U.S. Commander in Chief in the Pacific Admiral Chester Nimitz ordered a three-part American/Australian naval force to the Coral Sea. Aircraft carriers Lexington and Yorktown escorted by five cruisers and eleven destroyers provided two parts of the strike force while a contingency of Australian and American cruisers and destroyers made up the other. Both opposing fleet commanders sought each other out by aerial reconnaissance. Early the next morning the opposing fleets discovered each other's main force location and launched aerial strike forces focusing on the aircraft carriers. The Lexington's and Yorktown's aircraft struck Shokaku and Zuikaku unrelentingly, forcing the Shokaku to retreat for major repairs to the main Japanese Naval base in the island of Truk.

Although enemy torpedoes and bombs severely damaged the Lexington and the Yorktown they were able to land their returning pilots successfully.

Two hours after the last enemy plane departed, an internal explosion mortally damaged the Lexington. After the crew was evacuated safely, U.S. torpedoes sunk the unrepairable Lexington.

Although the Yorktown sustained severe damage, it was able to limp back to Pearl Harbor for repairs. Thanks to a miracle effort by ship repair personnel, it returned to duty within 48 hours!

*Strategic Outcomes*

The Japanese command called off the Port Moresby invasion because of its losses and uncertainty of the American/Allied military presence defending New Guinea.

The Japanese command faultily assumed that the Lexington and Yorktown were both sunk, thereby underestimating their strategic requirements for future engagements.

The Battle of Coral Sea marked the first time in naval history enemy ships never saw each other because the fighting was done completely by airplanes launched from opposing aircraft carriers.

*May 5-6, 1942*

Japanese Army launch attack on Corregidor

Following an artillery bombardment that left the once tree-covered island completely leveled; Japanese soldiers invade the minimally defended island by small boats. After overwhelming a small group of defender's they entered the underground passageways of the Malinta Tunnel and captured mostly bedridden injured, nurses and refugees from Bataan.

"With broken heart and head bowed in sadness but not in shame I report to your excellency that today I must arrange terms for the surrender of the fortified islands of Manila Bay…" Major General Jonathan Wainright wrote his final communiqué to President Roosevelt prior to his capitulation to the Imperial Japanese forces. He later surrendered the remainder of the American/Philippine forces on Corregidor to Japanese General Masaharu Homma. Most of POW's were convoyed by boats to shore then sent by truck to POW camp Cabanatuan north of Manila.

Captain Travis Perrenot was captured on Corregidor and was assigned to a different section of Cabanatuan than Frank Lovato. Burl A. Brewster, although he was captured on Bataan, had also been assigned to Captain Perrenot's section.

*June, 4-6,1942 (U.S.)*
*Midway Island*
*The Battle of Midway*

U.S. Intelligence (code breakers) discovered that a major Japanese naval task force was planning to strike the strategically located airstrip on Midway atoll. Not knowing the U.S. was aware of their plan to lure the remainder of the U.S. Pacific Fleet into a trap and total annihilation that had eluded them since Pearl Harbor, Admiral Yamamoto commenced an overly complex plan whose consequences would turn the tide of the Pacific War.

Although greatly outnumbered in ships and airplanes, the U.S. Midway Task Force plan was a surprise attack on Admiral Nagumo's Carrier Strike Force.

At 4:30 am Admiral Chuichi Nagumo launched a bombing strike at Midway's airstrip defenders. Midway's radar spotted the oncoming enemy planes and struck back with their own island based B-17 Flying Fortress bombers and old F-2F Buffalo fighter planes but did no damage to any of Nagumo's ships. Japanese antiaircraft fire and modern Mitsubishi Zero fighter planes, flying protective cover over the Japanese fleet, shot down most of the Marine fighter planes.

Nagumo's own attack planes struck Midway's coral island airstrip, dropped bombs and strafed the hopelessly overpowered Midway defenders. Upon parting review of the bombing run, Japanese Flight Leader Lt. Joichi Tomananga concluded Midway's runway was still operational and required another bomb strike to destroy it.

Nagumo's dilemma was whether or not to re-arm his carrier aircraft with bombs to strike Midway again or keep his planes armed with torpedoes and other anti-ship ordnance just in case the U.S. Pacific Fleet arrived earlier than expected. What Nagumo didn't know was that the U.S. carrier force was already nearby and prepared to strike once reconnaissance planes specifically located his aircraft carriers exact position.

Since the Midway based attack force did no damage to Nagumo's ships and none of his reconnaissance planes had spotted any of the U.S. aircraft carriers, he made the fatal decision that cost him the battle and changed the momentum of the naval war in the Pacific. Nagumo ordered his crews to rearm the attack planes with runway destroying bombs and re-attack Midway.

About fifteen minutes after his planes were sent below deck for rearming with runway busting bombs, one of Nagumo's reconnaissance plane reported spotting U.S. warships nearby. Unable to confirm with the whether or not the U.S. force included aircraft carriers that would necessitate changing back to torpedoes, Nagumo stopped the re-arming! Almost an hour later Nagumo's reconnaissance plane reported that the enemy (U.S.) is accompanied in what appears to be an aircraft carrier.

Finally, Nagumo opted to change his onboard aircraft back to torpedoes to destroy his principle targets, the U.S. aircraft carriers. In the hurry up chaos Nagumo's flight decks were left strewn with planes, bombs and torpedoes.

The first two attacks by U.S. "Vindicator" torpedo planes failed completely. Half the Marine "Dauntless" dive bombers were also shot down.

What appeared to be a overwhelming Japanese victory turned completely around when 50 "Dauntless" dive bombers from the Yorktown and Enterprise dived down and bombarded the vulnerable enemy carriers flight decks covered with the bombs that had just been removed. Hit after hit on Nagumo's Flagship Akagi, on Kaga and Soryu turned the three Japanese carriers into sinking blazing infernos as the exposed Japanese bombs continued to explode after the attack.

The sole surviving Japanese aircraft carrier Hiryu met a similar fate the next day after its attack planes had delivered a devastating attack on the resurrected Yorktown.

Later, Spruance's "Dauntless" dive-bombers caught the Hiryu and all of its aircraft parked conveniently on deck as the pilots and crews were eating supper. Four Imperial Japanese heavy aircraft carriers and their best pilots were destroyed at the Battle of Midway in the pivotal battle that changed the course of the Pacific War.

*June 6-7, 1942*
*Attu and Kisla, Alaska*

Japanese troops landed unopposed at Attu and Kiska, the two western most islands in the Aleutian chain capturing a remote weather station and its two inhabitants.

*Strategic Outcomes*

The Japanese Combined Fleets was never able to recover from its crippling losses at Midway. Hundreds of skilled pilots who had six months earlier participated in the attack on Pearl Harbor. Upon returning from their mission to attack the American aircraft carriers, they found their own aircraft carrier landing decks ablaze and sinking. Unable to land, the frustrated pilots, veterans of the Pearl Harbor Attack Force, crashed their out-of-fuel airplanes into the sea. Japan's finest pilots died along with Yamamoto's second attempt to annihilate the U.S. Pacific Fleet at the Battle of Midway. The Japanese public was not made aware of this first major defeat following their overwhelming succession of victories in the first six months of war with the United States, England, Holland and allies in the Pacific.

*June, 1942*
*North Africa*

German General Erwin "Desert Fox" Rommel's armored North Afrika Corps, stormed across North Africa with a plan to reach and capture the Suez Canal, in order to control all access to the Mediterranean Sea and Indian Ocean.

*June 22, 1942*
*Buna, New Guinea*

The Japanese military planners considered Port Moresby, New Guinea a strategic base to establish a launching point for an eventual invasion of Australia. After being thwarted in their first attempt at the Battle of Coral Sea, Japan's highly trained jungle-fighting troops were landed near the New Guinea village of Buna and began a arduous trek of men, artillery and packhorses across the Owens Stanley mountain range on the narrow Kodaka Trail. This backdoor strategy had worked effectively on their land invasion of Singapore and the Philippines.

*July 9th 1942*
*Russian Border*

German Army begins drive into Russia to capture key Russian cities of Leningrad and Stalingrad.

*July 21-22, 1942*
*Gona, New Guinea*

Another Japanese invasion force land near Gona, New Guinea to begin their offensive over the Owens Stanley Mountain Range on the treacherously dangerous Kodaka Trail.

*On the Home Front*

As young and military eligible age men signed up to Uncle Sam's call to duty, the vacuum in the workplace was quickly filled by American women wanting to do their part. Opportunities abounded in all facets of industry, academia, and jobs traditionally done by men. Young women from rural country towns poured into the cities to work in the factories building aircraft, tanks and machinery. Poster icons Rosie the Riveter and Wanda the Welder modeled the resolve of American women doing their part to win the war. When America's favorite pastime was suspended as players went to serve their country, the Women's Professional Baseball League was formed to fill the gap.

For the first time in history educated women had the opportunity to make major breakthroughs in institutions such as science, research, sports, and technologies traditionally dominated by men.

When Congress approved the establishment of female branches of the Armed Forces, they were assigned to essential but in predominantly non-combatant roles.

*August 7, 1942 (U.S.)*
*Guadacanal, Soloman Islands*

When the 1st U.S. Marine Division invaded Guadacanal Island in the southern Soloman Island chain, the surprised troops encountered little enemy resistance, easily capturing a Japanese airfield that they renamed after a Marine pilot who was shot down at Midway. Simultaneous. landings on Tulagi, Tananboro and Gavutu were met with fierce enemy resistance before the U.S. forces took the islets approximately 20 to 30 miles north of Guadacanal.

Defending Henderson Field, the base of the self-proclaimed 'Cactus. Air Force' on the sea, in the malaria infested jungles, and in the skies became a legendary six-month nightmare of attrition of men and materials as both sides fought valiantly and suffered heavy casualties.

*August 9, 1942*
*Battle of Savo Island, Soloman Islands*

The Imperial Japanese naval forces, specially trained in night fighting, surprised and destroyed seven U.S. and Australian navy ships guarding Guadacanal.

Japanese bombers from nearby air bases responded quickly to the aerial threat to their bases and ship harbors by delivering a heavy bombing attack on the runway and aircraft at Henderson Field.

*August 21, 1942*

Although the Japanese command was caught off guard and not prepared for an invasion they responded immediately by shuttling in highly trained troops to Guadacanal from bases in the North in heavily guarded transport ships down the slot between the Soloman Islands. With timetable regularity, the defending marines and sailors named these ships, the "Tokyo Express."

*Battle of the Ilu River*
*Guadacanal, Soloman Islands*

An enemy battalion of 815 jungle-trained, special assault troops attempted to retake Henderson Field. Charge after charge, the enemy ran into the marine defenders' machine guns, small artillery and aerial bombardment by the 'Cactus. Air Force'. Surrounded by U.S. Marines and unwilling to surrender, U.S. 'Stuart' tanks rumbled over Ichiki's remaining soldiers, crushing many under their metal treads. The surviving enemy troops retreated back to the beach where they had landed, and rather than be captured or killed by American bullets, committed hara-kiri with their own hand grenades. All 815 Japanese troops perished to the last man in the first attempt to retake Guadacanal.

*Strategic Outcomes*

Allied forces saw for he first time since Bataan the fanatic zealotry of the Japanese soldier. Death before dishonor was instilled in every Japanese child from birth, through school and finally into the military. The universally accepted national commandment was to live and die by the Code of Bushido.

*August 23-24, 1942*
*Naval Battle of the Eastern Soloman Islands*

For the third time Yamamoto devised a plan to deceive, trap and annihilate the U.S. aircraft carriers that had been his nemesis since he failed to destroy them in the Pearl Harbor attack and at the Battle of Midway. His strategy was to launch a massive naval task force led by the light-aircraft carrier Ryujo to lull Rear Admiral Frank J. Fletcher's task force to attack the 'sacrificial lamb' thereby exposing his aircraft carriers positions. As soon as the U.S. dive bombers screamed down on the Ryujo, sinking it quickly, Japanese dive bombers from the carriers Zuikaku and Shokaku, both veterans of the Pearl Harbor sneak attack, launched their strike aircraft toward the U.S. carriers.

Although Admiral Fletcher launched his dive-bombers and support fighter planes to destroy the Ryujo his two carriers Saratoga and Enterprise were well defended by over 50 F4 Grumman Wildcat fighter planes flying protective cover. Few Japanese planes broke through the aerial umbrella and heavy antiaircraft fire. The Saratoga survived unscathed while the Enterprise flight deck sustained only moderate damage.

Wild claims by returning enemy pilots claiming to have sunk three U.S. aircraft carriers were reported to Admiral Tanaka, Commander of the Japanese task force, giving him the confidence to attempt landing his troops on Guadacanal beaches the next morning.

As the sun broke over the horizon on August 25, dive-bombers from Henderson Field attacked Tanaka's flagship cruiser, troop landing ships, and destroyers, forcing them to beat a hasty retreat back to their main base in Rabual.

*Strategic Outcomes*

Yamamoto was foiled for the third time to annihilate the U.S. aircraft carriers in the Pacific.

Because the U.S. forces controlled the skies over Henderson Field and U.S. aircraft carriers continued to patrol the seas around the area, Tanaka realized that attempting to land troops on Guadacanal during daylight hours would be suicidal. Henceforth the 'Tokyo Express' would have to make its troop deliveries during the night.

*August 31-September 2, 1942*
*Alam el Halfa, El Alamein, Egypt*

For the first time after Rommel's army managed to 'Blitzkrieg' across North Africa, his armored Afrika Corps is driven back by British forces at Alam Halfa.

*September 12-14, 1942*
*Battle of Bloody Ridge, Guadacanal, Soloman Islands*

By the early September, over 5000 Japanese troops hand been landed at night and were ready to make an assault on Major General Alexander A. Vandergrift's greatly outnumbered 1st U.S. Marine Division defending Henderson Field. Vandergrift positioned the bulk of his marines on a ridge about 1 mile from the airfield. On the evening of September 12th the battle began with heavy shelling on the ridge by enemy ships. Less than half an hour later 2000 Japanese troops emerged out of the thick jungle into the heavy fire by the marines. Falling back to higher ground, the marines spent the next day fortifying their dug out emplacements with barbed wire in preparation for the next assault. At about 6:30 p.m. masses of enemy soldiers stormed at the marines screaming

" Marine, you die!" Partially overwhelmed by the sheer number of Japanese troops, the marines continued to hold the ridge with the help of artillery fire. By dawn 260 Americans and 600 Japanese lay dead on what the dauntless marines now called 'Bloody Ridge'.

U.S. defenders continued to retain their very shaky hold of Henderson Field during days and nights of heavy fighting while night after night ships from the 'Tokyo Express' shuttled in reinforcements and shelled the dug-in marine defenders.

Troops and supplies from both sides continued to pour into the bloody battlefield of carnage that was to become a legend in the annals of military history.

*October 11,12 1942*
*Naval Battle of Cape Esparance, Soloman Islands*

On the afternoon of October 11th, planes from the Hornet spotted an enemy cruiser and destroyer force headed toward Cape Esparance where Rear Admiral Norman Scott made the decision to wait and attack them at night. When radar registered their arrival, heavy rounds of artillery blazed into the night catching the Japanese ships off guard. Even though the U.S. considered the Battle of Cape Esparance a victory, more troops and equipment of the 'Tokyo Express' landed safely as the warships battled on the open sea.

*October 13,1942*
*Guadacanal, Soloman Islands*

After Scott landed the U.S. reinforcement troops they were continually barraged for three consecutive nights by artillery delivered by two Japanese battleships. Half of their airplanes were completely destroyed and the airfield completely perforated by large artillery shell holes.

Later, a two prong enemy offensive was foiled by faulty communication, near- impenetrable jungle conditions and spirited fighting by the exhausted Henderson Field defenders.

*October 26,1942*
*Naval Battle of Santa Cruz Islands, Soloman Islands*

Opposing carrier forces attacked each other near the Santa Cruz Islands east of Henderson Field. Although several Japanese carriers were severely damaged, the U.S.S. Hornet, veteran of the Doolittle raid on Tokyo, and U.S.S. Midway had to be abandoned and was sunk.

*November 4,1942*
*North Africa*

Unable to win against Field Marshall Montgomery's advancing forces, German troops begin retreat from El Alamein virtually assuring that the Suez Canal would not fall into German control.

*November 8, 1942*
*North Africa*

General Dwight D. Eisenhower lands troops in Morocco and Algeria.

The remainder of the Axis army is driven out of Egypt by combined Allied forces on November 11.

*November 12,13, 1942*
*Naval Battle of Guadacanal*

By November the Japanese command realized they were losing the battle by attrition of men and supplies against the Guadacanal defenders. To counter the U.S. forces hard fought successes, Yamamoto planned a massive three pronged attack that, if successful, would turn the tide and return Henderson Field and Guadacanal back to Japan. One of his naval forces would land thousands of reinforcements on the beaches, another would deliver an annihilating barrage of shells on Henderson Field, while the third would hold a position at sea to intercept any U.S. ships.

On the evening of November 12/13 the Henderson Field bombardment fleet ran head-on to an American cruiser and destroyer task force in 'Iron Bottom Sound'. The Americans named the sound after the large number of ships sunken there. U.S. destroyers crippled a battleship targeted to shell Henderson. Limping away from its intended destination, it was eventually sunk the next morning by dive-bombers from the Enterprise and B-17's from the base at Espirutu Santo. One prong of Yamamoto's plan had been diverted.

The next day, the second task force headed to bombard Henderson was cut off and although both sides suffered heavy losses in ship to ship fighting, Yamamoto's second prong of his grand plan to take Guadacanal was turned back.

Even though over half of the transports shuttling in soldiers were sunk, the remaining transports landed their troops on the shore only to be heavily bombed by the aircraft from the still operational Henderson Field.

*Strategic Outcome*

Yamamoto's plan had once failed again to destroy the American forces on the land, sea and in the air. His self-fulfilling prophecy issued after his strategic failure at Pearl Harbor to annihilate the U.S. fleet and its aircraft carriers continued to haunt him at Midway and now Guadacanal.

After six months of jungle fighting in wet malaria plagued conditions the greatly outnumbered, intrepid Australian defenders held the Japanese army until the U.S. and other Allied reinforcements arrived and pushed the Japanese back over the mountain to Buna. Port Moresby, considered the gateway to Australia, remained in Allied control.

November marked the turning point of World War II in Europe and in the Pacific.

Successive Allied victories on three fronts: the naval Battle of Guadacanal, the turning back of the German armies in North Africa, and victory at Stalingrad, inspired President Roosevelt to proclaim, "During the past two weeks we have had a great deal of good news, and it would seem that a turning point in this war has at last been reached,"

*October 1942*
*Siam (Thailand)*

Japan begins construction of the Siam-Burma railway using Australian and British prisoners of war through impassable rain forest jungles and over malarial swamps and rivers. Prime Minister Hidecki Tojo had decreed the previous. May a "no work, no food" policy to the over 300,000 Allied prisoners of war in camps. Japan had refU.S.ed to abide by the terms of the Hague Convention forbidding the working of military captives on industrial worksites, and rationalized their decision by citing they had not signed the Hague agreement. This executive action justified Japan's cruel and inhumane enslavement of allied prisoners of war in military and civilian industry. POW's were forced to build runways, load and unload ships, farm, and later coerced to work in underground mines and factories in Japan and China. Over 200,000 women POWs and civilian internees were forced to become sex slaves for the Japanese military and officials. Designated by the Japanese government as "Comfort Women," they endured or were killed.

*December 17, 1942*
*London, England*

Anthony Eden addressed the British House of Commons and made the first public statement referring to the extermination of Jews by the Nazi's in concentration camps.

*January 14-18,1943*
*Casablanca, Morrocco*

Allied leaders, Roosevelt, Churchill and Stalin together with their Chiefs of Staff met at Casablanca to outline a plan of action to win the war in Europe and the Pacific. Charged with the task of evaluating all available resources of men, material and strategic importance, it was decided that the 'Europe First' strategy would continue to take precedence over the war being waged in the Pacific.

*Priorities established in order:*

"Defeat of the (German) U-boats remains the first charge of resources."

"Russia must be sustained by the greatest volume of supplies."

Build up in Britain would continue or a possible full-scale invasion of France by 1944.

Increased heavy bombing raids of German targets

Planning was to begin for the invasion of Sicily following the defeat of Axis forces in North Africa.

Operations in the Pacific included securing New Guinea, the Solomans and an offensive against the Japanese strongholds on the Caroline and Marshall Islands and to recapture Attu and Kiska in the Aleutians.

The British agreed to organize an offensive in Burma by the end of the year.

*January 22, 1943*
*Buna, Papua, New Guinea*

In the final week of January 1943, after weeks of unrelenting tank and artillery supported fighting, allied forces crush the Japanese resistance almost to the last man.

*Strategic Outcomes*

For the first time in the Pacific War the Japanese Army had been completely stopped and defeated. New Guinea, the northern gateway to Australia, stood. The Japanese southern advances to dominate the South Pacific were forever halted. The myth of the invincibility of the Japanese soldier was dispelled in the jungles and remote beaches of New Guinea.

*February 1-8 1943*
*Guadacanal, Soloman Islands*

Unable to defeat Vandergrift's marines and retake their airfield, the Japanese command conceded Guadacanal and began evacuating their starving and diseased troops under the cover of darkness.

*Strategic Outcomes*

Guadacanal was the first Allied forces foothold in the outer defensive ring of enemy held island fortresses. The U.S. firmly established an island-based airfield in the southern Soloman Islands to launch aerial attacks on other Japanese held naval and airfields in the South Pacific. Guadacanal marked the first time the U.S. defeated and pushed the Japanese out of their own previously held territory.

In day and night sea battles surrounding Guadacanal, the U.S. Navy successfully weakened the might of the once seemingly invincible Imperial Japanese Navy.

Many of Japan's most skilled troops were killed on Guadacanal or in their transport ships by U.S. ships, bombers and submarines as they attempted to reinforce their fellow soldiers fighting a losing battle to retake Henderson Field.

*February 2, 1943*
*Stalingrad, Russia*

Hitler's starving and beaten Army is halted in frigid winter conditions at the doorstep to Stalingrad. The defeated German soldiers are captured by the Russian's and imprisoned in Stalag POW camps.

*March 1-4, 1943*
*Battle of the Bismarck Sea*

Yamamoto, determined to save his other island bases in New Guinea, sent a convoy of eight transport ships laden with 6,000 troops, escorted by eight destroyers, to reinforce his troops on Lae. The entire transport convoy as well as four of the destroyers were sunk by U.S. and British bombers that the Japanese later called the 'Bismark Sea Massacre'. The Battle of the Bismark Sea ended all Japanese major efforts to send troop reinforcements to New Guinea.

*March 1943*
*Atlantic Ocean*

More Allied merchantmen were lost to German U-boats than in any previous. month since the war had begun.

*April 18,1943*
*Northwest of Guadacanal, Soloman Islands*

Admiral Yamamoto killed

Naval Intelligence (code-breakers) intercepted a Japanese transmission outlining Admiral Yamamoto's flight itinerary of a morale-building inspection tour of his forces northwest of Guadacanal. From Washington, Navy Secretary Frank Knox ordered Major John W. Mitchell's P-38 Fighter Squadron to intercept and 'must at all costs reach and destroy Yamamoto and his staff'. In a daring sortie requiring extra fuel tanks, and special preparation, the fighter squadron intercepted and fired on Yamamoto's 'Betty' bomber sending it crashing into the trees.

Admiral Isoroku Yamamoto, Commander and Chief of the Japanese Combined Fleet, designer and planner of the Pearl Harbor Attack Force, the overly complex Midway/Aleutian island invasions, and all major Japanese naval operations in the Pacific, was found in the wreckage killed by a single bullet. Beginning at Pearl Harbor, Yamamoto was foiled in successive attempts to annihilate the U.S. Navy. Because of his firsthand knowledge of the vast resources of raw material, technology and human resources within the United States, Yamamoto forewarned that Prime Minister Tojo's and the ultranationalist military leadership in Japan was destined for an uphill battle following his failure to completely destroy the U.S. Naval Fleet (aircraft carriers) at Pearl Harbor.

His prediction that " we have only awakened a sleeping giant and given it a horrible resolve" had become his epithet.

*May 11-30, 1943*
*Attu, Aleutian Islands, Alaska*

U.S. troops land at Attu island and after a month of desperate charges by fanatical Japanese soldiers screaming 'Japanese drink blood like wine!' the U.S. 7th Infantry Division re-took Attu. The cost in lives to re-claim this remote, frozen outpost was high with over 1000 American soldiers killed. Almost all of the 2,500 enemy soldiers were killed in the bloody fighting to take back American soil from the Japanese.

*July 5, 1943*
*Russia*

Counterattacking Soviet forces destroy the might of Hitler's retreating army in the largest tank battle in history.

*July 28, 1943*
*Kiska, Aleutian Islands, Alaska*

Realizing that the U.S. would invade Kiska next, the Imperial Japanese Command under the cover of foul weather, evacuated over 5,000 Japanese troops before the surprised U.S. troops arrived to find only a few abandoned dogs.

PART III

# Slaves of the Rising Sun

*August 1943 – August 16, 1945*

CHAPTER 22

# Voyage of a Hell Ship

*August 1943*

One morning about eight hundred of us were notified that we were being transferred again, this time by ship to some unknown destination. It didn't take long to pack my possessions. I rolled up everything, except my canteen, in my GI-issue raincoat, tied it in a knot and reported to the central yard. Soon thereafter we were marched to trains to be transported to Manila.

The last time I had seen the deep blue ocean was on April 9th 1942, when we had our backs to the water and faced the Japanese for the final battle of Bataan. If we had had an inkling of the horrors that would ensue during the Death March and death camps, we probably would have disobeyed our orders to surrender and fought the enemy to the last standing man.

The freighter was an old gray tub about seventy-five yards long with no armament. Japanese merchant sailors in cotton thongs and long bandanas scurried about on the deck chattering to each other. They pointed at our POW group and shook their heads in disapproval like something was wrong. The guards forced us into a long single line to begin loading us in. Like ants slowly crawling on a food trail, we walked up the narrow wooden gangplank onto the deck and then descended down through a 6'X6' foot cargo hatch into another one of Emperor Hirohito's guest quarters.

Step by step, we climbed down a vertical, sixty-foot steel ladder through the level below the top deck that was filled with sugar cane to the lowest storage hold that was littered with straw. I realized why the deck hands were alarmed. The space in the hold could not accommodate eight hundred men, no matter how thin we had become. As we maneuvered for standing space in the rusty foul-smelling hold, men began to shout in the darkness, "We need more room! No more men! There's not enough room!" Everyone stared upward toward the tiny hole of daylight and watched in horror as the steady stream of prisoners continued to pour down the steel ladder. Frustration and panic spread through the sardine-can accommodations.

*"Hyacco! Hyacco!"* I could hear the cracking sound of poles beating the heads and backs of the descending men.

When the last prisoner had descended the long steel ladder into the cargo hold, no one dared sit down for fear of being trampled in the dangerously over-crowded sweltering hellhole.

"We need more air!" shrieked a terrified voice.

"We're going to suffocate," lamented another hopeless cry in the dark.

Angry, grumbling remarks about air, water, food and no latrine rumbled through the mass of packed humanity. The only source of fresh air was the narrow hold opening, at least fifty feet above us.

"There's no room to lay down and sleep," complained another voice in the darkness.

Gradually fatigue and the narcotic effect of reduced oxygen made it necessary for us to sit in the space where we stood, or risk falling down. The noisy diesel ship engines began to pound; the signal our journey out to the open sea from Manila Bay had begun.

I sat on the floor with my knees pulled up close to my chest and rested my head on my skinny folded forearms. *Boy! Out of the frying pan and into the fire. When is this hell going to subside even a little? Is there no end?*

When I realized the gravity of our situation, I wanted to pass out and sleep until it was over. If the rumor were true that the journey could take up to two weeks, I thought we were definitely goners.

"How in the world are we going to be able to lie down and sleep if we only have room to squat or sit cross-legged?" asked a gaunt-faced fellow on my right.

I shrugged my shoulders and shook my head. The lack of fresh air was making me queasy and confused. Once under way, the grumbling subsided and the ongoing process of survival began. It was clear that we needed to organize in order to survive the long journey that lay ahead. Some of the men stood and leaned against the steel hull so others could sleep sandwiched in like sardines. We each took a shift of standing, and likewise received a shift of sleep.

Before sailing on the transport ship from San Francisco to Manila, I had never been on a boat. The largest bodies of water I had ever seen in arid New Mexico were the lakes in the Jemez Mountains that were fed by snowmelt.

All day and night the diesel engines clanged away. Men were sullen and morose, and seemed resigned to their tragic fate.

Our captors were as stingy with the rice on board this ship as they were back at the camps. Water and food were lowered down through the hatch in steel buckets. As the water bucket made its sixty-foot journey down, some spilled out. Thirsty men stood beneath the descending bucket with their mouths wide open and their tongues out, hoping to catch the precious fluid before it landed on the prone body of a sleeping prisoner. The Japanese sailors looked down through the hatch laughed and mocked us, as if we were circus animals performing a trick. Water was no laughing matter to those of us suffering from dehydration. At night the guards made the air worse when they shut the hatch, which left only a small 4X4 foot square. All of us panted like tired dogs after chasing rabbits.

Our grimy, half-naked bodies touched on all sides all the time. Some of the prisoners suffered from dysentery and defecated uncontrollably as they tried to crawl over bodies to get to the bucket. All we could do was to wipe the mess off with straw. We all were affected and I knew there was nothing one could do when their bowels were purging. From the beginning of the march to this very moment, the Japanese forced us to live with human filth, dysentery, and bacteria.

From out of the darkness someone screamed, "Get off me, you big fat son of a bitch!"

We knew he was yelling at one of the huge ship rats that shared storage with us because there weren't any fat prisoners. The rats ran across our bodies on their way to and from the sugar cane in the other holds. During the night little rats followed their fat parents across the sea of bare backs and bellies of those who slept. Their sharp claws dug into our bodies whenever they became frightened. Often men would toss them off their bodies, but the rats would land on other POWs. Occasionally someone would catch one of the furry rodents, snap its neck, skin it, and included it in our soup. We had a small coal-fired stove to heat our rice, weeds and rat-flavored broth. Occasionally, the topside crew tossed a few fish heads into the food buckets. Those fish heads and the rats were the closest thing to meat protein we got. Learning to survive in a gigantic sewer with only two handfuls of cooked rice per day, made the difference between those who lived and those who didn't.

The guards did not venture down into the reeking hold, nor did they have to. They controlled the ladder that was our only access to the outer world. The 'honey buckets' (excrement containers) in our hold were always full. Occasionally they allowed the strongest of the POW's to climb the long ladder to topside and use the *benjo* that hung over the water. Unfortunately, the thin pipe ladder rungs were always slippery because they were coated with the defecation of the poor guys who weren't able to hold it long enough to get up the sixty-foot ladder. They also let some of us go topside long enough for them to torment us with degrading games. Their favorite was forcing a group of us to stand in line while holding our bladders, until it hurt so bad that everyone was grimacing and squirming in agony. There was always a loser in this game who eventually broke down and soiled himself. The guards then forced him to his knees and gave him a severe beating. Only when they finished beating the loser did they give permission for the rest of us to urinate over the edge of the ship while they roared with laughter and mocking gestures. Almost everyone moaned in agony as we sprayed dark-yellow streams of urine into the sea.

"Damn cowardly Japs. They're just pretenders," mumbled one of the guys from the line as we descended the ladder back into the pit.

"Look at them. Little, piss ant army rejects who haven't seen a day of real battle since this whole mess began," I replied.

"Yeah, it's easy for them to be tough when we're unarmed, weak and beat up," he said, while taking another careful step down the shaky ladder.

"Back in Bataan we fought against real soldiers," I said. "The fighting Jap soldiers who guarded us the first day treated us with more respect."

"Sickos, maniacs, and 4Fs trying to prove something," he complained, loud enough for the guards on top to hear.

"Yeah, same kind of jerks at the camps," I acknowledged as we approached the bottom rung.

A breath of the fresh ocean air was worth the aching pain in my burning bladder.

"Good luck, Buddy," he sighed as he disappeared into the dim recesses of the hold.

My guess was that the real Japanese soldiers with fighting experience were more likely to be in combat situations. Why would the Japanese waste the experienced soldiers on broken down prisoners? Many of the prison camp guards were older, some were partially disabled, but all of them were crazy. They reminded me of the Spencer Tracy movie, "Dr. Jeckel and Mr. Hyde." Under normal conditions, people control their emotions and actions reasonably well. The good side is the predominant side of their personality. Under conditions like war, death, fear and survival the darker sinister side of the personality becomes dominant. Helplessly we caught the brunt of the guards' dark sides with no chance to fight back for fear of instant death.

*Second week in the Hellship*

There were over eight hundred of us in the Emperor's floating cesspool, and it was a miracle that no one had died or been killed since we started. I heard the rumor that we were selected from the general population of Cabanatuan because we were the healthiest prisoners, which explained our surprising survival.

Sometime in the mid-afternoon of the ninth or tenth day, the guards started screaming at about dozen or so prisoners topside to hurry and climb down the ladder. The guards pushed them down the hatch as fast as they could and continued to hit the ones they could reach.

*What the Hell is going on?* I wondered as I watched the commotion from under the ladder.

"Our planes are out there!" announced the first POW before he reached the bottom.

Apparently, American aircraft had been spotted flying overhead and the guards rushed the POWs down the hatch to avoid them being spotted on deck.

"What kind of planes were they? Bombers? Fighters? What? Who saw them? How many?" pleaded a fast talking guy with an East Coast accent.

"Hard to tell. As soon as the Japs saw them they started hitting us and herding us down the hatch," replied the witness.

"Why the hell did they do that?" asked another.

"It seems to me that letting the pilots know that allied POWs are on board would be good insurance for an unarmed, Nip freighter," remarked a fellow standing by the ladder.

I said in disgust, "Who knows why the Japs do anything?"

But looking around me I saw faces of hope for the first time since we surrendered. Our excitement built with the discussion of our planes near us.

"Thank God the planes didn't try to sink our sorry asses," blurted another voice in the crowd.

"I saw them! They were bombers. Two engines and twin tails," panted one of the men who had been topside.

"B-25s," blurted out another from the packed crowd of excited faces. "Maybe they'll radio our position and rescue us?"

"How many?" questioned another voice in the darkness.

"Seven maybe ten. Real high! Heading southeast," remarked someone. We clamored for all the information we could get about our fellow soldiers in the Pacific.

One thing was sure, it was good to know American forces were in the vicinity of Japan. The last secret radio news I had heard at Cabanatuan was that the enemy had incurred some big losses on land and sea. But I never knew for sure. Nothing was ever official on the rumor hotline in camp. This was the first legitimate sighting of our guys in one and a half years.

"Why in the hell don't the Japanese have any markings on this ship to indicate they are transporting POWs?" I asked the obvious question.

"What if one of our planes or subs spotted this defenseless freighter between here and Japan and decided to sink us?" asked someone in the crowd.

A voice out of the darkness replied, "We would be the first to be killed. We're trapped below the water line. We'd sink with the cargo and the rats."

The following day I heard a new rumor that we had changed course to avoid detection and would be out at sea longer. It was hard to know what was true, considering the source of information was always unknown. I often wondered how our informants got their news. I heard that some of the guards could be bribed with food or favors. Since I never gambled or bartered for money or food in camp, I never ever had any cash to buy anything from the guards.

Day after day we watched the sky through the hatch, hoping for a tiny glimpse of free Americans, our fighting buddies, those who one day would liberate us from the cruel hands of the Japanese.

But as each day ended without another sighting of our planes, the excitement in the hole diminished. It had been a long week since the bombers flew high over our ship.

"Did they really see our planes?" I overheard someone asking his buddies, while I lay resting half-awake on my side.

"Oh, yeah, I'm sure they did," answered another.

"They probably didn't even see us. Wasn't it real cloudy that day?" retorted another.

I lay there wide-awake and listened to the changing mood of the prisoners. All of us aboard that hell ship fought in Bataan without contact or reinforcements or supplies, until we were backed into this same ocean and surrendered. It was easy to understand the feelings of abandonment, since we hadn't seen any of our planes in the sky but those B-25s since our capture almost two years earlier.

*September 1943 — Arrival At Moji, Japan*

Nearly three weeks after being herded into the dark, filthy innards of the hell ship the rumor circulated that we were going to arrive in Japan by day's end. I ignored the mumbled speculations of what might happen next. I knew that whatever it was, I needed to keep my head together if I was going to survive.

When the ship's diesel engines stopped for the first time in twenty days, the sound of the ocean waves lapping the freighter's steel hull triggered an eerie silence among the men.

"We're in Japan," someone speculated. Another prisoner, a sailor, said we would be towed by tugs into the harbor. Rumblings of conjecture commenced. The next phase of survival was about to begin.

"Thank God we made it to land without being sunk by our own submarines or bombers," I said, staring upward to the hatch hole along with everyone else.

"With no thanks to the Japs," remarked a fellow beside me.

When we finally arrived at the dock of the huge shipping port of Moji, Japan, we had spent twenty days at sea and survived not only Japanese cruelty, but also our own self-doubts. What lay ahead for us now that we were in Japan was a giant mystery.

We crawled up the shaky ladder out of the pigsty, and down a long steel gangplank onto the wooden dock. I heard sighs of relief mixed with a "Thank God," and "I thought it would never end," and an occasional "I'll never go on another boat again as long as I live."

As our eyes adjusted to the bright sunlight, what we saw of each other was not a pretty picture. We looked more like zombies than human beings. Bearded, gaunt faced, skeletal men in clothing so damp and soiled the fabric rotted off in irregular pieces. Everyone of us had dirty straw stuck to our skin, our hair or falling out of our pockets and boots. It felt good to be on solid ground again and gulp deep breaths of fresh air. I said another prayer of thanks that I survived one more of the Emperor's guest quarters. "Thank God, they haven't got me yet," I repeated quietly as I stretched my muscles in the sun.

The Japanese guards and sailors, on the other hand, must have cleaned up and changed uniforms before landing, because they looked as neat as pins. On the dock we were then divided into groups and herded into open railroad cars.

CHAPTER 23

# Under the Earth

*Fukuoka Camp No.17 — Mitsui coal mine, Omuta, Japan*

As the train chugged along the narrow track, I looked in amazement at the majestic Japanese landscape. Lush rice fields formed a verdant tapestry of blue and green. Towering volcanoes reached up through thin, wispy clouds against a turquoise blue sky. Everything looked so serenely peaceful, and in perfect order, unlike the charred, bombed-out remains of the Philippine countryside. From what we could see from the train, Japan had not been touched by our bombs for it was stunningly beautiful and immaculately clean, as though every tree and leaf were perfectly placed in the manicured rice paddies, orchards and landscaped homes. For the first time in almost two horrifically painful years I felt a few moments of peace. I watched people going about their daily work without barbed wire fences or armed soldiers prodding or beating them. Tears welled up inside as I reminisced of happier days before this insanity. I saw common people planting and cultivating rice that had become more valuable than gold to us. The visual images of peaceful living must have touched the other prisoners as powerfully, for they too were silent except for a sniffle or quiet sob. I prayed that conditions would be better now that we were in Japan and out of the war zone. Being on the train reminded me of the sounds I used to hear working late at the bowling alley near the Albuquerque train station.

After about an hour, the slow moving train's iron wheels screeched to a halt at the front gate of Mitsui Coal Mine Camp 17. Smokestacks towered over multiple rows of barrack-style buildings that were over 150 feet long. With the addition of our group, there were over fifteen hundred American, English, Dutch, Australian, and New Zealander prisoners. Like everything else we saw since entering Japan, cleanliness and order prevailed throughout the huge industrial complex. Compared to the filth and overcrowded conditions back at O'Donnell and Cabanatuan, it appeared that we might finally get decent housing and treatment.

Once again we stood at attention to listen to the camp commander deliver his 'welcome speech'. He reminded us that we were less than animals for surrendering. He also outlined the camp rules we were to follow without exception, and emphasized all punishment would be severe.

Imperial Japanese Army Camp Commander Fukahara repeated in English, "You are here to work. You no work, you not eat same as worker." He had originally ordered that we salute the Japanese flag, which we all adamantly refused to do. It was one thing to be humiliated by constant whippings and beatings but we would never salute the flag of the enemy that had killed and maimed thousands of unarmed POWs and now enslaved us. He rescinded his order because he understood that we would all refuse and choose to be shot rather than degrade our dead and ourselves by obeying that command.

Following a four-day training period on how to use mining equipment and an indoctrination on prison camp rules, we began our enslavement as coal miners for Baron Mitsui and the Imperial Japanese government. Civilian engineers from Mitsui Corporation directed the daily mining operations with the persuasive backing of Japanese army guards. These guards were more unfit, both physically and mentally, for regular army duty than any we had met so far. As in the other camps, we gave the guards nicknames like One-Arm and Hop-a-Long, to describe their physically disabled condition. We thought it was a good sign that the Japanese were so desperate for prison guards that they had to use disabled and older men to guard us, rather than the young and healthy. Unfortunately appearances can be deceiving, because the guards of Mitsui Coal Mine Camp 17 made up for their lack of physical abilities with cruelty and proved to be the most brutal of all the Japanese we had encountered so far.

After a brief orientation by an English-speaking Mitsui engineer, we were divided into specific work details and trained by an engineer to work on one of four specific work details: Exploration, Excavation, Preparation, and Exportation.

The Exploration job description involved drilling a pattern of deep holes into solid rock walls with air-powered drill motors and long bits. The second step was to insert sticks of dynamite and burnable fuses into the drilled holes, twist the fuses together, light with a match and run. This slow but effective process blasted new tunnels or extended spurs beneath the earth to find the black coal veins. The Excavation crew came next and loaded the heavy rock rubble in wheelbarrow-like carts to take to the nearest mine cart that traveled on a railroad-like track. Sometimes, larger rocks had to be dynamited again or broken up with an air-powered jackhammer, drill and sledgehammers before they could be lifted and carried across the uneven floor. The Excavation crew also carved out the floor and busted up the rough edges of the tunnel-like spur. There wasn't much room to maneuver until we blasted, chipped, and carried out more rock. Both of these early stages were perhaps the most dangerous because there was no ceiling support or adequate lighting in the newly dug spurs.

As soon as the new tunnel floor was flat, wide, and clear enough, a Preparation crew strung electrical wire and bare light bulbs overhead, and set up a long conveyor belt. Iron pipes carrying the high-pressure air were installed along the wall to power the heavy drills and jackhammers. Smaller rocks were loaded on the belt and moved to the wheelbarrows or carts. The Extraction crew shoveled and loaded the rock and coal onto the conveyor that carried it out of the mine to waiting railroad cars.

Topside of Mitsui Coal Mine at Fukuoka POW Camp 17
*Ex-POW Ben Steele*

Every day following *tenko* and chow, the topside guards marched each work shift to the mine entrance to get onto the mainshaft sled that descended down a shaft on rails to the level we were working on that day. Depending on the distance of the level below the ground, the ride took about eight minutes. The cramped, cable-car on the rickety rails was like a roller coaster grinding down at about a sixty-degree grade in a narrow hole surrounded by solid rock.

Upon reaching the main shaft, we broke off into our various crew assignments and began the twelve to fourteen hour shifts.

Guards rarely ventured into the unsafe areas of the mine unless they were asked to by one of the Mitsui engineers. They usually remained in the well-lit main tunnels to avoid possible cave-in hazards. Anyway, we were trapped deep in the mine with nowhere to go but past them.

The first time I went down in the mine with a shift of prisoners, Mitsui engineers, and guards, I was not prepared mentally or physically for the conditions beneath the earth and Nagasaki Bay. We were dressed in Japanese issue, rubber-soled canvas shoes and gauze-thin pants and shirts that offered no protection from the jagged rock or heavy steel machinery and tools.

The main shaft ceilings were supported with thick wooden beams at regular intervals that looked strong and well built. Mitsui Mining had professionally constructed the shafts and main tunnels many years before the war started. Narrow-gauge railroad tracks ran through the middle of the main tunnels for the rusty steel carts that carried the coal and rock out of the mine. Mitsui engineers led us down the old, worked out main shafts into dimly lit spurs. The farther we were led down the narrow spurs, the less we saw of the heavy wooden support beams. Icy cold water dripped from the ceiling and walls and formed black puddles of irregular depth that made walking on the uneven floor difficult and dangerous. With only our gas-powered miner's headlamps to light the way through the darkness, we often sloshed through waist-high underground pools to get to our work site.

I was assigned to work to an Exploration crew that was responsible for drilling and blasting new spurs or extending abandoned spurs left by Mitsui several years earlier. Because the space was small and the job technically more specific, only three people were required for our crew: a Mitsui engineer, and two POWs — myself and a British POW named Jack. The engineer decided how deep to drill and how much dynamite to use. If we used too little, we made a mess. If we used too much, we made a really big mess. The job was simple but extremely dangerous. The thought of the whole mine shaft collapsing and burying me deep in Japan was a thought I had to put out of my mind each I lit the detonation fuse. We worked in the dark with only the carbide gas beam of our miner's headlamps to illuminate the area in front of us. The Mitsui engineer and sometimes a guard stood in the back recesses of the dark tunnel and watched as my partner, Jack and I did all the work. They often drank saki and got drunk together as we drilled. The deafening whine of the air drill rang in my ears long after the motor stopped. But an even louder ring left by the next phase of Exploration soon replaced the blasting. Once we lit the thin wire gunpowder-coated fuse we ran for cover wherever we could find any. The Mitsui engineer and the guard were usually a long distance away whenever we did the blasting. Jack and I often huddled behind a large boulder or a bend in the tunnel and waited for the explosion. We watched the bright, red-yellow burning fuse snake through the pitch-black tunnel like a Fourth of July sparkler. It cracked and hissed through the dense silence that one finds only in a cave or mine deep in the earth. Its burning flame stunk the spur with pungent clouds of burnt

Excavating rock in coal mine *Ex-POW Ben Steele*

gunpowder. To make the smallest available target for the unpredictable barrage of debris, Jack and I squatted, tucked our knees into our chests and covered our ears with our hands.

The ensuing blast often rocked us off our feet as splintered rocks and pulverized dust ricocheted through the narrow mine shaft off the floor, walls, and ceiling. For a brief moment our headlamps streamed through the smoke and dust like fog lights in the gray haze. There was an eerie stillness that followed the earth shaking as we waited for any loose rocks that might fall from the unsupported ceiling. After each explosion I sighed with relief, made a sign of the cross, and thanked God for surviving one more time. We waited a minute or so until the dust settled or until the engineer came to examine the results. We coughed a lot because all we had were the thin Mitsui-issued handkerchiefs for dust and smoke protection.

We usually worked on ten day, twelve hour cycles. The eleventh day was considered a rest day or yasume. But there was never time to rest for a prisoner of the Japanese. Instead of going down the mine to work, on yasume we were required to wash our clothes and clean the barracks. We also had to clean the benjo and were forced to do an hour of Japanese style exercises. Following tenko and breakfast lugao, we marched to the exercise area, stripped to our waists and followed the directions of the Japanese exercise leader. As an athlete in high school I was used to exercising daily. We did pushups, side straddle hops, sit-ups, toe-touches and deep knee bends. The first time our yasume group had to follow the exercise leader's "reach for the sun" motions to a bouncy Japanese melody on the scratchy phonograph record, we all started laughing. That outburst brought a hail of whippings on our bare backs from the attendant guards who didn't see the humor.

By November 1943, frost-covered mornings warned of colder days ahead. It had been almost three years since most of us had experienced any frigid weather. Standing in line for morning tenko, I felt the brisk autumn air cut through my paper-thin Mitsui uniform. The gauze short pants and short sleeved shirts were not going to be warm enough for the winter season in Japan. For the first time since coming to the South Pacific two years ago, I could see puffs of warm air come from the men's mouths when we barked off roll call. The disappearing clouds of breath reminded me of another place and time that seemed so long ago.

I remembered rabbit and quail hunting with my father and brothers, Abel, A.T., and Joe, on frosty fall mornings on the high desert plains west of Albuquerque. We huddled in a tight circle and our warm breath condensed into clouds in the cold, dry New Mexican air as we waited patiently for the autumn dawn. Daybreak's first golden rays emanated skyward from behind the deep purple Manzano Mountains twenty-five miles to the east across the Rio Grande Valley. The emerging daylight made the frosted tumbleweeds and sagebrush glow like fresh snow in the moonlight. Hunting for wild game helped augment our food supply during the Great Depression years when money was scarce. Our family was fortunate because Dad had a steady job as a machinist at the railroad. He made axle parts that needed replacing often, which assured him continuous employment. His regular income, eggs from the chickens I raised, and successful hunting trips guaranteed that our family ate when others were not so blessed. Our family shared some of the meat with our neighbors who were having difficult times putting food on their tables. Fresh meat was a luxury that many couldn't afford. Often we returned on Saturday afternoons with over a dozen rabbits strapped to the wooden rack Dad had rigged on the side of his 1927 Chevy. On a good day, we brought home a few doves and quails which were delicacies. Mother served them on rice that evening. The tiny breasts of the wild birds were tender, and melted in our mouths like warm sweet butter. Nothing was wasted of the rabbits we killed. Mother prepared the soft fur pelts for coat collars, small purses, and earmuffs. She used rabbit skins to make riding chaps that became the envy of every cowboy at the New Mexico State Fair.

Each day that I hung onto my life as a POW, I appreciated more fully the meaning of freedom. I missed the days filled with simple, rich moments spent doing ordinary activities like eating Sunday dinner, playing a game of football at the park, going to a Saturday matinee with my buddies, and being free to do whatever I wanted with the people I love.

Even though we knew that forcing POWs forced to mine coal or do any work for the enemy was against the rules of the Geneva Convention, we continued to do so because we wanted to live rather than be killed through starvation or beatings. The war we now fought wasn't a game with referees who gave penalties for breaking the rules of war. Instead it was more like a crime wave. I could not forget the brave officers at Camp O'Donnell who had asked for quinine and medical supplies and had received a bullet in the head. There were no rules of war other than the rules that the camp commanders invented or the Mitsui Corporation engineers created for their own benefit.

On the whole, the Camp 17 guards were the bottom-of-the-barrel of the Emperor's army. Many were sadistic mental cases who perversely enjoyed hurting and physically damaging anyone in their path. It was rumored that most of them were recruited from mental hospitals and correctional prisons. Although every guard would whip a POW if he were provoked, it was a foregone certainty that someone was going to get severely beaten when one of the known psychopaths approached. Some of the worst were the Sailor, Screamer, One-Arm Bandit, Billy the Kid, and Slime. Often, they continued beating a man after he was unconscious. They clearly enjoyed beating a man down and leaving him bloodied and bruised. POWs whispered warnings when of one of them approached a work crew.

After two long years of being a prisoner of the Japanese, I could sense when a whipping would commence and learned how to best take a strike. All Japanese guards carried sticks or pieces of wooden two-by-four boards. In the coal mine the guards used round poles that were tools for probing wall and ceiling surfaces for looseness. Some guards carried hand-carved clubs the size of baseball bats. There was no escaping the inevitable strikes, but a bent head and shrugged shoulder posture seemed to result in the least long-term damage.

Those prisoners who raised their arms and hands to ward off the blows would be hit harder. Hits across the thighs or hamstring muscles hurt the most and often resulted in a crippling injury. Just as in the Death March, when a soldier was unable to make it to the next appointed task, the end was near. Staying in a work detail was the best way to ensure receiving the daily ration of rice.

A guard we nicknamed Bucktooth often used his shift as guard in the mine for the opportunity to catch a little sleep in the narrow, dim-lit tunnels. We watched out of the corner of our eyes as Bucktooth sat perched on a boulder in a shadowed recess with his back against the wall. When his mouth drooped open, we knew Bucktooth was asleep. Our rate of work slowed down at least seventy five percent during his nap, which could last a few seconds or a few minutes. We watched his mouth carefully. If it started to close it was time to get back to work.

The Mitsui coal mine was inexcusably unsafe. The Japanese priority was to extract as much coal as possible in the shortest amount of time. The Mitsui engineers knew better than anyone else did the degree of danger that existed in the mine. They continually looked up at the fractured ceilings with worried expressions. Often the engineers showed up drunk or got that way on the job. High on saki was perhaps how that they faced the eminent danger of cave-ins.

Following every shift the injured and wounded limped out of the dark hellhole, exhausted from the backbreaking work. The fear of dying or being crushed under a thousand-pound slab of rock weighed heavily on our minds. When we first began mining, we had no idea how unsafe the process was. None of the prisoners had had any experience in coal mining. It didn't take long to learn of the peril, as falling rocks crushed men almost daily. The existing thick wooden ceiling support posts, hefty cross-beams, and wire mesh in the main shafts should have been used throughout the new areas to prevent cave-ins. Whenever we asked for wood posts or wire, the answer was always the same, "Ni, ni, ni." I heard a rumor that the Mitsui coal mine had been condemned because of safety issues. The Japanese only reopened the mine when they had a steady supply of expendable workers –us!

Some of the prisoners were so afraid of dying in the mine that they intentionally injured themselves to get off the detail. One of the tricks a soldier used was sprinkling lime powder on an open wound so that it would fester and bleed profusely. We could get the lime from the benjo, where it was used to help break down the solid waste. Other prisoners would intentionally drop a large rock on their own feet to break them. This careless method could possibly leave the man permanently disabled. On the other hand, if one wanted results that would not be permanent, a POW known as Bone Crusher could break an arm or a leg in a manner that was less painful and would repair over time.

There was no way I would hurt myself when at the same time I was I praying to God to protect me. I did not judge others for what they did in the face of madness and cruelty. Survival was what mattered.

Keeping personal possessions required a watchful eye or a good hiding place. Anything not hidden would disappear. Food, clothing, boots, medicine, writing paper, pencils, and old photographs had value on the black market. Some prisoners bartered for food, cigarettes, and sometimes sake. I took my harmonica with me wherever I went because I didn't trust anyone, especially those who gambled away their meager rice rations. Once I witnessed a man steal food from his dying younger brother. "He doesn't need it. He's going to die anyway," he said. It was tough to watch men squabbling over a dying man's clothing or boots while he was still alive. That was the nature of survival.

Being a loner by nature, I kept to myself rather than socialize in the small, clannish groups of men from the same fighting unit or the same city back in their home countries. I never found my former comrades from G-Battery after I was captured. The Filipinos were separated from us at the start of the death march, imprisoned in separate camps, and were not sent to Japan to work as slaves. My only close friend who made it out of the Philippines alive to Japan was Herman Tafoya, and I constantly watch out for him. He frequently faded in and out of consciousness and ended up in sickbay on reduced rations. It was as though Herman's mind reacted to the fear and pain he had to face and turned his eyes off. When he was in one of those altered states he was unable to recognize me. I begged him, "Come on, Herman. Snap out of it. You've got to wake up, Buddy. Herman! Think of your mother and father back home. Even if you don't care, they want you to come home." I knew the kind-hearted Tafoyas and it would kill them if they could see Herman wasting away in the dark, dingy prison hospital. I'm glad there were no mirrors for me to see my own emaciated condition. Herman was my only reflection. I couldn't let him die, so I visited him each day after my shift. I fed him what little rice I had and encouraged him to fight to live.

Miraculously he recovered again. When I asked him if he remembered anything that happened in the hospital, he just shook his head and answered, "No, nothing."

"You had me worried, Buddy." I said with relief. "I don't want to take you home to your mother in a little box, *comprende?*"

*"Si, yo comprendo, amigo."*

The Japanese cremated those who died in Camp 17 and stored their ashes in a warehouse rather than burying them in Japanese ground. A guard once said, "No foreigners in Japanese sacred soil. Only Japanese." But in the Philippines it didn't matter who they buried, because it wasn't their homeland.

Sleep was the only respite from the constant danger of collapsing mine-shafts, drunken Mitsui engineers, or vicious guards. During those brief hours I could finally drop my emotional armor and the defensive, on-guard attitude. In my dreams I could go home and sit on the front porch and listen to the crickets with my mother and father. I watched my younger brothers and sisters playing games in the yard. I could smell the sweet, hot aroma of green chilies roasting in neighbors' kitchens. In my dreams, I could hear Mother playing happy melodies on the piano and encouraging me to sing along to the words of *"La Paloma,"* and *"Celito Lindo."* The song I sang all day while I worked the screeching rock drill was "God Bless America." I felt safe in my dreams because I was in the arms of my dear mother and my beloved country.

Until I met Big Speedo, I had not met a Japanese officer, soldier, or civilian who showed any sense of respect or compassion toward the POWs. We dug the coal that heated their homes and fueled their factories. All we wanted was to be treated as human beings. We worked steadily, on starvation-level food rations moving the heaviest material on God's earth. The consequences of not following the Geneva Convention resulted in the unwarranted death of thousands of prisoners as Red Cross medical supplies, food, and water piled up outside the prisons fences. It would have made a significant difference in the death toll if we had been allowed access to them. It would have cost the Japanese nothing to give us what we needed to survive.

Of the hundreds of Japanese officers, guards, and Mitsui engineers I had encountered, only Big Speedo showed any semblance of fairness or compassion. His nickname referred to his lightening fast movements whether it was his sudden appearance at a work detail or his equally quick departure. Compared to the average, short and wiry Japanese men, he was almost seven feet tall. His long legs and powerful strides would have made him a Jim Thorpe-style running back. He was a Sergeant Major and no one doubted he could whip out his enormous sword and lop off a head or two with blinding speed. We could tell by the other guards' behavior when Big Speedo was coming.

"Here comes Big Speedo," whispered a prisoner, as he spotted the guards straightening their uniforms and posture and nervously fidgeting with buttons as they prepared for the big man's arrival. He stormed into the work detail area with the force of a tornado and his underlings trailed respectfully several steps behind him. Tall and perfectly erect, he towered ominously above his minions. A silent hush descended on the scene as Big Speedo stood as still as a statue and allowed everyone the opportunity to acknowledge his entrance and commanding position. According to my Mitsui supervisor, Big Speedo was born of the Samurai, or warrior class.

Under a heavy mane of coarse, jet-black hair, his piercing coal-black eyes cast an ominous glare at every guard. His long, full-faced beard extended to the middle of his barrel chest and form-fitting uniform. We kept working as the guards bowed their heads and kept an eye on the towering giant of a man. They feared to arouse Big Speedo's wrath and the enormous Samurai sword that hung from his waist at their eye levels.

Once a drunken Mitsui engineer was beating me on the back for not being able to lift an enormous rock and put it into the mine cart. I tried every way possible to lift, lean, and wedge that boulder into the cart, but it was not possible.

"Hyacco!" barked the Mitsui engineer. He whipped me again and again, as I tried to move it. The solid chunk of mine rock must have weighed almost to two hundred pounds. Suddenly, from out of the dark Big Speedo appeared and yelled at the engineer. Big Speedo bent down, grabbed the rock, and said, "Now!" He lifted the whole rock by himself, while all I did was hold on to it. He roared something to the shaking Mitsui engineer, turned his giant head toward me, nodded, smiled, and then sped away as fast as he had arrived. He was the one Japanese soldier I respected. I hoped that I would get to meet him outside of this hellhole someday. Never again did that Mitsui engineer beat me for not being able to do the impossible.

I had heard that Big Speedo had been a policeman in Tokyo. I had also heard from some of the others that he had been directly responsible for helping many prisoners survive in the Philippine camps. When Big Speedo was around, I felt somewhat safer from the sadistic guards and Mitsui supervisors who took out their fears and frustrations on the prisoners. He stood above the inhumane, thoughtless behavior of the rest.

I did not understand the Japanese hatred and animosity toward the prisoners. These soldiers and engineers who beat and tortured us must have been about ten years old when the fighting between Japan and China had begun. They had grown up with war as a way of life and maybe family members died in the fighting, fueling additional hatred.

No one beat us when Big Speedo was in the vicinity. I had begun to believe that all the Japanese were bad — that their way of life, their religion and their beliefs were more savage than any other race I had read about in history. It was good to know that I might be wrong and that there could be more humane Japanese like Big Speedo.

CHAPTER 24

# Surviving Mitsui

*December 1943*

As the first cold winter in Japan progressed, all the days began to look and feel like a continuous dark night. All I got was a fleeting glimpse of sunlight while walking between my sleeping quarters and the mineshafts. By the time my shift was over, the sun had already set and it was dark again. The continual darkness was a prison within a prison for me, a native of New Mexico, where the sun shines over three hundred days a year.

Everyone coughed incessantly even after the shift was over. Our feet were constantly bruised and sore because we only had a thin layer of canvas to protect our feet. Most of us received head injuries and many men died from falling rocks. Only when someone was seriously injured did he end up in sick bay where he had to live on reduced food rations. Night and day we risked our lives mining their precious coal. The Japanese didn't care if a POW died. He could be replaced with another suffering Battling Bastard of Bataan.

The worst mine accident from which anyone survived occurred while a crew was working in a new spur. I was returning from a benjo break when I saw a solitary carbide light streaking toward me through the darkness. I heard someone screaming in a panic for help. Suddenly, a rotund Japanese engineer appeared from around the bend and almost ran over me in his hysteria. He waved his hands for me to follow him and clamored in English and Japanese, "*Hyacco!* Now! Must help! *Hyacco!*"

I nodded and said, "Yeah, let's go!" Quickly, he turned and ran back through the narrow tunnel from where he had come and turned into a side tunnel about twenty-five feet away. We ran and stumbled over small boulders and rock fragments with only our headlamps to illuminate the way. Suddenly he stopped by an eight-foot long slab of rock and started yelling at me to grab and lift it. For a moment, I didn't understand why he wanted to lift that huge slab from the floor until I saw the lone beam of light shining from beneath it.

*"Ichi, ni, sun, go!"* (1-2-3-GO), shouted the Japanese engineer as he motioned me to lift at a certain point of the slab. Together we grunted and struggled with all our might to lift a corner of the rock from the pinned victim. Slowly the rock began to move, as if it were balancing on a fulcrum. Just about the time we moved it, four other prisoners rushed into the narrow tunnel and helped hold up the tilted slab. We pulled the smashed body out. Blood oozed from the unconscious man's eyes, mouth, ears, nose, and the multiple punctures in his body. He was a pitiful sight and I didn't recognize him at first because of all the blood. He was a buddy of mine from the 200th, Agapito "Gap" Silva.

"Oh God," I said.

"He's got to be dead," said another.

Our miner's lamps shined down on the pools of blood forming around Gap's head on the cold mine floor. The lamp on his forehead cast an eerie beam of light across the blood and rock. For a moment we stared in silence at his crushed body. I didn't see how he could still be alive. He was smashed under a rock the size of a mattress.

One of the guys knelt down, put his ear by Gap's bleeding nose and mouth and listened for a breath.

"He's still breathing, but just barely," he reported.

"Let's get him topside and to the medic," I yelled. "Get a stretcher." I wondered how Gap was not completely flattened under that huge rock. The Mitsui engineer and I shined our lamps under the rock and found the answer. Apparently he had been operating the Stoper drill when the roof caved in on him. The heavy cast iron hammer and some large rocks had provided about eighteen inches of space and saved him from being totally crushed. The Japanese engineer and I looked at each other and smiled.

*"Arigato,"* his voice quivered and I could tell from his eyes that he meant it.

"Thank you," I replied. We felt the camaraderie miners feel who share the constant threat of being buried alive. We were human beings caught up in a horrible war that neither of us wanted. The Japanese engineer didn't have to rescue Gap. He was driven by a higher ideal to save a life.

"Thank you very much. Thank you." All the prisoners thanked the engineer for his determination to save one of us.

The only means we had available to take Gap to the hospital was a wheelbarrow. Six of us knelt beside him and placed our hands beneath his broken frame. In one motion we lifted him onto the wheelbarrow and tried to keep him as level and as motionless as possible.

He had several broken ribs, a fractured pelvis, and back injuries. Dr. Frank Hewlett treated Gap as best he could with the limited facilities and supplies the Japanese allowed him to have. Dr. Hewlett assigned two corpsmen to assist Gap in his recovery by taking him to the communal hot bath and to massage his sore muscles. Gap recuperated in the prison hospital and returned to the work-site about six weeks later.

Accidents occurred on a daily basis that resulted in minor injuries and sometimes death. The once-condemned coal mine needed reinforcement throughout the shafts. There were hundreds of railroad ties stacked outside the mine.

"Why can't we use those piles of railroad ties to shore up the ceiling and walls?" I asked the Mitsui supervisor.

*"Ni, ni,* not can do," he said shaking his head. *"Ni, ni."*

"Why not?" I had to ask.

*"Ni, Ni,* not for mine. Only for tracks."

"They're just sitting there not being used, while parts of the mine collapse daily," I argued.

In order to protect all of us from more cave-ins, we implemented a technique of stacking pilings into floor-to-ceiling columns along the shafts to support the unstable ceilings. The thick rock columns also served as our hiding place for the dynamite we 'liberated' when the guards weren't looking. The guards and engineers always made themselves scarce when it was time for the actual blasting. They came into the mine drunk and usually stayed drunk throughout the shift, which was helpful when we needed to sneak a stick of dynamite into our trousers. As we waited for the lit fuse to reach its charge, we hid the stick of dynamite in the rock column in case we needed it at a later time to escape or fight.

One of the most serious accidents that happened on my crew actually injured our Mitsui engineer. He was particularly irritable and drunk one day. As Jack and I packed dynamite into a hole with a long steel rod, he came running up to us in the darkness.

*"Ni! Ni! Ni! Ni!"* he screamed. "I show how to do right!" He took the packing rod in both hands, and continued to curse and shout. He shoved a foot-long piece of dynamite into the hole carelessly. I had an uneasy feeling as he fum-

bled with the next piece of dynamite and poked the powerful explosive into the second hole. Jack and I backed away from him as he slammed the packing rod into the hole again and again as he screamed unrecognizable Japanese words. Without any warning, a thundering blast hit Jack and me like a train that blew us off our feet onto our backs on the tunnel floor. In his drunken haste and carelessness, the engineer had detonated the dynamite. His blood-curdling shriek pierced through the ringing in my ears. Jack and I watched him wail incoherently and run around in circles like a chicken with its head cut off. The beam projecting from his miner's lamps, reflected off the walls and ceiling like an out of control pinwheel.

Jack and I looked at each other and without speaking rushed over to the hysterical engineer to do what we could to help him. He had multiple cuts all over his body and one of his arms was completely blown off at the shoulder, while the other dangled broken and bloodied from the elbow. I lunged at him and wrapped both my arms around his chest to stop him before he fell and injured himself further. He screamed hysterically, obviously in shock from the blast. I pulled off my shirt and pressed it into his bloody shoulder to stop the spurting blood that pumped with each heartbeat. His screaming faded into garbled whimpers and then into silence as he passed out in my arms. For a moment Jack and I watched as his blood dripped onto the mine floor. If he were not dead, he would be shortly unless we could do something quickly.

"Get his legs, Jack," I said as I felt him go limp in my arms. "We've got to get him topside in a hurry!"

Jack grabbed his legs and together we lifted him and started to carry him up the tunnel to the main shaft. From the beam of my headlamp I spotted the supervisor's severed arm on the jagged rock floor. I picked it up and stuffed the bloody limb down his pant leg. The bloody stump was almost his complete arm, and his hand was curled as though still holding the steel tamping rod.

After a brief explanation of the accident to another Mitsui engineer, the guards ordered us to get back to work. As Jack and I turned around and headed back to our work site, we decided not to tell any of the other prisoners that we had tried to save the engineer from bleeding to death.

"People can be strange. If they think we saved a Jap's life, they might give us hell for it," I said.

"I just hope he lives to tell his superiors what really happened," Jack commented. "Hell, our heads could be on the chopping block if they think we sabotaged him on purpose!"

"You just can't win sometimes, huh?" I said as I shook my head.

Jack and I returned to the site of the accident and found the steel tamping rod that the engineer had been using. Apparently, when the dynamite ignited, it shot the rod out the hole like a cannon projectile, ripping off the hapless man's arm. Bloody pieces of the supervisor's flesh stuck to the cold rock surface. They were vivid reminders of how not to handle dynamite. Though he worked us like slaves, I felt sorry for the engineer. He had lost an arm, maybe two, perhaps even his life to work in that Mitsui hellhole. If he lived, maybe his supervisors wouldn't make him come back down into the Mitsui deathtrap again.

*April 1943*

Everywhere in the Mitsui coal mine was unsafe, but the crudely cut channels burrowed out of solid rock had to be some of the most dangerous. If the rock had had an even consistency like concrete, cutting tunnels through it would be safe. Unfortunately, rock breaks and splits like wood. When that happens on a ceiling, it spells disaster for anyone underneath.

One day I was thinking that I had been in the Mitsui coal mines for eight months without sustaining any serious injuries. No sooner had I applauded my luck, than I heard a small piece of rock strike the floor directly on my right. Based on intuition and a disciplined education in the college of hard knocks and rocks, I knew that sound meant trouble overhead. I immediately looked up and saw that a large chunk of rock was breaking loose from the ceiling. Instinctively, I jumped to my left as the slab came crashing down onto the outer edge of my right foot. A bolt of excruciating pain shot up my leg as I stood with my eyes closed. I pressed against the cold tunnel wall and trembled like a leaf in the wind. The pain pulsed with every heartbeat and I tried to pull my foot from under the rock, but it didn't budge. It was pinned to the rock floor.

"Oh, God, it hurts!" I screamed. I waited a moment before I shined the light down. I was afraid to see the actual damage. I took a couple of deep breaths and looked down at my throbbing foot. In the yellow carbide light, I could see that a three foot-by-five foot slab had smashed and pinned my right foot. I almost passed out from pain as I lifted the rock and dragged my bloody foot from under the slab. Blood oozed out of the porous cloth of my canvas shoe. I knew that I probably would not get to see a medic for a while, so I left on the shoe for support in case I had broken any bones.

Slowly, I hobbled back to my supervisor and showed him my bloody shoe.

"*Ni! Segato!* (No! Keep working)!" There was no arguing with a Mitsui engineer once he made up his mind and if I'd tried, he would call over one of the guards to administer a beating. I hurt enough already and the last thing I wanted was more pain. I went back to my detail and finished the shift. Walking back to my barracks was even more painful because it was so cold outside and I had lost so much blood.

*"I have made it so far by putting one foot in front of the other. One more step will get me closer to getting out of this hellhole and home again, so help me God."* I was shivering from the biting cold and throbbing pain but luckily, I hadn't broken any bones as far as I could tell, so I cleaned the blood off my foot and shoe. For the next few weeks I hobbled on the injured foot rather than going to sick bay and getting the half-ration of food ration that was allocated to those who didn't work.

The things I witnessed could never have been imagined in my most terrifying nightmares. No history books, magazines, or movies had ever described how horrible one man could be to another. Even Dad, who was a Great War veteran, could have prepared me for the heinous things I'd witnessed. My nightmares were real and there seemed to be no hope that things would get any better. Only my love for my family and country, and my faith in God kept me focused and alive.

One day one of the prisoners snapped and hanged himself in the benjo. Apparently, he owed a big gambling debt and had lost most of his rice rations. The gambling in our prison camp reminded me of the stories of Mother's first husband. He gambled away the family's food and rent money, and lost everything, including his wife and family. My mother, on the other hand, was a kind and generous person who would do anything for her family. I knew not to gamble my meager rations with the professional gamblers in camp. They were the ones who were lucky most of the time. I had made it this far on my wormy weed and rice slop without dying of hunger. I was a skeleton now compared to what I looked like three years ago, but at least I was a living skeleton.

## CHAPTER 25

# Gratitude

Several hundred tons of rock and coal had passed through our hands since our Mitsui engineer's accident. One day Jack and I were talking about him while we worked. "I wonder whatever happened to the poor guy. Do you think he made it?" asked Jack.

I answered, "God, I don't know how. His entire arm blew off, including the bone that goes into the socket. When I stuffed my shirt into his bloody shoulder, there was nothing but a hole and open veins. I'll never forget the smell of his burnt flesh when we carried him up." I shuddered as I remembered the gruesome experience.

Jack lifted the big drill to the wall and reminded me, "It was his own fault he blew himself up. He almost took us with him. He was drunk and in a hurry and he wasn't careful with the dynamite."

"Hell, it can happen even if we *are* careful," I grumbled loud enough for Jack to hear, but not loud enough for the guard to hear.

"If they would feed us better, and the guards didn't beat us, maybe we could get more done," Jack commented with a sigh.

"Does Mitsui Mining treat their employees the way they are treating us?" He asked.

*"San be yaku ju hachi!"* shouted a guard. We turned around to see the guard waving at us to stop working and to go with him. He barked out Jack's POW number and a barrage of *hyaccos.*

"What now?" Jack asked me.

As we left the mine, the guard said, "You go to Camp Commander!"

"The camp commander? What the hell did we do now?" I whispered to Jack.

"I'm sure he's not having us over for lunch it would be nice though," he joked.

The guard prodded us as we made the long walk out of the mine into the light of day. A million thoughts raced through my mind as we were led up the steps and onto the deck of the camp commander's headquarters. Guards stood at attention outside his door. One guard barked a loud command that I didn't understand, and then he opened the door for us to enter. We were filthy and covered in powdery rock, dust, and sweat. We stopped just inside the doorway. The stone-faced Camp Commander Fukuhara stood behind his desk and to our surprise the Mitsui engineer who had lost his arm stood beside him. The door shut and the four of us stared at each other.

Our former supervisor looked well fed and neatly dressed in civilian clothing. He had a big smile on his face and made a short bow. He walked around to the front of Fukuhara's desk. The shirtsleeve of his missing arm was neatly folded and pinned up. He proudly lifted his other arm that had been severely damaged and moved it to show us its range of motion. The engineer had made it through that horrible accident and was in good spirits. For a moment we stood in silence, smiling at one another. For one brief, glorious moment I forgot about the war and the hell in which we lived. Here was a man who represented our cruel enemy, an enemy who had tortured, mutilated, starved, and brutally killed thousands of my countrymen and allies. Yet as we stood there, face to face, I was sorry that he lost his arm, and I was happy that he was alive and looking well.

He stood directly in front of us. Then we were shocked as he ceremoniously knelt down on both knees and bowed three times and said, *"Domo arigato gomen mashita* (Thank you very much)." Stunned, Jack and I stood silently. Earlier in the day a guard had beaten us for not bowing to Japanese authority now in the afternoon, in the headquarters of the Japanese camp commander, Japanese authority was bowing to us! Fukuhara stood like a cast iron statue and stared at Jack and me as the Mitsui engineer went through his ceremony of gratitude. Thoughts raced through my head about the outcome of this highly unusual behavior. These people have proved themselves in the past to be completely unpredictable.

The engineer slowly stood up and walked over to a table which held a teapot, two tiny cups, and plate of rice balls. With his usable arm, he poured the green tea into the cups and replaced the teapot on the table. The elegant formality of every move he made was like a religious ceremony. This was all too unreal to be true, but my mouth watered at the thought of having a snack in the middle of the day. I would have assumed that I were dreaming if my muscles didn't ache so badly, or my nicks and cuts didn't sting from the sweat and rock dust. Slowly, the one-armed man brought the teacups and rice balls to us on a tray. He graciously bowed again, then offered the tea and rice balls to us.

For the first time in almost three years a Japanese person treated us like human beings. For those few minutes we were honored and appreciated guests.

After we ate the delicious rice balls and drank our cups of tea, the grateful Mitsui engineer bowed goodbye and Fukuhara ordered the guards to escort us back to the mine to complete our shift. It was business as usual, as if nothing had changed. Jack nudged me and jokingly asked in his British accent, "Frank, do you think we should have asked him if we could meet him again tomorrow for tea?"

"Hell, yeah. Those rice balls were delicious," I muttered. "I could have eaten a few hundred more."

Jack laughed out loud for the first time since I met him six months earlier. The sweet taste of the little rice balls lingered in my mouth long after my shift was over.

CHAPTER 26

# Deliverance

*August 1944*

One day my buddy Jack was so sick that he could hardly stand. He was weak from a fever and couldn't eat his meager rice allotment. I was worried that he couldn't keep working much longer. Without warning, an enraged Mitsui engineer lashed out at Jack with a metal rod, knocking Jack to the floor of the mine with a series of strikes that sounded like Jack's bones were breaking. Jack lay curled on the hard floor, crying out for help as blood seeped out of his open wounds. The Mitsui engineer towered above him and screamed for Jack to get up while he continued to savagely beat him.

"Get up! Get up!" screeched the obviously drunken Mitsui supervisor as he mercilessly kicked Jack. I was afraid he was about to kill Jack on the spot, so without thinking of the consequences, I picked up a rock about the size of softball and threw it as hard as I could at the enraged engineer. The rock whizzed by his head. *Oh God! What have I done? I've tried to knock him out and missed!*

As the rock hit the floor, the engineer spun around and stared at me in disbelief. We were less than five feet apart as we stood staring at each other through the dim yellow beams of our headlamps. Then his face transformed to that of a crazed maniac. His bulging black eyes and ominous scowl were now directed at me, not Jack. At first, I froze in my tracks, petrified at the thought of what he might do. Then I turned toward the narrow opening of the tunnel and bolted away from his screams of "I going to kill you! You dead man!" My heart was pounding like a freight train as I ran as fast as I could from the drunken supervisor past other startled crews and guards.

Everyone must have been shocked to see a prisoner running away because that usually meant certain death. Before anyone could catch me, I made it out of the mine and into the daylight, but was captured quickly by guards, who beat me to the ground. They quit when the screaming engineer made it to the surface to claim me as his own. He grabbed a rifle with a mounted bayonet from a guard then stomped over to me and shrieked, "I going to kill you *San-be yaku-ju-hachi!*" Two guards picked me up out of the dirt, held my arms back, and waited for the crazed Mitsui supervisor to run me through. I knew that pleading for help or mercy was hopeless with these madmen. How many times before had I seen their counterparts kill a POW for even less an offense than mine? As he raged inches from my face, I smelled the distinctly foul odor of fish, rice and saki from the Mitsui man's hot breath. Although somewhat dazed from the pounding by the guards, I stared into his jet black eyes now totally oblivious to everyone else around me. *He's really going to kill me. After all the near misses and escapes, this is it! The Jap infantry didn't kill me in the battle at Lingayen Gulf or in Bataan, the march, or even the firing squad. Damn! This drunken Jap civilian is going to get me!* Suddenly, the guards snapped to attention when camp Commander Fukuhara and his entourage appeared.

Fukuhara shouted in Japanese, "What is this?" The Mitsui engineer first blurted out his version of the story. Fukuhara then asked me. I admitted to him that I lost my head for a moment when I saw how mercilessly he was beating Jack. "He was going to kill him. It's not Jack's fault he could not work very fast. He is deathly ill. I had to do something to stop the Mitsui man."

You could hear a pin drop as Camp Commander Fukuhara walked slowly up to me. *Does he recognized me from when Jack and I were served tea and rice balls in his office?* The last thing I remember was the blur of his fist crashing into my face.

When I woke up I realized that I had been stripped naked and tied to a pole near the entrance of the mine. They had strapped a bamboo pole behind my knees and propped me up in a kneeling position so by the time I awoke, my knees ached. Guards and engineers had urinated and spit on me while I was unconscious. For the rest of the day I knelt tied up in the cold without water or food. Several of the guards and engineers hit me with their sticks as they passed by. I feared what later was in store for me. My body was battered and my muscles and joints ached. I felt like lying down and letting them bayonet me from my wretched existence as a slave but Dad's words, "Never, never give up," kept echoing in my head.

"*Atama beoshi* (crazy in head),"remarked of the Japanese guards and

Mitsui supervisors that filed in and out of the mine throughout the day. When the other shifts of POW's passed by, many would nod their heads and say, "Hang in their buddy." Even some of the Japanese guards nodded at me with a sigh of compassion, but I knew they too could do nothing to assist me.

I had seen other POWs killed for lesser offenses so I wondered why Fukuhara had let me live this long. I didn't know of anybody who had to tried to kill a Japanese citizen and got away with it. I hoped Jack had made it back but I was unable to ask any of the other POWs because I was off limits to them. Nobody was allowed to talk to me.

Form approved
Budget Bureau No. 76-R063.1

VETERANS ADMINISTRATION

**STATEMENT IN SUPPORT OF CLAIM**

*NOTE.--If additional space is needed, use reverse.*

CLAIM NO.

C.

LAST NAME - FIRST NAME - MIDDLE NAME OF VETERAN (Type or print)

Lovato, Frank Natoniel

The following statement is made in connection with a claim for benefits in the case of the above named veteran:

I was a prisoner of war with Mr. Frank Lovato in Camp #17 in Fukuoka, Omuta, Japan from August 1943 through the surrender of the Japs in August 1945. During this time while in Japan, they had us working in a coal mine, forcing us to work from 12 to 14 hours a shift. In the fall of 1944 Mr. Lovato was severely beaten by one of the civilian oversoers who was drunk. The Jap overseer used a pick handle and shovel to strike Mr. Lovato over the head and all joints of his body. If Mr. Lovato had not run away this Jap would have killed him. Mr. Lovato went to the mine shaft where the Japanese interperter stopped him and also started beating him until he was unconcious. His hands were tied and a stick was placed behind his knees in a squat position until the rest of the men on the shift joined him on top side. Since his joints were swollen and being in this position for several hours, he could not stand up. They started to beat on him again forcibly making him stand up Finally Mr. Lovato got up and with his hands still tied behind him, they made him run ahead of the group to camp which was about 1 mile away. Mr. Lovato was beaten several times, but this one stands clearly in my mind as one of the worst beatings he received.

I CERTIFY that the foregoing statements are true and correct to the best of my knowledge and belief.

| DATE SIGNED | SIGNATURE |
|---|---|
| 1 July 1970 | AGAPITO E. SILVA<br>SIGN HERE ▷ Agapito E. Silva |

ADDRESS
1620 La Poblana N. W., Albuquerque, New Mexico 87104

PENALTY - The law provides severe penalties which include fine or imprisonment, or both, for the willful submission of any statement or evidence of a material fact, knowing it to be false.

VA FORM JAN 1967 21-4138 EXISTING STOCK OF VA FORM 21-4138, JAN 1963, WILL BE USED. ☆GPO : 1967 O - 252-132 (219)

Copy of Veterans Administration Claim Form

As daylight faded into dusk my body began to shiver uncontrollably. I curled into a ball to conserve as much heat as possible as the night's temperature plummeted. Every part of me hurt. I was unable to stand because my wrists and ankles were tied together behind me, so I had to lie on my side. I had taken a beating like none since I'd been captured.

Later in the night three guards prodded me awake with their whipping sticks. *Oh great. Now I get another beating before going to sleep.*

*"Hyacco! Atama beoki. Hyacco!"*

"Phew, you smell like animal," they laughed. They pinched their noses in disgust from the smell of my defiled body. They laughed and chattered from a safe distance as they prodded me to the large community bath to wash the filth and blood off my body. When they cut the rope from my wrists I could barely move my cramped arms. I bent over and shook my arms to get the blood flowing before I crawled into the hot bath. The hot water stung my open wounds like needles but at the same time it felt like heaven to my aching and bruised muscles. *If they are going to kill me tonight, at least I will be clean.*

Surprisingly, they gave me a new set of clothes and returned me to my five-man sleeping barrack and left me alone, except for a guard that marched back and forth in front of the open door. I thought they would have put me in the stockade. "It's another miracle," I whispered to myself, "another one in a string of extraordinary miracles." I was alive and had been left alone for the night. I crept softly to my dried grass mat and tried not to wake the others. I pulled the rice-paper sheet over my exhausted body and lay staring out the open door.

As I lay awake unable to sleep, I wondered why I was alive when so many others had died. As I ran out of the mine with the Mitsui engineer chasing me, I thought that was the day my prayers ran out. But I was in my barrack, safe from another near-death experience. My guardian angel was surely working overtime.

Five other prisoners were sleeping in my small cubicle. Each prisoner worked on a different shift and detail, so getting to know any of them was difficult. I liked to lie near the open doorway in case I had to get out in a hurry.

I couldn't sleep even though my body was exhausted and in pain. Instead, I kept thinking about the engineer who had vowed to kill me. I kept seeing in my mind the vivid image of his sweat covered face screaming, "I going to kill you! I going to kill you!" I stared at the open doorway and wondered if each moving shadow that passed through the barracks door might be him coming to get me. *Why didn't they toss me in the brig? It would have been safer than in these open barracks. Maybe they sent me here so he could sneak in during the night and knife me while I sleep?*

While those terrible these images and thoughts raced in my head, a baseball-size brilliant white light suddenly appeared in the center of the doorway as though it was suspended in thin air! At first I was terrified at the sight of something so strange and intense, so I covered my head with my rice paper blanket and hoped that whatever I was seeing would vanish. But the loosely woven fibers couldn't stop the bright glowing light from shining through. Astonished, but no longer afraid, I sat up and looked at the other prisoners to see if the mysterious light had awakened them, but they were fast asleep.

"What the hell," I started to say, but then I stopped because I had this feeling that whatever I was seeing must be a good thing. I started to pray out loud, "Hail Mary, full of grace, the Lord is with Thee." The oval, radiant light grew until it filled the entire doorway.

As I prayed, the light seemed to speak to me, not with spoken words but with thoughts. Those feelings told me to relax and not be afraid that everything was going to be all right. I sensed I was not going to die, at least not soon. I pinched myself to wake up, but realized I was awake and whatever I was seeing was not a dream. The light surrounded me and filled me with a sense of safety and peace. Outside, the solitary guard paced back and forth completely unaware of what I was seeing. Miraculously, the brilliant light transformed slowly into the glowing image of Our Lady of Guadalupe, the Virgin Mary. She softly pressed her hands over her heart, fingers pointing to Heaven in solemn prayer. Her gentle gaze, so sweet and kind, looked upon me like my own dear mother's smile. Bluish-white rays of pure light radiated around her like images I had seen on prayer cards and paintings. My mother always prayed to the Lady of the Roses and said that the Holy Mother always answered her prayers.

For the first time since the war began, I felt no fear. She emanated the wonderful feeling of serenity and it filled me with peace. I knew beyond any doubt that I was going to make it out of this hell on earth and return to my family and to the country that I loved. It felt wonderful to know that all this horror would end. Once I fully embraced that message she was telling me, the vision faded away slowly until her image and the light was gone. What she left behind was an understanding of my destiny and a feeling of confidence, safety and peace. Although my body hurt from head to toe, I had never felt so wonderful within my heart and mind. I had no fear of the Mitsui engineer or of the mine caving in on me. I no longer had fear of anything or anyone. She left me with a positive feeling for the future and I knew she would always be with me. I closed my tired eyes and saw the beautiful blue-white image of the Holy Mother as I prayed and drifted off to sleep.

Before dawn I was rudely awakened by the sharp poke of a guards bamboo pole.

*"San be yaku ju hachi.* Stay in barracks today. Not go in mine." The guard grinned from ear to ear and spoke in a foreboding tone "You go to bad boy camp. You think this bad? Ni! Bad boy camp very bad!" He pointed a finger at me, squealed a hideous high-pitched laugh, and then stomped down the wooden steps. In the dark stillness of the early morning, I could still hear him laughing in the distance. *How bizarre. It isn't time to get up and yet the guard decided to deliver my orders in the middle of the night and he woke everyone else in the process. So here I am again, out of the frying pan into the fire. At least I wouldn't be going down into that Baron Mitsui hellhole today.* My cellmates mumbled good luck wishes and then rolled over and fell back asleep.

The next morning, I returned to my barrack after tenko to rest and to wait further orders about my transfer. It was hard to walk because every muscle ached each time I moved in any direction. Since I didn't have to go down into the mine, I decided to give my body as much rest as possible before the next phase of hell. As I stepped up the barrack steps a guard called my number and delivered an unexpected surprise.

*"San be yaku ju hachi,* this for you!" a guard barked as he handed a neatly tied bundle of letters addressed to me.

In the past two years of captivity I hadn't received any communication from home even though I knew my family had written. I felt both joy and fear as I held the ten letters. Although I wanted to read their loving words I was worried that maybe a tragedy had befallen one of them. All of the letters had been opened, probably by inspectors, and left unsealed. I untied the coarse string that bound them together, spread them out on my blanket and picked one to open first.

As I lifted the open envelope, a solitary rosary card of Our Lady of Guadalupe fell out and landed face up on the blanket. A chill shot through me as I saw the brightly colored picture of the Holy Mother. Just hours ago I had seen her vision in the doorway, and now I was holding her picture in my hands. I said a Hail Mary and placed the prayer card on my small rag pillow. *Another miracle!*

After reading all of the letters I was greatly relieved to learn that everyone back home was healthy and doing well. All references to the war and items deemed inappropriate by the censors had been blocked out by black ink.

Again, the next day I was allowed to rest and recover from the beating. My body felt like it had been in a fight with both Jack Dempsey and Gene Tunney. I was covered with new sores and deep black and blue bruises on every visible part of my body; however, nothing seemed broken, including my spirit. *Thank*

*God Fukuhara knocked me out before the engineer got to me.* My knees were very swollen from kneeling on the hard ground with the pole strapped behind them. I could barely bend them more than a few inches. Every muscle ached and throbbed.

At *tenko* I asked whether anyone knew if Jack had made it out of the hole, but no one knew. Although he and I worked every shift together, we slept and ate in different sectors of the camp. Since the blasting crew was the smallest work detail, we often did our job alone, except for an engineer who directed our work and an occasional guard who wanted to catch a snooze. I asked other POWs to pass the word to Jack to tough it out and that I'd try to see him soon.

The messenger guard had told me they would be taking me to another camp designed for troublemakers. It was hard to believe the Japanese would create a camp especially for problem prisoners. Usually the Japanese tortured or killed anybody that was deemed a troublemaker. I wasn't afraid of anything they planned because the Holy Mother told me I was going to survive. I could take anything they could dish out. I had no fear, because I knew everything would be all right.

The morning of the third day, I was ordered to quickly remove my few belongings from my barracks. All I had was a handmade comb and toothbrush, my harmonica, the letters, a rice paper blanket, and my GI raincoat. I bundled everything in the raincoat except my harmonica, which I put in my pocket for safekeeping. A guard used the point of a bayonet to escort me to the narrow gauge train that ran into the camp. I was shoved into an empty boxcar to begin my passage to the bad boy camp. As they slammed the big doors shut, I thought of those unfortunate ones entombed in that the Mitsui mine.

As the train chugged along the bumpy track, I huddled in a corner, leaned my tired back against the cold wooden walls and wondered how I made it alive up until know. *How did I make it through the death march delirious from malaria? Why didn't they shoot me at Camp O'Donnell when I unconsciously broke rank and ambled towards Camp Commander Tsuneyoshi? How did I survive the night of the "Blood Squad" execution? I'm sure I'd have been killed if the Cabanatuan guards knew it was me who had started the singing of "God Bless America." How do I have all my body parts after all the dynamite I set or avoid being squashed under a slab of solid rock like Agapito Silva? Why didn't Fukuhara let the Mitsui engineer kill me? Did he spare my life because he remembered the gratitude ceremony by my former supervisor? Thank God for my good friend, partner, and guardian angel, The Chillicothe Kid, wherever you are. I've had one close call after another, yet I'm still alive and in one piece by the grace of God, my guardian angel, and Our Lady of Guadalupe.*

After the train came to a stop, the guards opened the doors to let me out at my new prison camp. Although the ride had been less than an hour, I didn't know the camp's official name or exact location. *"Hyacco! Hyacco!"* barked the guards. They used their pointed bayonets to encourage me to disembark.

Small, newly constructed wooden buildings nestled in the hills made this prison look more like a mountain summer camp. Of course, the tall wooden guard towers with machine guns and the multi-strand barbed wire fence around the perimeters made it clear I was not on a vacation. This camp was tiny in comparison to Mitsui Camp 17. I didn't see any continuous lines of prisoners marching to and from work details.

As two guards escorted me through the camp, I noticed an anti-aircraft emplacement surrounded by sandbags and manned by Japanese soldiers who scanned the skies occasionally. Nestled in the trees were two long barrack structures that appeared to be unfinished. The boards that covered the outside walls were uneven with large cracks between them. I figured the cracks would soon be filled with mud, cement mortar, or tar. A large creek ran through the camp and flowed toward the city of Fukuoka. Everything in the camp appeared to be in order and comparatively relaxed, compared to the constant hustle and the twenty-four hour work schedule at the Mitsui mines.

The attendant guard released me to an officer at the camp commander's headquarters and was then taken to a construction work site. I was turned over to a Japanese sergeant and promptly handed a handsaw. A group of about fifty POWs looked at me without stopping work. They appeared to represent several different nationalities: dark Pacific Islanders, Orientals, and a few white people who were American, English, Australian, or Dutch; I couldn't tell by their clothing, because at this stage of the war everyone's uniform had deteriorated into shreds.

The sergeant led me to a long rough-cut timber log and demonstrated with his open hand a three-angled cut. He gruffly commanded in Japanese, "Cut here, cut here, cut here!" I nodded that I understood his directions, and then began my new job assignment. Each POW had a specific task in the preparation of the large timbers for a new barrack facility. This didn't seem too bad considering my death-defying duties at the Mitsui coal mine. The construction of wooden buildings in the fresh air was much better than going down into a hole filled with falling rocks. I sensed my relief was premature, but so far the Japanese guards had been treating me better than the Mitsui civilian engineers. Since the guard had told me this was a "bad boy" camp, I had expected that this camp would be worse than the coal mine.

After a short time, an older fellow with thinning hair I guessed to be in his late forties handed me a ladle of water from a bucket he was carrying and said with a slight Spanish accent, "Welcome to Fukuoka 1, my friend. I am Garcia. What is your name?" His gentle, soothing voice reached into my soul like silk.

*Fukuoka 1, so that's where I am.* Before answering, I drank the precious liquid and handed the ladle back to the smiling fellow and said, "My name is Sergeant Frank N. Lovato, US Army. Thank you. Thanks a lot."

*"De nada,"* he replied. He probably recognized that I was a Spanish-American by my accent and dark skin.

I smiled and repeated my gratitude to the special man with a heartfelt *"Gracias, muchas gracias!"*

That was the first sip of water I'd had all day. I was perplexed at the quieter, business-like attitude of the guards, who so far seemed content at the steady pace at which we worked. Everything so far was better than any good day at the Mitsui hellhole. I wondered if the food would be better too. I found out soon enough at evening meal. The rice was just as tasteless and the quantity as meager. I closed my eyes and chewed each crunchy grain of rice slowly to make it last as long as possible. *Maybe I could fool my growling stomach.* Every muscle, joint, and cut still ached from the beating. Both of my knee joints were painfully difficult to move after I sat still, even for a few minutes.

There were less than a hundred POWs in Fukuoka 1, compared to the two thousand plus in Mitsui Camp 17. *How could we all be the "bad boys" from every other camp?* All the POWs worked methodically, with no major incidents or beatings from the guards. *Was I the only "bad boy" in the bunch? But why did Fukuhara send me here?* The living conditions and the temperament of the guards were better than at the coal mine. The workings of the Japanese mind confounded me again as my life as a POW moved into the fourth year of captivity.

I found it strange that there weren't any other Americans among the Australians, New Zealanders, British, Dutch, Javanese, and Pacific Islanders. Everyone got along. Whenever they had the chance to be with POWs of their own ethnic group (chow time or after work detail), they congregated together and spoke their native languages. Mr. Garcia was the only individual that mingled among all the groups with ease. He could speak most of the languages in our multi-national camp.

In a few short days, the new barrack building was completed. Remarkably, no nails are used in the Japanese-style of construction. They used a technique similar to the notches and joints of the American toys called Lincoln Logs, but their system was more sophisticated and stronger. For the first time since being a POW I enjoyed working, partly because I was making something for our own use, not for a giant Japanese corporation. The mere fact that I didn't have a Mitsui engineer hovering at my back raised my spirits considerably. Although the Japanese construction site foreman didn't use the word "camouflage," it was clear that he wanted the buildings to blend into the natural landscape of rolling hills and thick trees.

Because he always had an answer for everything, I asked Mr. Garcia, "Why do you think the Japs want us to tuck the buildings into the trees?"

He stood back and gazed at the building, the walls of which were being covered with vertical pieces of natural bark that gave the appearance of trees. He replied, "Hum, I never thought about it, Frank. Maybe the Japanese want them well-camouflaged from aerial detection or bombing."

"But our pilots wouldn't bomb barracks with POWs," I said.

He shook his head and plunged the water ladle into the bucket. "Maybe the Japanese plan to use them for themselves when our planes invade Japan."

"But what about us? What are the Japs going to do with us if..." I realized the answer to my own question. So far we have been useful to the Japanese Army and civilian population. We farmed their food and mined their coal, but POWs were dispensable in the grand scheme of things. *When we become a liability, our days will be numbered.*

"Could our forces be closing in on Japan?"I asked. Mr. Garcia shrugged his shoulders and went to fill his bucket.

I had been at Fukuoka Camp One ten days when I heard that we would be getting mail from home. Because I had just received the ten letters before coming to Fukuoka 1, I didn't expect anything.

The camp commander stood on a stepstool and spoke in English. He apologized for the length of time it took the mail to reach the camps, citing priorities and wartime conditions. Following his speech, guards emptied gunnysacks of bundled letters and small packages on the ground for us to sort through.

Men shouted their buddies' names as they dug through the bundles looking for one with their own name. It was odd to hear our names instead of Japanese numbers called out "Lovato," shouted an Aussie fellow as he held a box above his head with both hands and searched the crowd of anxious POWs.

"My God," I gasped. I was shocked to hear my name. I never imagined I would be receiving anything more, especially a package. I couldn't take my eyes off of the brown paper package that was loosely re-tied with coarse dark string. Mother had said in one of her letters that she had sent several packages and asked if I had received any of them. I figured the Japanese kept the food and clothing she sent because I had not rcccivcd anything. When I lifted the cardboard flaps I saw the treasures mixed in cookie crumbs and bars of soap. I was overwhelmed by the sweet smell of anise seeds in homemade *biscochito* cookies and the fresh-scented soap. For a moment the all American smells took me ten thousand miles back home to my family. My hands trembled as I pulled out a pair of soft flannel pajama bottoms and held them up to my waist. Next I saw the pajama top with pearly buttons and cookie crumbs in the pockets. After three years of Mitsui-issued clothing I had forgotten what new clothes felt like. I caressed the soft flannel with my chapped hands and pressed the bundle of sweet aromas from home to my face and cried my first tears since singing "God Bless America" so long ago at Camp O'Donnell. I knew my dear mother had held these pajamas close to her heart before packing them and that made me indescribably happy.

Fall's chilly temperatures lingered longer in the shadows of the many trees at Fukuoka 1. Though I was glad to be far away from the deadly Mitsui coal mine, I missed the coal-fired baths that warmed me after my shift in the mineshafts. I started wearing my new flannel pajamas all the time to stave off the cold and conserve as much internal heat as possible. Each day the sun rose lower on the horizon and the shortened daylight hours prompted the Japanese to push us faster to complete the construction.

After we finished the barracks, our next project was to construct a concrete ammunition storage site fifty yards from a similarly constructed ammo dump. Working with heavy concrete and digging deep holes in the rocky soil was much harder on our malnourished bodies than constructing the wooden structure. Mixing and transporting the concrete was done by hand with shovels, buckets, and wheelbarrows. We moved tons of concrete, one thirty-pound metal pail load at a time, to create the floor, ceiling, and walls. As soon as the new dump was finished and the concrete was dry, we were ordered to move the wooden crates of ammo from the old dump to the new one. The ammo and weapon boxes were extremely heavy and everyone was exhausted by the end of the shift. The strange thing was that nothing else was moved into the old site. No one could figure out why they made us move tons of ammo from one site to the other, fifty yards away. The old dump was as large and as well constructed as the new one.

I asked Mr. Garcia, "Why are we moving everything from one building to the other?"

He shook his head and said, "The Japs don't have anything else for us to do, I guess."

"Maybe the Jap Army is preparing to defend Japan from a land invasion," I guessed.

"Maybe so, Lovato. Maybe so," he replied. "The men at the anti-aircraft batteries are continually scanning the sky. They weren't so vigilant before."

An Aussie said, "Aye, that's right. Our boys must be getting closer to Japan. That's why the Nips are so nervous!"

Every morning we were woken before the sun rose. The Japanese participated in a morning prayer ceremony each day and I realized that they were a people of strong discipline. The guards led us in calisthenics every morning. Regardless of the chilly weather, we had to take off our shirts for exercise.

"Hell, we're going to catch pneumonia screwing around out here without our clothes. It feels like its ready to snow," grumbled one of the prisoners.

"It's freezing, can we please put on our shirts?" asked Mr. Garcia in perfect Japanese.

*"Ni!* It better for you!" answered the exercise leader. We nicknamed him "Charles Atlas" because of his well-developed physique.

I didn't understand how doing exercises the chilly air with my shirt off was going to do me any good.

*January 1945*

According to the rumors around camp, someone had built a radio receiver. We heard the great news that the allied forces were defeating the Japanese on land, sea, and in the air. These messages filled us with hope that a final showdown was fast approaching. Whoever had the radio receiver remained anonymous for fear a loose tongue might reveal his identity. I had heard hundreds of rumors, so I was reluctant to put too much faith in the messages. If the news were true it was great; if it were false it was still good to believe in something positive.

If MacArthur were coming back, I hoped his troops were better prepared than we were. We had been given no information on Japanese soldiers in Bataan except the joke that the Japanese soldier was so short that he could barely carry his heavy rifle. We were told the 6.5-mm Arisaka rifle, the standard issue for the Japanese infantry soldier, was more like a .22-caliber. I had seen cartoons that depicted the Japanese soldier as buck-toothed with thick glasses because he was so cross-eyed that he couldn't shoot straight. The soldier wore baggy pants and carried a sword way too long for his height. Many believed the cartoons that portrayed the Japanese Mitsubishi Zero fighter planes were built from flimsy bamboo and cloth, their tanks were made of wood, and that their ships were designed to look like pagodas and were top heavy. The Battling Bastards of Bataan were the first to discover that all these rumors were painfully false. The Japanese Army was a thoroughly prepared and equipped fighting force that brought the battle to us with a fury no one could have predicted.

I learned from the beginning of the war not to believe any of the rumors I heard; at best they only boosted our morale temporarily. Captain Perrenot told me to forget about the rumors, to expect the worst, and to do my best to win each daily battle to stay alive and defeat the enemy.

The Japanese guards wore insulated winter uniforms and boots, huddled around fire barrels, and complained about how cold it was. None of the POWs had socks and our tattered boots never seemed to dry from the constant wet conditions. We wrapped our bodies with strips of cloth and cement bag paper sandwiched together for added insulation from the biting cold. I salvaged a piece of material and tied it around my waist like many of the Japanese did. It seemed to help a little, but nothing was enough for me to feel warm during the coldest period from December through February. Occasional rays of sunshine felt like warm kisses from God on my chilled skin.

When we returned to our barracks to sleep, we were as cold as outside. The only protection the barracks offered was from rain or snow, but not cold or light. Uneven patterns of yellow light from the guard tower streamed through the cracks in the barracks walls and cast an eerie glow . We were given only a single, flimsy blanket to cover our bodies, and a thin woven grass mat to insulate us from the cold wooden floor. The outside walls of our barracks were a single layer of tree bark left over from cutting lumber. Without coal or wood to burn, our sleeping barracks was more like a giant refrigerator with frosty cold air blowing in. When Mr. Garcia pleaded with the camp commander to allow us to fill the cracks with mud and sticks, the camp commander refused him without a reason.

In late January when the temperature dropped to its lowest, lengthy immobility could result in painful frostbite or worse. Several prisoners lost fingers, toes, or ears to frostbite while the weakest or the ill froze solid during the night. Mr. Garcia assembled the men together and devised a plan to keep us from freezing to death. We agreed that the only way to save our lives was to keep our bodies moving to keep our blood circulating. Dad always said, "Moving water doesn't freeze, until it stops." I figured the same applied to people since our bodies were mostly liquid. Throughout the frigid nights we took turns sleeping in thirty-minute shifts - surviving the bitter cold was a higher priority than getting sleep . In the heart of winter we needed restful sleep the most to rebuild our tired bodies, but we hopped up and down and rubbed our fingers, noses, and toes. We sacrificed precious sleep time to keep from freezing to death.

Night after night I vowed I will find my way home, and once there I would take at least two hot showers every day. I hadn't valued the simple things in my life like warm blankets, a hot shower, and a bar of sudsy soap until they were stripped away. "Count your blessings" will always have a deeper meaning for me because I will never take the simple treasures for granted again.

*January 29, 1945*

"HellShip" survivors of the ill-fated *Oryko Maru* arrive in Moji and were removed the next morning from the ship on to the dock in freezing winds. The near-dead POW's were then stripped of their tattered clothes and sprayed with a noxious disinfectant before given new clothes. Of the original 1,619 POW's that started the nightmarish journey from the Philippines, only 450 made it to the dock. Over 100 died soon thereafter.

According to a letter written by a fellow POW to the Perrenot relatives after the war, Captain Travis Edward Perrenot died shortly after arriving of injuries, malnutrition, and disease sustained in the tragic journey.

CHAPTER 27

# Angel amongst us

Most of us had been prisoners for over three years and had seen, heard, felt, and smelled the Grim Reaper knocking at our door at least once. Fortunately, we had a good angel to keep us going when all hope seemed to slip out of reach. Mr. Garcia was a shining example of pure human spirit that gave everything he had to encourage us to hang on, pick ourselves up and live another day. His sacred mission seemed to be to keep us alive and our morale high.

The majority of the POWs were in their early twenties, but Mr. Garcia was an "old guy" who was at least forty. He was born in South America and he served as a Merchant Marine until the Japanese sank his supply ship and he was captured. He spoke most of the Asian languages including Japanese, as well as a number of European languages. Since Fukuoka Camp 1 was comprised of prisoners from all over the world, he was able to help them communicate with each other. Everyone looked forward to his arrival. He always had a new joke or story to tell that was both funny and uplifting. He chuckled at my Albuquerque Barelas version of Spanish. I knew he wasn't laughing at me in a derogatory way, but was laughing at how the Spanish language had been reinterpreted in the States.

The prisoners all loved and respected generous Mr. Garcia. We had few older role models; most of the older prisoners had already died because they were the first to resist the Japanese and could not take the physical neglect and abuse. Most of us were teenagers when the war began so when we needed the advice or a man to trust, we turned to Mr. Garcia. Wherever he went his presence alone encouraged everyone to smile and talk more openly. He was like a shining light who comforted us because he always knew what to say.

A fellow from Australia became increasingly depressed because his broken leg had healed crooked and could no longer tolerate the freezing nights, the lack of sleep, and the inadequate food. As he lay deliriously in pain in his bunk he mournfully wept the names of his family back home and his fallen buddies before him. He had reached his personal breaking point and stopped eating his daily ration. His closest buddies tried to get him to respond but every effort failed.

During this war I had seen that distant look countless times before: a resigned, far away stare that seemed to say"Enough of this hell. Staying alive is no longer worth the pain."Another POW slapped his face to try and break the death spell, but it were as though he was in a trance; he was alive yet he was deaf and blind to the world around him.

Mr. Garcia cradled the Australian in his arms and began to tell him a story as he rocked him gently. "I can hardly wait to get home. When I get home I am going to make a carpet of soft fur. This carpet will be covered with hundreds of bumps shaped like women's breasts." Garcia dreamed out loud, "There will be big ones, tiny cute ones, pointed ones, full and rounded ones, all shapes and all sizes. Every day I am going to take off all my clothes and crawl naked onto my carpet and feel every one of those soft delicious bumps." He began to writhe like a snake, rocked from side to side and moaned as if lost in a lusty trance.

What initially began as a mortally serious incident turned into hysteria. Peels of laughter erupted throughout the packed room at the idea of a naked Mr. Garcia crawling on his imaginary breast carpet. Perhaps it was our laughter or the humorous erotic story; whatever it was, the boy started grinning and rocked his head in astonished disbelief at Mr. Garcia's far-fetched tale. "Get him some food!" someone yelled. Within minutes he was drinking water and eating his gifts of love, and life-sustaining nourishment. Thankfully, he recovered over the next few weeks because his will to live had been reawakened by the unconventional but effective efforts of our resident angel, *Señor* Garcia.

---

*August 1, 1943*
*Soloman Islands*

PT 109, commanded by Lieutenant John F. Kennedy following a torpedo attack on a Japanese destroyer convoy, was sliced in half by a Japanese destroyer. Kennedy managed to rescue several of his surviving crewmembers before finally reaching the shore of a small island. Realizing that he had to attract the attention of passing PT boats, he risked his life by swimming several miles on the open water between the islands. After six days Kennedy was spotted by an Australian "Coastwatcher" on a neighboring island and he and his exhausted and hungry crew were rescued by another PT boat.

The Coastwatching Service, a secret Australian organization originating in 1919 and expanded when the war began, was designed to observe and report naval traffic. The dedicated Coastwatchers were comprised of plantation owners, merchants, and other civilians who knew their immediate territory well. From secret lookout hideaways they radioed vital information regarding enemy movements between the islands.

*August 17, 1943*
*Wewak, New Guinea*

The U.S. 5th Air Force, using information provided by Ultra Intelligence, (codebreakers) surprise attacked and destroyed 200 Japanese aircraft on the ground.

The Japanese called this date "The Black Day" when virtually all their air power in New Georgia had been destroyed almost to the last plane.

*On the Home Front*

For the first time in history, motion picture technology brought the war home, to the big screen. People of all ages and backgrounds, flocked to the movie theaters to see actual footage of aerial combat, beachhead landings and all the sounds and sights of the war. Motion picture studios produced popular, full-length war stories such as Casablanca, Wake Island, and Bataan.

*September 8, 1943*

Eisenhower announced an unconditional surrender by the Italians.

*September 16, 1943*
*Lae, New Guinea*

Allies take Lae, once considered a Japanese air base stronghold that possessed a squadron of some of the highest skilled fighter pilots in Japan's arsenal. Pilots from Lae frequently sank Allied boats, strafed ports, shot down bombers and scored numerous. victories in dogfights with Allied fighter pilots.

*November 1, 1943*
*Bougainville, Soloman Islands*

U.S. forces land on Bougainville, largest of the Soloman islands and closest strategic location to launch land-based aircraft for an all out attack on Japan's principal stronghold on Rabaul, New Guinea.

In a clever plan to deceive the Japanese forces defending their important base on Bougainville, U.S. and New Zealand forces fein a diversionary landing, supported by ship bombardment and aircraft bombing while the main invasion force landed at Empress Augusta Bay almost fifty miles from the nearest enemy defenders. A Japanese naval counter-attacking force of warships and troops, hoping to catch the dug-in U.S. troops on the beachhead, were intercepted and attacked. Coastwatchers, once again, had alerted The U.S. Navy that the Japanese were on route to destroy the Empress Augusta Bay landing.

*November 2-11 1943*

On November 11, Admiral Chester Nimitz dispatched three new carriers to join Admiral William ("Bull") Halsey's Saratoga and the Independence, to combine for the biggest air strike ever delivered by the U.S. Navy.

U.S. aircraft carrier and land-based bombers from Bougainville attacked the Japanese stronghold in Rabaul, forcing the Japanese naval command to withdraw their ships and retreat.

*November 20-23, 1943*
*Gilbert Islands*

Following stiff resistance by Japanese defenders dug in protective coral emplacements, U.S. forces take Tarawa, Makin and Gilbert Islands.

*November 28-30, 1943*
*Teheran, Persia (Iran)*
*Teheran Conference*

Roosevelt, Churchill And Stalin discuss need for a second front in Europe, and post war division of Europe.

*January 22, 1944*

Allies land on Anzio, Italy

*February, 1944*

Throughout the month, U.S. Naval forces and Marines attack and destroy Japanese strongholds on Kwajalein, Eniwetok, and Engebi in the Marshall Islands as well as the huge Japanese Naval base at Truk, in the Caroline Islands.

*Strategic Outcomes*

Japan's outer perimeter defense ring had been effectively crushed by combined allied naval aircraft, ship, and troop assaults. This allowed the Allied command to focus. on the inner defense ring located in the Marianas Islands.

*June 6, 1944*
*D-Day*

Combined Allied aerial, naval and infantry forces embark on the largest invasion ever planned to liberate Hitler's heavily defended,"Fortress Europe." Allied troops land on six French beaches that extended from Calais to Normandy to unseat Germany's firm grip on countries it had conquered by its earlier military "blitzkriegs." Secretly dubbed "Operation Overlord" by military planners, took three long and bloody months to unseat Hitler's forces and establish a firm grip on Europe's Western front.

*June 14-15, 1944*

The first high-altitude B-29 bombing raids on Japan take off from bases in China. The Boeing B-29 "Super Fortress" outfitted with the top secret Norden bomb sight, was capable of delivering its load of bombs at an altitude above the effective range of Japanese antiaircraft.

*Strategic Outcome*

The high-altitude, blanket-bombing had little effect on reducing Japanese war material production because most of their factories were now small assembly facilities hidden in residential neighborhoods.

*June 11 - July 9, 1944*

Saipan was the first Japanese island fortress in the Marianas chain that includes Tinian and Guam, to be conquered by combined naval and land forces. Fierce resistance on land by enemy troops resulted in one of the highest casualty counts in the war.

*Strategic Outcome*

Saipan, Tinian and Guam were considered strategically necessary for the inevitable invasion of the mainland of Japan. B-29 bombers, capable of reaching Japan from airstrips on Tinian eliminated supply difficulties encountered in China. It was from an airstrip on Tinian, that one year later, the B-29" Enola Gay" sortie dropped the atomic bombs on Hiroshima and Nagasaki.

Massive civilian suicides on Saipan revealed a gruesome forecast of what to expect as Allied forces closed in on the mainland of Japan.

*June 19-22, 1944*

Battle of the Philippine Sea "The Great Marianas Turkey Shoot."

What appeared to the Japanese Naval staff as an opportunity to lull and defeat the U.S. task force supporting the invasion of Saipan, Tinian and Guam, resulted in the final blow that destroyed any chance the Japanese Imperial had to stop the Allied forces from the air. U.S. Navy pilots, in the newly developed Grumman F-6 Hellcat fighter, handily shot down over 400 outmatched enemy Zero's. Additionally, the Japanese lost three heavy aircraft carriers and support aircraft in the battle.

*Strategic Outcome*

By now, Japan had lost virtually all of its experienced fighter pilots and the once invincible Mitsubishi "Zero" was no match against the more powerful, heavily armored, and highly maneuverable Hellcat.

Any Japanese naval aerial threat was crushed once and forever at the Battle of the Philippine Sea.

*July 18, 1944*
*Tokyo, Japan*

Following successive defeats on land and sea and just as Admiral Yamamoto had predicted, Imperial Army General Hidecki Tojo resigns as Prime Minister of Japan. Tojo, an ardent military nationalist and avowed enemy of the West, was considered the principle driving force that brought about the plan for war with the United States, Great Britain and their allies China, Australia, New Zealand, Canada, India, Netherlands, Burma, Java, Philippines, and eventually Russia.

*September – October 1944*

MacArthur's forces close in on the Philippines by taking the Japanese held islands of Morotai, Pelielu, Anguar and Palau. Unfortunately, his troops suffered heavy casualties in what proved to be strategically unnecessary to invade and retake the Philippines.

*October 20, 1944 (U.S.)*

MacArthur lands on Leyte

*October 23-25, 1944 (U.S.)*
*Battle of Leyte Gulf*

In a last ditch attempt to thwart the allied forces landings on Leyte, the Japanese Naval command mounted a multi-pronged attack force to decimate the allied troops on the shore and in their troop carrier ships before they could move inland. The elaborate plan consisted of luring Admiral "Bull" Halsey's aircraft carriers away from the San Bernardino Straits with a sacrificial diversionary force. This would leave the San Bernadino Straits clear for the main force of Japanese battleships, cruisers and destroyers to bombard the U.S. troops landing from the sea. The third prong of the attack planned to converge at the Leyte landings in a coordinated pincer movement from the south.

Fortunately for the Allies, two U.S. submarines on patrol discovered the Japanese southern force. The subs partially damaged the enemy vessels with torpedoes and reported their heading to the Allied command. Later, Admiral Kincaid's southern defenders were able to block and defeat the enemy in the Surigao Straits using a flotilla of PT boats, destroyers, cruisers and battleships. The enemy's main northern force, after being turned back once before by allied aircraft, stormed back down the San Bernardino Straits with only a small defending force of light aircraft carriers and destroyers. Daring smokescreen torpedo attacks by the U.S. destroyers, together with a constant barrage of strafing runs by the light-carrier aircraft pilots, confused and frustrated the enemy fleet commander enough that he called off the attack and retreated. Although Halsey's heavy carriers were unable to return in time to assist the outgunned defenders, the bold and intrepid actions of Admiral Sprague's Taffy 3 defenders turned back the enemy for the last time.

The appearance of the recently organized Japanese Special Attack Corps of suicide bombers marked the beginning of a new weapon of terror and destruction. Enemy bombers and fighter planes heavily loaded with additional bombs attempted to crash-dive on to the decks and hulls of U.S. ships from bases on the mainland. Their principle targets were aircraft carriers, battleships and cruisers. The terrified defenders fought back against the suicide bombers they named 'devil-divers' with antiaircraft fire and evasive maneuvers. The U.S. aircraft carrier St. Lo was the first U.S. aircraft carrier sunk solely by suicide airplanes.

Young and mostly unskilled pilots assumed the proud role of Kamikaze, meaning Divine Wind, named after the legendary typhoon that decimated the massive Mongol invasion in 1281 saving Japan from eminent defeat.

The Taffy 3 defenders' defensive and offensive actions have since become a classic model studied by naval academies throughout the world.

*Strategic Outcome*

Following the Battle of Leyte Gulf, Japan ceased to be a naval power.

Thanks to the dauntless U.S. Navy Commanders, pilots and sailors courageous. actions, MacArthur's forces were able to land with a minimum of casualties. The emergence of the new 'Kamikaze' suicide corps marked a new level of desperate measures by the Imperial Japanese leadership. The final battle for the Philippines would end for the Japanese as it had for the defenders of Bataan and Corregidor three years earlier, on land.

*November 24,1944*

B-29 Superfortress bombers bomb Tokyo from bases in the Mariana Islands. Throughout December, B-29's continued to bomb key Japanese bases and weapons factories, U.S. submarines sank an increasing number of japanese merchant ships, and aerial bombing choked off Japan's material resources supply line and its ability to wage a war that could be won.

*December 16, 1944*

*Battle of the Bulge*

The last major German offensive literally ran out of gas before reaching fuel storage tanks. General George Patton mounted a counter offensive that put the remaining German tanks on the run. When heavy overhead cloud cover subsided, Allied aircraft pummeled what was left of Hitler's once lauded Panzer Division.

*January 9, 1945*

U.S. forces land unopposed by ground forces at Lingayen Gulf where three years earlier Japanese General Homma's invasion force landed and began their march to Manila and into Bataan.

*January 27, 1945*

The 'Burma Road' supply route to China reopened.

*January 29,1945*

Although MacArthur's forces met fierce enemy resistance inland they successfully reached Manila and began a rooting out campaign that proved to be particularly costly in Filipino civilian lives. MacArthur opted not to aerial bomb the city because of the residents within. The entrenched Japanese soldiers, realizing that they were surrounded and their fate was sealed, went on a rampage of rape, murder and destruction that took the lives of over 100,000 Filipino men, women, and children.

*January 29,1945*

"HellShip" survivors of the ill-fated Oryko Maru arrive in Moji and were removed the next morning from the ship on to the dock in freezing winds. The near-dead POWs were then stripped of their tattered clothes and sprayed with a noxious. disinfectant before given new clothes. Of the original 1,619 POWs that started the nightmarish journey from the Philippines, only 450 made it to the dock. Over 100 died soon thereafter one of whom was Captain Perrenot.

According to a letter written by a fellow POW to the Perrenot relatives after the war, Captain Travis Edward Perrenot succumbed to injuries, malnutrition, and disease sustained in the tragic journey.

*January 29, 1945*

*Cabanatuan POW Camp, Philippines*

Following a diversionary aerial distraction by an attacking U.S. fighter plane, 121 soldiers of the 6th Ranger Battalion, stormed into Cabanatuan and rescued 513 Allied POWs. Within an hour, the frail but appreciative POWs were evacuated from the camp with protective cover and assistance by Philippine guerilla troops. The other eight thousand plus. POWs once imprisoned in Cabanatuan had already been transported in the "Hell Ships" to slave labor camps throughout Japan and Imperial Japanese conquered countries such as China and Thailand. Their eventual liberation would have to wait until after war's end in the late summer of 1945.

*February 3, 1945*

American tank forces burst through the gates at Santo Thomas University and freed over 5,000 American civilian held captive following the fall of the Philippines in 1942.

*February 16-26, 1945*

U.S. forces retake Corregidor

*February 19, 1945*
*Iwo Jima*

U.S. troops land on Iwo Jima after an extensive naval and B-29 bombardment of the deeply entrenched Japanese defenders. The kidney-shaped, volcanic sand island was considered an important possible emergency landing site for returning damaged B-29 bombers because it was strategically located about half way between the main base at Tinian and targets in Japan. Only 216 remained of the over 20,000 Japanese killed or took their own lives in its defense. U.S. Marine casualties numbered over 25,000 wounded and 6,000 killed. On February 24th, a forty man combat patrol reached the crest of Mount Surabachi and raised the first Stars and Stripes above the bloody battlefield. Associated Press photographer, Joe Rosenthal, later captured the raising of the larger flag. In honor of the brave American soldiers, Admiral Chester Nimitz proclaimed "Among the Americans who served on Iwo Island, uncommon valor was a common virtue."

*Strategic Outcomes*

Native American Navaho Marines, trained at Camp Pendleton to use their language as a secret code, baffled the enemy throughout the Iwo Jima campaign. The Japanese never broke this code.

Once again, as witnessed many times before on Saipan and other islands and atolls, the Japanese Code of Bushido to fight and die for their emperor and country, made it painfully evident that the cost in human lives to bring Japan to surrender would be astronomically high.

*March 9/10,1945*
*Tokyo*

Over 300 low flying U.S. B-29 bombers drop first incendiary bombs on Tokyo. The Napalm style bombs spread fiery infernos through the predominantly wood and paper suburbs that were home to small neighborhood factories generating war materials. Over 100,000 persons were incinerated in the raging blaze.

*Strategic Outcomes*

The earlier high-altitude bombing of major cities, although monumentally destructive, had proved ineffective in destroying or disabling Japanese war materials production. This prompted General Curtis LeMay to adopt this new incredibly devastating strategy. Attacks on most major cities, although monumentally destructive in both property and human lives, still did not bring about a surrender or any communications to that effect.

*March 20, 1945*

British troops capture Mandalay.

PART IV

# Liberation

*April 1, 1945 – September 15, 1945*

CHAPTER 28

# Hail to the Chief

*April 13, 1945 (April 12 in the US)*

I was unloading wood from a train, when I heard the guards shouting, *"Roosevelto batai! Roosevelto batai!"*

The prisoners asked each other, "What the hell's going on? Why are they running around cheering and yelling? What are they so happy about?"

"Roosevelto dead! Roosevelto dead," cheered a guard as pumped his rifle above his head in a triumphant gesture. I was so shocked and saddened to hear the sudden announcement, I dropped the load of wood I was carrying. I bowed my head and thought, *Oh my God! Our Commander and Chief is dead.* President Roosevelt was a great man who was an inspiration to the common people during the Great Depression. His leadership had given us more than empty words. He had created jobs for anyone willing to work. His death was a great loss to Americans and free people all over the world. *Did the Japs think America is going to lose the war because our president died?*

Most of the men took the bad news in stride and were not concerned that it would affect the outcome of the war. I felt sad for Roosevelt's family. "President Roosevelt may be dead, but America is not," I murmured, as the guards whooped and danced as if they had just won the war. According to our secret radio information, the Japanese hadn't had any victories in a long time. The reports indicated that they had lost all of their major island bases, including the Philippines. We heard that Tokyo had been bombed by a new kind of super-bomber called a B29. An operation that size would need to be located close to Japan because a large bomber like that would need long runways and fuel depots. The Japanese must no longer be capable of preventing attacks. Their defense must have been made ineffective.

The guards began yelling, prodding us with their sticks to assemble in the big yard. *"Hyacco! Hyacco!"*

"What the hell are they up to now?" I asked Mr. Garcia.

He looked at me and shrugged his shoulders. "They're acting like something big is happening. They don't seem particularly angry. I think it has something to do with the death of President Roosevelt."

I was astonished when I heard a fellow say, "The Japs are handing out beer — one beer for each POW. They must think America will fall apart without the same president. Man, they have a lot to learn about Americans." Mr. Garcia took a swallow of the brown, unlabeled bottle of Japanese beer and remarked with a grin, "This beer must be from the brewery in Fukuoka. I've seen the guards drink it."

Regardless of the sad occasion, the prisoners were happy to get a work break and a beer. I didn't feel like drinking beer with the Japanese to celebrate the death of my president. I gave my beer to Mr. Garcia who had already finished his. I knew he would appreciate it. For the first time since becoming a POW I was awestruck to see the Japanese behave like children at a party. Thinking about President Roosevelt reminded me of all that was good back home. I only wanted to get back to my country as soon as possible. *God bless you, Mr. Roosevelt and God bless America.*

CHAPTER 29

# Countdown to Freedom

*May 1945*

After the death of President Roosevelt, we needed something to hold onto. Mr. Garcia knew this and created a new vision for us. The second week in May he announced enthusiastically in every language spoken in the camp, "One hundred days and we all go home!" He went from group to group and recited his revelation to everyone, including the guards. "Yes! Be happy! Only one hundred days left and we all go home to our families."

"You're crazy, old man! We'll all be dead by then. The Japs too!" one of the prisoners shouted. Although some of the men doubted Mr. Garcia, most found our angel's proclamation amusing. Once again he was the shining light of hope when everything around us looked dark and bleak. It was as though God had given us Mr. Garcia to rally our spirits when we were ready to give up.

A few weeks later we were unloading canvas sacks filled with concrete mix from a rail car when a lone aircraft streaked across the sky. Pointing at the aircraft cruising less than one thousand feet overhead, one of the Aussie's shouted, "Look! It's one of ours! It's one of our boys!" Even the Japanese guards stood motionless and stared at the odd-shaped fighter plane that zigzagged back and forth over Fukuoka. The aircraft didn't drop any bombs, fire any rockets or shoot machine guns as it cruised over. Perhaps the pilot's mission was primarily reconnaissance and photography, I thought.

"Where are the Nip interceptors?" asked a curious prisoner.

The bearded Aussie replied, "They haven't got any."

Sightings of Japanese airplanes had decreased with each passing month since I had arrived at Fukuoka 1. Now in May 1945, sleek, new American aircraft were flying unopposed over Japan.

"Silence! Back to work! *Hyacco!*" yelled the scowling guard.

I could feel the prisoners' excitement as we awaited our fate. The sight of one of our shiny new airplanes cruising unchallenged lifted our spirits to the highest level since this ugly war began. We didn't cheer and we hid our joy for fear of what the guards might do. It was clear they too knew they were losing the war. All the prisoners wondered what the Japanese would do with us when the invasion began. One of the Japanese guards said we would all be killed if Allied land forces invaded Japan. Every Japanese man, woman, and child would take up arms to fight to defend their sacred land. *What if they lined us up and shot us? No prisoners — no stories of atrocities. Dead men don't talk.*

As we stood on the loading dock, we saw old men and women on the street practicing thrusting movements with long, pointed bamboo poles. Loud screams accompanied each forward thrust as they practiced in unison. Their primitive weapons were not going to save Japan from the power of the Allied Army.

After three years of war, we were the last survivors of entire divisions and battalions. We had survived sunken ships, disease, neglect and abuse. The Japanese kept us near starvation, exhausted, and weak from beatings. They used us as slaves for mining and moving tons of cement, iron, and wood. There were no friends or allies on the other side of the camps' barbed wire who would help us escape. We were stuck in Japan.

According to the rumors, B-29 bombers were regularly destroying Japanese cities and factories. How long could the Japanese cities and people hold out before they surrendered? One of the guards once me that Japan had not lost a war in over two thousand years and they would never surrender because it was their duty to die for their emperor.

*Will the allied forces liberate us? Will the Japanese let us go as they retreated to the hills to fight their last battle? Will they line us up and execute us? Perhaps this is the most dangerous time of all. We are a threat to them as our forces close in. This is their sacred home, so sacred that our dead could not be buried in Japanese soil.* Wooden boxes of unmarked, cremated remains lay stacked in a storehouse awaiting shipment home.

Each day we continued our routine but every day there were fewer guards than before. The camp was reduced to only twenty guards instead of forty. We wondered why the guards were disappearing. *Were they going AWOL, or were they being called to combat duty?* The expressions of the remaining guards told us the direction the war had taken. They looked like we had when Japanese tanks and infantry surrounded us on Bataan. I knew from the beginning of the death march that somehow, someway this day would come. I just didn't know it would take so many years and so many lives. Living with death made me appreciate every sunrise, each breath of air, and each living moment. If there were a lesson I learned in this horrible ordeal, it was that life and everything in it is precious.

"Sixty-five," Mr. Garcia announced with a cheery smile. "Sixty-five days left before this is all over and we can go home to our sweethearts." Since the day we saw the US airplane flying in Japanese airspace, his enthusiastic predictions made believers out of the toughest skeptics.

"Sixty-one!" shouted a group of Aussies before Mr. Garcia had the opportunity to say the day's magic number. The group laughed at the notion that they believed the war would be over in Mr. Garcia's timeframe, but it didn't matter. The fun was playing along with the game he had created.

## CHAPTER 30

# Shared Tears

*June 19, 1945*

*"Hyacco! Hyacco!* Go now!" shouted the lone Japanese guard as he rushed through our dark barracks, prodding sleeping prisoners with his rifle butt. "Must go now! *Hyacco!"*

"What the devil is going on?" I asked half-asleep. I wondered if this were another bad dream. It was obvious this was not another work detail or torture session. Something big was going on. All the lights in the prison camp yard were off, so we stumbled through the darkness toward the outer perimeter of the camp. "Where in hell is he taking us?" questioned a voice in the darkness.

Hideki was one of the better guards in the camp. He seemed concerned that we get out of the barracks so we followed him to wherever he was taking us. Above the chaotic chatter, the distinctive drone of approaching planes rumbled in the heavens as we made our way through the darkness.

Hideki led us to one of the underground shelters we had constructed and motioned us to quickly enter. Just as we began to file into the dark cave-like structure, six B29 bombers thundered into view. "Damn," echoed the stunned onlookers as we craned our necks upward. The shadowed underbellies of the multi-engine aircraft blocked the half-moon lit night sky like giant flying dinosaurs. Their unfortunate target was the city of Fukuoka located below us in the valley. Everyone, including Hideki stood awestruck at the sight of the enormous airplanes as they began to circle over Fukuoka more like birds of prey than man-made mechanical airships. It was difficult to comprehend how something made of metal as large as a B29 could actually fly. Glints of moonlight reflected off their wings as they banked in a circling formation, and made a low-level bombing raid over Fukuoka. Thunderous explosions drowned out the air raid sirens as the first load of bombs burst into brilliant flames. In an instant, the dark night skyline of the city burst into fiery yellow and red rolling waves of flames. Thunderous shock waves rocked the ground beneath our bare feet and the trees wavered from the concussion heat wave that followed. These were not ordinary bombs, but specially designed incendiary bombs that spread a blanket of solid flames. Bomber after bomber made their runs, spreading an inferno on Fukuoka's factories, railroad depots, and population center. Although we would have preferred to see the attack, Hideki ordered us to get inside the bomb shelter. We sat on the dirt floor, leaned against the earthen walls of the bomb shelter and watched Hideki as he stood motionless outside the open doorway gazing at the fiery inferno unfold. Each bomb burst cast a red glow on his pie-shaped face as it exploded below. Sharp images of the burning city reflected off his round, wire-rimmed glasses like little motion picture screens.

We all felt his pain as tears rolled down his cheeks and he began to cry. He told us that his whole family was in the city. His mother, father, sisters, and brothers all lived there and they were probably facing a horrible fiery death.

I felt no victory as I watched him cry for his family. We all shared Hidecki's grief as intermittent sniffles broke the silence within the dark shelter. This was beyond hating the enemy. "Go to your family," we said. "We'll cover for you. We won't leave. Go on. We'll stay right here."

*"Ni,* I cannot go. *Domo arigato,"* he said. I'm sure the Japanese code of honor and fear of reprisal from his superiors prevented him from going.

After the bombers departed we slowly walked back to our barracks and watched Fukuoka burn. I wondered why Hideki had roused us from our sleep to take shelter. It would have made no difference if we had been destroyed. Nothing made sense anymore. I realized how horrible war was. Everyone gets hurt, not only the soldiers, but also their families. I wanted all the madness to be over. Throughout the remainder of the night, we saw the flames of Fukuoka flicker through the cracks of our barracks walls.

If the bombing of Fukuoka were any indication of what US bombers were unleashing on other cities of Japan, it was obvious that an allied invasion was forthcoming. Prior to our first sighting of an American airplane, all we ever heard the guards speak about was their overwhelming victories, beginning at Pearl Harbor. Our secret radio reports indicated that the Japanese had suffered devastating losses, both on land and sea, the US was able to rebuild bases and airfields within striking distance of Japan.

But as the dream of freedom seemed possible, a new fear gripped the hearts of every prisoner. They might kill us to prevent us from supporting our invasion troops or for revealing the atrocities they committed. Even with the excitement of the chance of liberation there existed the underlying anxiety of being killed. So like for the past three and a half years we went about our daily lives combating fear like we all ways have-distraction. Some found relief by loosing their minds like Herman did, others by channeling it into other activities like the gamblers. I preferred comic relief and humor.

"Forty-two and soon I'll be home with you,"

"Look at them, walking about cowering, like beaten dogs with their tails tucked between their legs," said one of the Englishmen. "Their hearts are not in it anymore."

According to Mr. Garcia's prediction, there was only one month left in this miserable war. The closer we got to the final day, the more exciting the countdown was. Whether it happened as he forecast or not, it was a great morale builder. The gamblers were betting on how accurate Mr. Garcia's count would be. There was no question that the end was near. The real question was whether we would be around to celebrate. What was the Japanese high command's plan for us when our troops invaded the mainland?

*July 1945*

During morning *tenko,* we heard the drone of several powerful engines approaching from the foothills behind us. Everyone, including the Japanese, turned toward the rumbling whine that was getting louder by the second. Suddenly, eight dark blue fighter planes with bent wings crested the hill at treetop level and swooped down the hillside in our direction. The sight of the approaching war birds caused the Japanese guards to scatter.

Most of the POWs stood in the open yard and watched the fighter plane attack without any concern for their own safety. I was ecstatic when I saw the Stars and Stripes emblazoned on the wings overhead. Other prisoners waved their arms, cheered and threw kisses to the low-flying aviators, who responded by tipping their wings.

The Japanese anti-aircraft gun shot only a few times before it was destroyed in a spectacular blast of flames and exploding ammunition. We behaved more like spectators at a football game than prisoners as we stood in the open yard area and blocked the bright sun out of our eyes with open hands. Flying less than a hundred feet off the ground, the planes strafed the camp headquarters, the ammo dump, and the few remaining vehicles. Anything with a Japanese rising sun was fair game to the intrepid pilots, including the Camp

Work Status Board. A volley of .50-caliber bullets exploded it into a pile of splinters. The remains of the mutilated board brought some fellows to their knees and provoked peals of unbridled laughter. The status board was used by the Japanese foreman to record work progress. No matter how hard or fast we worked, we never achieved his expected level of performance, which gave the foreman justification for a more strenuous work regime. After their red and white rising sun flag, the status board was the most despised symbol of their dominance over our lives

In less than ten minutes the raid was over. The pilots tipped their wings at us for the last time and peeled back over the hilly horizon. Their attack left a pile of burning rubble and smoke. It was a miracle that not one POW was injured.

The raid lifted our morale so much that we talked into the night like schoolboys. We retold every strafe run and roared with laughter at every mention of the status board. The Japanese guards didn't even enforce the evening curfew.

"The attack was absolutely gorgeous," said one soldier.

"Did you see what they did to the status board? Tore it right up," laughed a prisoner. "It looks like the pilots blew it up on purpose."

"They showed those Nips a thing or two," said an Aussie.

The final battle was approaching Japan. The raid brought up new questions. Unless Japan surrendered before a land invasion, we might be considered an unnecessary problem. *Since they didn't abide by the terms of the Geneva Convention, why would they consider sparing our lives?* The only reason they brought us to Japan was to work us as slaves for their war industry.

## CHAPTER 31

# "…rain of ruin"

*August 7, 1945 (August 6 in the US)*

The Japanese guards dejectedly ambled through their duties. Their heads hung down and they didn't care how fast we worked. Their uniforms were wrinkled and soiled and some had buttons missing. Theirs were the faces of the defeated and shamed. They had lost their will to win. I will never forget the feelings of loss, anger, and fear when we surrendered on Bataan. It was their turn now to ponder the broken dream. I'd waited three and half years to see their defeat. They had started this war in Hawaii, but the battle was being brought to their home with horrifying reality.

There were rumors that the Japanese were preparing for the invasion by building fortifications in the mountains. One of the guards told us that Japan would never surrender. Surrendering was not a part of their sacred code of Bushido. They would defend their homeland and their honor to the death. Women and children would fight for their emperor with sticks and stones, if necessary. He said, "We will kill ourselves before surrendering." If they were willing to take their own lives, what value would they put on our lives when we were no longer useful?

Our work detail was unloading wooden slats from a railroad car when a messenger rode up on a bicycle and delivered a verbal message that shocked our three guards. One of the distraught guards began walking around in circles with his hands on his head and repeated, *"Ni! Ni! Ni!"* The other two shook their heads in disbelief. Something big had just happened that left them stunned.

From a distance I could make out the words, "Hiroshima . . . destroyed . . . atom bomb . . . many, many dead." They kept repeating, "Atom bomb, Atom bomb."

We looked at each other and wondered what they were so upset about. "What the hell's an Atom bomb?" I had no idea what they were talking about.

Mr. Garcia approached one of the guards who was trying to tune in his battery-operated radio. Finally, a tinny-voice broadcaster came through the whine and hiss repeating the same message again and again. I couldn't understand anything but the words "Hiroshima" and "Atom bomb." Apparently a large bomb had been dropped on Hiroshima that destroyed a large part of the city and population. Mr. Garcia stood with his hands on his hips and stared at the black radio. He shook his head in disbelief.

I walked over to Mr. Garcia and asked him what was going on.

Without looking up he replied, "An American B29 has dropped a new kind of bomb on Hiroshima. It's called an atomic bomb. It destroyed the entire city. Everything for miles around has been destroyed. All the people." It was the first time I had ever seen Mr. Garcia look so serious.

"Are the Japanese ready to surrender?" I asked him.

"I don't know, Lovato. There's no talk about that on the radio. I don't know."

*"Segoto! Hyacco!"* snapped the head guard. " Hurry-up! Back to work!" We were still their slaves until the Emperor surrendered or our forces destroyed every last one of them.

The evening rumors centered on the news of the atomic bombing of Hiroshima and what it might mean to our situation. Mr. Garcia, who usually knew everything, was hard pressed to explain. No one could understand how a single bomb could cause so much destruction. Mr. Garcia said the radio reported the atomic bomb contained the energy like the fire in our sun.

I prayed this would end the war quickly, and that no more lives would be lost on either side. The mood throughout the camp was somber. I figured the bombing of Hiroshima demonstrated what the US would do to end the war.

"Seven days left and we can all go home. One week is seven days. Isn't that right Mr. Garcia?" asked a Brit. Mr. Garcia nodded his head, smiled, and said nothing. He had been acting strangely since we heard the news of the atomic bomb. He seemed serious and pensive in a time that should have been a time for celebration if his prediction was accurate.

Mr. Garcia predicted we would be freed on August 16th. The gamblers in the camp were betting heavily on what would be the exact date.

Each morning we anticipated another news broadcast that would change the course of our lives. There were fewer guards on duty and their behavior toward us was almost what one would expect in a normal work environment. It was business as usual; we had breakfast *lugao, tenko* roll count, then we went off to the loading docks for another day of slave labor for the government of Japan.

The camp commander had been silent about the future. He and his guards had been the most humane that I had encountered as a POW. When I was told I was going to be sent to the bad boy's camp, I didn't realize that Commander Fukuhara had done me a favor. The Mitsui supervisor would have killed me if I had gone down in that coal mine again.

An Aussie asked, "Are the Yanks going to keep dropping atomic bombs on Japanese cities until the Emperor screams uncle?"

"Will our land forces invade Japan and fight it out to the bitter end?" I asked.

"If they do, we'll be goners for sure. Our lives would be over, no matter who won the war," said another.

"They would use every man, woman and child to fight," he continued.

"Yeah, we saw them training with bamboo spears in the street by the loading docks."

"We are dispensable. We're no use to them."

"Let's pray it doesn't come to that."

Only four more days were left in the countdown. It was uncanny how each day felt closer to the end. It felt as if we were going to be set free on August 16th, just as Mr. Garcia had predicted. Whatever the exact day, it wouldn't be much longer. Mr. Garcia kept us focused on the end of this hell to give us hope. He helped us believe there was a chance. He kept us smiling, laughing, and joking.

It was a misty overcast day as we headed out to our work detail. We walked slowly, worked slower, and handled fewer items in each load. The guards didn't seem to care that we worked at a reduced speed. They seemed lost in their own defeated thoughts. They looked sullen, speaking very little among themselves. Gone were the brash, cocky laughter and screaming commands. They just pointed now to the railroad car for unloading and let us work. We had done it enough times to know how. The past three and a half years we had done it all. We had grown their food, built their camps, mined their coal, and loaded and unloaded their ships and trains. We knew how to work better than they did.

Suddenly, an intense flash of light lit the hazy day as though a giant flash bulb had exploded from the heavens. "What the hell was that?" asked a prisoner. We looked into the high gray clouds and searched for the source of the lightening flash that had startled us. I shrugged my shoulders and went back to carrying the wooden slats to the dock. I figured it was probably lightening-what else could it have been? A minute or so later a thunderous blast almost knocked us off our feet.

We looked into the empty sky for the source of the deafening explosion. The prisoners exclaimed, "God damn! What the hell was that? Jesus! What the hell's going on?" I saw the Japanese guards were also looking up and questioning each other. Nobody moved for about a minute. All we could do was stare up at the high clouds over Fukuoka. This explosion was unlike anything we had ever experienced. Then it occurred to me that it must have been an atomic bomb. It must have been fairly close for us to see the flash and hear the explosion. One of the guards pulled a black radio out of his sack, extended the antenna, and tuned in a faint Japanese broadcast. The guards huddled around the radio to listen. "Nagasaki had been destroyed by another atomic bomb. The destruction is total!" yelled an English-speaking Japanese soldier. Nagasaki was less than fifty miles from Fukuoka Camp 1. The guards were stunned. They wandered around aimlessly and their dazed faces revealed the horror of this tragic news.

The guards and officers lost their composure. Some were openly weeping.

"We did it again."whispered a prisoner. "We completely destroyed another city with a single bomb." The Japanese had existed for over two thousand, five hundred years and had never lost a war, but that was before atomic bombs that could annihilate an entire city. None of the POWs showed any outward excitement. We knew the guards could easily kill us in a matter of minutes. Now was not the time to challenge their authority. We were winning the war and that was enough to lift our spirits.

Later in the day Mr. Garcia was jumping up and down, excited about the latest news. He knew it was over now and was not afraid to openly celebrate, nor was he afraid of any retaliation. I had never met anyone like him before. He was a wise man with a child-like personality that lifted our spirits when no one else could. I didn't know if it was a game he played to keep his sanity, or one to help us keep ours. Either way, all of us, including the Japanese, were eternally grateful for his friendship and support.

CHAPTER 32

# Over

*August 15, 1945*

When I woke at dawn, I couldn't help but think that today was the day that we were to be freed. It was hard to believe that Mr. Garcia could be right. It was even harder to believe that atomic bombs had been dropped on Hiroshima and Nagasaki. When Mr. Garcia started his countdown, there had been no hope. Hope was now much more than an old man's dream.

"Today's the day!" shouted out one of the prisoners from his bunk.

"It's time for everyone to collect his bet!" yelled out another. "We have waited for exactly one hundred days."

If Mr. Garcia were correct, it was the day we had prayed for. I had endured three and a half years of dirty rice, foul water and horrors I would never forget.

Mr. Garcia arrived with a big smile on his face. "This is it, guys! Thank God. The day has finally come," he announced with certainty and an air of relief and calm. Everyone waited silently.

"Well, what happened?" someone finally asked. Just then the guards herded us out to the work area. Strangely, the perimeter guards, instead of facing inward towards us, were facing outward, and they were spaced every 25 to 50 yards apart. This was the first time they had ever done that. Nobody talked. We began to work. About noon several guards came running up to the worksite with two radios blaring. *"Hyacco! Hyacco! Mae susume!* (quick march) Back to camp. Now!" They didn't have to tell us twice.

"What's going on? Why are we being taken back to camp so early? What the hell are they saying on the radio?" the prisoners asked.

"The Emperor is on the radio announcing the war is over!" said one of the prisoners.

With no explanation or speech from the camp commander, the guards released us into the main yard and continued to stand facing outward along the perimeter of the grounds. Whoops and cheers exploded from the prisoners as we realized it was actually true. The war was really over and we were still alive. Some prisoners began hugging each other while others danced, ran, and leapt with unbridled exuberance. Others collapsed to their knees and wept. One fainted and had to be revived.

"It's over! It's over! The war is really over!" men shouted in their native language. I heard every language but Japanese. The Japanese officers quietly returned to their headquarters, shut the door, and were not seen for the rest of the day. None of the guards left their posts along the perimeter.

"What do you suppose the Nips are going to do now that they've lost?" asked an Australian fellow.

"I don't know, but it's sure strange they haven't moved all day from their posts," I answered. I wondered why the guards turned their backs to us. * It is a Japanese custom to face backward as a sign of ultimate respect and usually reserved for the Emperor.

"Didn't like looking at their ugly mugs anyway!" He laughed.

*August 17, 1945*

The next morning we found that the Japanese had evacuated during the night. They left their rifles, pistols and sabers stacked in front of their headquarters. There was not a trace of any of the Japanese anywhere. We cautiously looked around and found that they had packed up every bit of paperwork in headquarters. All of the ammunition for the pistols and rifles was gone.

It was eerie to be alone in camp without a single Japanese guard in sight. I walked over to the pile of rifles and picked one up for a souvenir. It was in pretty good condition because it was probably used only to guard us and was never fired. I wondered if Hideki had found his family. I prayed for him. I hoped he could get his life back together again. He had given me a notebook with Japanese lettering and photos when he had seen me writing in the paper cement bag notebook I had bound together with a string. It was a gesture of friendship. He could have been severely reprimanded for giving anything to a POW.

A few of us strolled down to the nearby beach because we didn't have anything to do. Nobody knew how or when we were going to be rescued so we waited for our forces to let us know what to do next. I knew that one of our planes would drop information to us because they knew where we were. It was hard to believe that Mr. Garcia had been right to the day. *This stinking war is over; our imprisonment is over; and it will soon be time to go home.*

With no one around to watch their every move we walked around freely, with nothing to do but entertain ourselves. Some walked off to be alone. Others looked for a routine to keep focused. Some couldn't leave the camp or the familiar surroundings. It would take some time to get over this hell. I knew I would never, ever forget it.

Tears rolled down gaunt faces. There were tears for the physical pain we endured when they beat us unmercifully. There were tears for the nightmarish horrors levied on our brothers who were killed without mercy. There were tears of relief for the freedom from the cruel hands of the war machine that had made us slaves. There were tears of joy that the war was finally over. There were tears because we could let down and cry.

Some of the men stayed in their bunks late into the morning. Small quiet groups milled about almost in slow motion. My wish to never again hear the infernal Japanese word of *Hyacco* was finally granted. From now on I would hurry only when I felt like it. It was so peaceful and serene in the camp without the Japanese soldiers.

Around midday, five US fighter planes buzzed the camp. The planes were close enough that we saw the pilots in their open cockpits enthusiastically saluting us. I burst into tears of pure, ecstatic joy at the sight of free Americans. I could see their happy smiles and white teeth. The glorious blue planes, with their Stars and Stripes, swooped back and forth over us as we wildly hopped and danced in our victory celebration. After about five minutes, the pilots veered off, tipped their wings in one last gesture of brotherhood, and disappeared into the east. It felt great to see our boys in the Japanese sky.

*August 18, 1945*

Early the next day four of our war birds returned, circled the small airstrip about a half-mile from the camp, lowered their landing gear, and dropped below the tree line out of our view. Several of us were outside the camp exploring for possible caches of Red Cross food and medicine. We rushed toward the airstrip to greet the pilots and to hear their news. It occurred to me as we ran down the narrow road toward the pilots, that we looked like starving hobos with our scraggly beards and tattered clothes. I wondered if we would ever recover from the time we spent as guests of Emperor Hirohito. His hospitality had taken an extraordinary toll on our bodies. It might take us the rest of our lives to heal. A couple of the men hobbled on makeshift crutches and walking sticks.

About halfway to the airstrip four pilots emerged from around a bend in the road, and walked toward us with big smiles.

"Holy smoke. Look at the size of those guys," remarked an English fellow who was awed by the well-nourished physiques of the Marine pilots. "They're bloody giants!"

The closer they got, the more unreal (by our standards) they appeared. Even the smallest pilot weighed twice as much as any of us. The healthy young men were the first non-POWs we had seen in three and one-half years. It was like a dream to see our men in their flight uniforms with polished leather gun belts and boots. The weapons they carried were smaller and lighter than the ancient WW1 Springfield rifles we had used in Bataan.

The approaching pilots walked proud, with the nonchalant, devil-be-damned swagger of victors. When we met them face-to-face on that dusty road, it was too much for us to hold back our tears. Quivering, bony hands reached out to shake the smooth, strong hands of the American pilots. Handshakes gave way to hugs and sobbing. We shared camaraderie known only by men who have put their lives on the line and survived.

"Anybody want a cigarette or chewing gum?" asked one of the pilots.

"How about a candy bar?" I asked, hoping for the impossible.

"Sure, here, Buddy," he said, as he reached into his gas-mask case and handed me a Hershey chocolate bar. At first I just stared at the shiny brown paper package. Then I took the precious gift in both hands and held it like it was a treat from God. It was wonderful to hold something from America, my home.

We walked with the pilots back to camp. We asked questions about everything from MacArthur to baseball. The pilots did their best to answer us. Of course, the main thing that we all wanted to hear was when we were going home.

"Hey Buddy, when are we getting out of here?" asked one anxious fellow.

"We're here to instruct you on how the United States Armed Forces plans to evacuate all of you to your respective countries," said one pilot. "It might take a few weeks, so be patient. We've scheduled food, clothing, and medical supply drops, starting tomorrow. A lot of preparation has gone into getting you guys out of here safely. Mines need to be cleared from the harbors so we can get hospital ships and transport ships into the dock. We've also got to make sure the Japs haven't booby-trapped the trains and bridges before we send in troops."

As men from the camp came forward to greet the flyers, another pilot remarked, "You sure have a mixed bunch of allied soldiers in this camp."

I said, "Yeah, we got Dutch, British, Javanese, Korean, Australian, South American, Balinese, and of course, Albuquerque New Mexico's only representative, yours truly."

Though the Japanese had evacuated the camp, the pilots scanned the surroundings for possible danger. They carried lightweight carbines by their straps at waist level, ready for use. We had not seen hide nor hair of the Japanese soldiers since the night before, but it was far better to be cautious in a land whose people were our sworn enemies. After the bizarre behaviors I had seen in the past forty months, the last thing I could predict was what a fanatical Japanese soldier might do. We had been reminded repeatedly that their code of Bushido did not allow for surrender. Until I was on the ship headed home, I made certain to keep my eyes and ears open.

"Is it really over?" yelled the Aussie we called Roo.

"Yeah, it's over. The Jap Navy is completely wiped out. They have almost no aircraft and their army is in rags," replied a tall blonde pilot. "Our atomic bombs flattened two of their cities as a warning of what they could expect if they continued to fight."

"It's over. It's really over," reiterated a tall Marine pilot who looked like Gary Cooper. "Let's just get you all home in one piece. So hold on a little bit longer, and before you know it, you'll be stateside and on the train home."

To hear our boys speak with such calm authority and confidence was almost too good to be true. They explained that the medical supplies, food, and clothing would be dropped by parachute from B-29s, C-47s and other specially rigged transport planes.

"Is there anything you absolutely need that can't wait until you get medical attention or help?" asked a pilot.

"Girls," joked a handful of guys at about the same time, eliciting roars of laughter and cheers.

"If we had any, you guys would be the first to get them — by parachute! Okay?" the pilot answered.

More cheers and whoops echoed off the wooden buildings in the main yard. It had been too long since we had laughed in merriment. It had been too long since we had anything to cheer about. It felt unreal to laugh without fear of reprisal.

The leader of the flight squadron lifted his hands and announced, "It has been great meeting all of you men today, but it's time for us to return to base before nightfall."

A voice from the group yelled out, " Yeah, back to the waiting girls."

We walked back to their planes with them, and we thanked them in our native languages and blessed their return journey. One by one, the fighter planes roared off the runway, circled over the waving band of grateful survivors, and tipped their wings in the traditional aerial salute before they disappeared into the hazy, high clouds in the east.

The thought of eating food other than rice, weeds, and bugs, made my mouth water and my stomach growl. It had been forty months since my last full meal. Whatever the planes dropped, it had to be better than what we had been eating.

CHAPTER 33

# Manna from Heaven

*August 20th, 1945*

Two days after the pilots gave us the good news; bombers, and cargo planes cruised so low overhead we could see the crew waving at us from their windows. Dozens of brightly colored parachutes began to stream out of the airplanes. Their precious cargo of medicine and food landed in the camp and in the surrounding fields. The beautiful sight of the billowing silk parachutes against the blue sky turned into a fiasco. Fifty-five gallon drums and wooden cargo boxes crashed into camp buildings and onto the hard earth. Apparently, the planes were too low or the parachutes were not strong enough to prevent the containers from breaking on impact. Cheering and laughing like children, we ran under the plummeting packages, anxious to get at the life-saving contents.

Someone, who understood the danger yelled over the enthusiastic cheers, "Look out, the canisters are falling too fast!" A fifty-five gallon-drum of food crashed to the ground, burst open, and exploded its contents in a colorful cloud of white flour, yellow powdered eggs, and brown cocoa. The men fell to their hands and knees to pick through the mounds of powdered food. They devoured the chocolate and laughed hysterically at each other covered from head to toe in the powdered food.

By nightfall we had salvaged enough to make scrambled eggs, along with a new canned meat called Spam. Unsure of how to cook the meat, we fried the chunky slices in its own gelatinous gravy like sausage until it was brown. We were unused to eating anything but rice and the smell of the cooking food caused several of the men to throw up. Throughout the night the rest of us ended up with severe bellyaches.

The planes dropped khaki fatigues that were too big for our skinny bodies. We looked like little kids dressed up in our parents clothing, but it felt wonderful to be wearing thick American cotton against my skin.

CHAPTER 34

# Taps for an Angel

*August 21, 1945*

Far in the distance we heard a B-29 rumble in the morning silence. "More chocolate," someone said which made everyone laugh.

"No more Spam," moaned another poor fellow who had diarrhea and stomach cramps. Unfortunately, our systems couldn't yet handle the large quantities of American food.

I looked up to see the low flying aircraft crest the hilly horizon, bomb bays open, ready to make a drop. "I hope we get some different food today - as well as stomach medicine," I said.

The men ran out and stood in the open field gazing upward at the parachutes drifting toward us. Crates came crashing down into the camp's building area, smashing roofs, walls and a storage depot we had made to organize the food. A crate slammed into a tree, disintegrating its wooden frame. Its contents of large steel cans of peaches shot out like silver cannon balls into the yard. One can struck our beloved Mr. Garcia squarely in the back of his head. The can split open his skull and killed him so suddenly he never made a sound. Those of us who saw it happen stood stunned at the horrible sight of this great gentleman, face down, his head split wide open. I was shocked at this horrible twist of fate that seemed so unfair. It wasn't long before the others discovered what had happened. Tears returned to Fukuoka 1 as an abysmal grief gripped our hearts. We were speechless. I wondered how this could happen to the one man who had always been there for us. Mr. Garcia was the shining beacon of hope when there was no hope in sight. He was the one man who could talk and joke with every POW in their native tongues. He was the playful angel who could jump up and down to make us smile and laugh when our heavy hearts cried. Mr. Garcia's war was over.

Sadness hovered over the camp the rest of the day as we gathered the food crates and stacked them. No one ate or talked much. We mourned the loss of an angel. His memory would live on in me forever. *God bless you Mr. Garcia, wherever you are.*

Now there were no restrictions, I took out my harmonica and played many of our favorite songs. The men sang along, but few could sing when I played The Prisoner's Song. "Oh I wish I had wings of an angel. Over these prison walls I would fly. I would fly to the arms of my loved ones, and I'd leave these prison walls far behind."

The camp's officer in charge notified the civilian Japanese officials in Fukuoka of Mr. Garcia's death. They took his body to Fukuoka and his ashes returned in a small wooden box. I prayed they were eventually returned to his native South America.

*August 22, 1945*

On the day following the tragic death of Mr. Garcia, the pall that hung heavily over the camp was broken by the surprise visit of a group of Japanese civilians whose kind and benevolent manner lifted many of our saddened hearts. The group comprised of about twenty elderly men and mothers with young children. They approached the camp, huddled together cautiously, and waited for a gesture of invitation from us to. We waved them into the camp and welcomed the local residents who carried brooms and gifts of live chickens and fresh eggs. They were dressed in simple, neat, working class clothing. They bowed to each of us in a respectful manner and offered the chickens and eggs in a gesture of peace and good will. I recognized one of the ladies as the kind person who had slipped me a rice ball on the dock at Moji when we were unloading a shipment of cement. I did not know if she recognized me, but I walked over to her and offered her and her children a handful of candy and gum. She bowed in gratitude and without words, demonstrated her willingness to sweep anything we wanted with the handmade broom she was carrying.

"They want to clean our bloody camp," remarked an English chap.

The camp was a wreck following the last delivery of supplies. Earlier this morning, we were mourning the death of Mr. Garcia, and decided to make a large X in the middle of an open field for the pilots to use as a guide.

I couldn't believe the Japanese civilians were so friendly after what our bombers and firebombs had done to Fukuoka. I had seen the charred remains of the city from the loading docks. Thousands of civilians must have been killed, but these civilians, like us, were the survivors of the war.

The children must have found our appearances humorous because they giggled when we approached them with treats. It had been over three years since I had seen a child's angelic face. Their rosy cheeks and smiling faces showed no hostility, fear or prejudice toward us. We offered them candy bars and chewing gum. While their mothers and grandfathers cleaned the camp, the children played with many of us. They lit up the gloomy landscape with laughter and joy. After three and a half years of using every ounce of energy to stay alive, it was difficult to be frivolous, play hide and seek, or just have fun. When survival dominates every thought and action, there is no room for anything else. Those happy Japanese children reminded us how to play again. I wondered if they would remember us as those funny-looking men with round eyes who lived up on the hill, who only ate candy bars, chewing gum, and liked to play.

With simple hand gestures and a barrage of Japanese instructions, the Japanese women transformed the dreary atmosphere of the prison camp. A tiny woman crawled under one of the brightly-colored parachutes, placed a long pole in the center of it, and then raised the pole vertically. Several of the other women untangled and tied the nylon cords to wooden stakes that the Japanese men had cut and hammered into the ground. We now had a beautiful sunshade made from a salvaged parachute. For the rest of the afternoon we worked side by side with the Japanese civilians. We erected more of the colored silk parachutes and created a circus-like compound. We all felt pure joy watching the children jump up and down and wave their arms, as each tent puffed up to its full balloon-like appearance. The bright sun lit up the silk structures that created a colorful kaleidoscope of shade.

"God, look at those Nips work, " remarked an Aussie. "They're so fast. No wonder the guards accused us of being slow and lazy." We had never seen any of the Japanese military guards or civilian supervisors do any manual labor.

As the tents rose, the feeling of the prison camp began to change as it took on a festive look. Our world had been dark and gray for too long. The colored canopies made us feel like we were at a party. We stacked the supplies in the tents for protection and easy access. We installed electric wire and light bulbs and were finished by nightfall.

The next day the Japanese brought colorful paper lanterns to cover the bare bulbs that created a softer light after dark.

We stood under the tents and turned on the lights. Like magic, the hardened look on our faces began to melt away in the warm glow of the pastel lights. Together, the Japanese civilians and we now ex-POWs had built a new environment out of the old – one that was beautiful and peaceful.

Before the Japanese civilians left for their homes in Fukuoka, we filled their baskets with a variety of foodstuffs, and of course, candy for the kids. What had begun as a sad day following the death of Mr. Garcia, was magically transformed into a feast of sharing and celebration. That's just the way Mr. Garcia would have liked it to happen.

Several days passed without word from our liberation forces headquarters. We had plenty of food, medicine, magazines and clean clothing. The navy pilots had said our evacuation might take several weeks. An English fellow and I decided to go back to Mitsui Camp 17 to visit the fellows we knew there.

We filled our fatigue jacket pockets with snacks and took full canteens of water. We walked to the nearest railroad station to catch a train to the Mitsui industrial mining facilities in Omuta. Both of us were surprised when we boarded the train and every Japanese man, woman and child stood up, bowed and offered us their seats on the crowded train. *"Ni, Ni, Arigato,"* we thanked them for their generous hospitality. Two adjacent seats materialized so we could sit together. Most of the adults kept their heads slightly lowered and avoided eye contact. The children couldn't take their curious eyes off us. When we offered the children handfuls of chewing gum and candy, the parents nodded approvingly, and broke the ice with smiles.

The narrow gauge train chugged through the beautiful Japanese countryside, but everyone stopped talking when the train passed by the charred remains of buildings and vehicles left by the B-29 fire-bombings. Only muffled sobs or whispers broke the silence.

When our train arrived at the station a short distance outside the steel gates of Camp 17, we were shocked at the specter of death that hung over the Mitsui coal mine. Guard posts towers and fences lay crumpled on the ground. The putrid stench of rotting bodies wafted through the air as we approached the main gate. Howling dogs yelled on both sides of the road and added to the grim atmosphere. After over three years of being close to death, I developed a sixth sense of imminent mortal danger. I felt that something horrible must have occurred. My English buddy and I looked at each and briefly discussed whether we should turn back, but decided to push forward. We had to know what had happened at Camp 17.

As we approached the perimeter fence, a loud voice shouted, "What the bloody hell are you guys doing here?"

I was almost too surprised to answer the guard's question. I looked at my partner incredulously. We were shocked at the cold welcome from one of our own men. I answered, "We came to see some friends of ours."

"Yeah, we were POWs here. Let us in," asked my companion.

One of the guards ran off to notify someone of authority that we had arrived. We, former prisoners of Camp 17, waited for permission to enter.

"What the hell's going on here?" I asked the guard that remained. I was puzzled at their strange behavior. "We're not the enemy, Buddy."

"I can't let anyone in without orders," he answered. "No one. Just wait until our commanding officer gives the okay."

"Yeah, okay, we can wait. I waited two years to get out of here, now I've got to wait to get back in," I retorted.

An English officer marched up to the gate and without asking anything shouted, "Go back to where you came from. I cannot let you in. This camp is under Marshall Law." He explained that when they had heard the war was over, several of the POWs had formed death squads and killed some of the guards. There was no doubt that many of the guards deserved to die but that was not our responsibility.

"May we come in and visit some of our friends?" my companion asked politely.

The officer answered, "Absolutely not. Go back to your own camp and wait until this bloody war is over. Then you'll have plenty of time to visit your friends."

I looked at him and said, "I thought this bloody war was over."

"Get on, I say," ordered the pompous Brit.

There were no tents or Japanese lanterns glowing at Camp 17. I thought about how different our experience had been. Our guards evacuated under the cover of darkness before anything could happen to them. I don't believe our small camp would have reacted the same way, and killed any of the guards.

"Get back to your own camp and wait to be officially liberated," ordered the officer.

"Please, Commander," I pleaded. "It's getting late and it'll be dark soon. Just let us stay overnight, Sir."

"You heard my orders. Now get away with you," he replied flatly.

We took one last look at the slave factory then turned around and began to walk back down the road. I was grateful to God that I didn't die in Camp 17. The time I spent underground was more than enough for one lifetime. I would never forget those days of slavery. I prayed I would be able to put those nightmarish memories away in a safe place when I got back home; a place where they would not interfere with making my dream come true.

"God bless you, men of Camp 17," I whispered as I turned my back forever on the Japanese underground gate down to hell.

The train ride back to camp was quiet and uneventful. We knew we had it better at Fukuoka 1 than those poor guys did back at the coal mines. It felt good to walk back to camp knowing we were not under Marshall Law.

While we were gone, the Japanese civilians had rigged up a shower for us. It was only cold water, but it still felt good to lather up with American soap and to shave and put on a brand new pair of all-American khaki fatigues. The B-29 packages even included mirrors; it was a good thing we didn't have them sooner, because I saw how bad I looked. I could actually see guys gaining weight after a few days of full meals. A full stomach was easy to accept. That night we had chipped beef, gravy and toast for dinner. As we ate, we laughed and told stories about what we would do when we got home.

"When I get home I'm going to eat so many cheeseburgers and fries that I will pass out,"one soldier said as he pushed out his belly like a pregnant woman."

The next morning fighter pilots returned to tell us that we would soon receive specific information regarding our liberation. One of the pilots joked, "We saw your tents from the air and thought you guys were having a carnival."

The other pilot remarked with a grin, "You guys keep it up and you're not going to want to leave." We all laughed and knew they were kidding.

"A hospital ship is en route to Nagasaki Bay and should arrive there in about a week," one of the young pilots informed us. "Meanwhile, enjoy your picnic. You've earned it."

"Why is it taking so long for them to get us out of here? It's been one whole week since the war's been over," complained one of the guys.

The navy pilot explained, "Before the war was over the Japanese expected a naval invasion and laid a series of submerged sea mines around the island. The navy has had to clear all the major bays and harbors before bringing in any hospital ships and transports." He said that the hospital ships that would process our evacuation would probably dock at either Moji or Nagasaki.

A pilot, sensing our anxiety, added, "We'll let you know the exact time and specifics as soon as we know from the operations unit. Hang in there, buddies, you've gotten through the hard part. It won't be much longer."

The US fighter pilots were our only direct contact with the Allied Command. Now that Mr. Garcia was gone, it was difficult to communicate the specific details to all the other men in our international camp but we did our best.

We stood in the open field and watched the messengers from home soar into the sky in their shiny blue fighter planes. They looked like blue angels returning home somewhere over the rainbow. We strolled back to our camp and saw the big X the open field, which designated the drop zone. We bowed our heads in a silent prayer in memory of Mr. Garcia.

On the way back to the camp, the Japanese children from Fukuoka who had adopted us as their playmates met us on the road. I never understood the mentality of the Japanese officers and most of the guards. But playing with the children of Fukuoka convinced me that we were all the same. When I was growing up, I was in awe of the local National Guard Cavalry who had highly trained horses and practiced maneuvers by Jefferson Junior High School. They looked so impressive on their mounts. When I had the chance, I joined the National Guard like most of my classmates at Albuquerque High School. At the time, I was only a few years older than the oldest kids of Fukuoka were. I was young and full of illusions, but that changed quickly when the bombs began to fall and the Zeros attacked us on December 8, 1941. From then on we paid the consequences for not being fully prepared. What kind of world lay ahead for these young Japanese children? I knew that I would someday have children of my own. I hoped these kids and my kids might be friends and allies one day.

The days passed slowly as we anxiously waited for our liberation. There were many sick soldiers who needed professional medical attention. The new medical supplies helped keep their wounds clean and sterilized and there was finally enough food, but it had been three weeks since the war had ended and they were still weak. It would be a horrible tragedy if they didn't make it after knowing we were free. We encouraged them to be patient and hang in there just a little longer.

## CHAPTER 35

# Out of the Ashes

*September 1, 1945*

The day we were waiting for finally came. The navy pilots brought instructions for each nationality regarding which train would take us to the various locations of our respective countries' checkpoints. Of the forty-eight prisoners of the Fukuoka Camp 1, there were only four United States servicemen. In broken English, Spanish, Javanese, and Burmese, we made our farewells to the men we would probably never see again. We were the last survivors. I placed the Japanese rifle into my duffel bag along with the raincoat I had inherited at Cabanatuan, the notebook the Japanese guard had given me, my little cement bag notebook, and my oldest possession and friend, the Marine Band harmonica. I would never forget that hot night at Camp O'Donnell when we sang our hearts out to honor the land we missed and loved. So many had died since that night.

I knew Camp Commander Tsunyoshi was wrong when he said, "Those of you who died were the lucky ones." *Those who have survived and are going home to build a better world were the lucky ones.* I didn't always feel that way when the pain and suffering was unbearable. We paid for our freedom and liberty with a piece of our lives.

I felt sad saying goodbye to the children of Fukuoka. Their lack of hatred and prejudice created a bridge from war to peace. I would never forget the atrocities, none of us could. Perhaps when the children grew into adults they would remember with smiles and affection, the friendly men who lived on the hill in colorful tents.

We loaded the bedridden on stretchers and big-wheeled wagons that the airplanes dropped by parachute. The wagons looked like a larger version of an American Radio Flyer red wagon. I thought the kids would have some great wagons to play with when we left them at the train station. Slowly, we walked away from Camp Fukuoka 1 and left the bright colored tents and children behind us. The only things we took were memories and the few possessions we could carry in a duffel bag.

We Americans were being sent to Nagasaki to be processed for our boat home. All of us were going to different parts of the globe. When the train pulled out of Fukuoka, I looked back for the last time at the children and their mothers. I prayed our countries would someday find peaceful ways to resolve our differences. I gazed out the window and thought about how all this had come to pass. I prayed that my children would never experience what I had, just as Dad had done when he came back from the Great War.

The slow-moving train crested the burnt grass rolling hills that bordered what was once the thriving port of Nagasaki. Nagasaki had been flattened into piles of charred concrete, twisted steel girders and burnt debris. In the aftermath of the atomic bomb, the industrial seaport city was no more.

"My God, it's no wonder they surrendered," I said to the soldier beside me.

He replied, "Imagine how many people died. There's nothing left standing."

"I can't believe a single bomb could be so powerful," I said in amazement.

The train crept slowly through the blackened rubble toward the waiting ship that would be our refuge from the terrible consequences of the bomb.

My heart felt like it would pound out of my chest when I saw Old Glory flying proudly from the white hospital ship docked in Nagasaki Bay. I couldn't take my tear-filled eyes off the Stars and Stripes flapping in the ocean breeze. Three and a half long, painful years had passed since the Imperial Japanese Army tore down our proud Stars and Stripes in Bataan, and stripped us of everything that identified us as Americans. They took our weapons, our food, our wedding rings, and so many lives. But they never took my pride in being an American.

When the train stopped at the dockside station, nobody on board moved for a brief moment. A military band began playing "Hail, Hail the Gang's All Here" as the doors opened. I was one of the lucky ones who could walk; others were transported on stretchers directly into sickbay. Many of my fallen buddies were in boxes of ashes marked with the name of the camp and the word AMERICAN.

As soon as I stood on the dock, I squared my shoulders and gave Old Glory the salute of a lifetime. I will remember sight of our flag flying in the clear blue sky atop the mast of the hospital ship until the day I die. We were in our beloved country's arms again. We had made it. Our country had come to take us home.

The music, the flag, and the healthy American soldiers in fresh uniforms seemed like a beautiful dream. When the band played "God Bless America," the anthem that rallied us that hot night in camp, I closed my eyes and wept for all the thousands of POWs who didn't make it to this dock.

"This way please, soldiers," a stout, young American GI directed us onto the boat. I hadn't heard the word "please" in years. It had been *"hyacco"* for the past three and a half years. Thank God, I would never have to hear that word again. We were sent into makeshift dressing rooms where we undressed for a de-lousing shower and fresh khakis.

"I want my duffel bag in sight at all times," I requested.

"I'll carry it for you through the line so you can see it," offered a sailor.

I didn't want to lose the few things that I had left. I had the Japanese rifle, some Japanese money, the little secret notebook I had made from the cement bags, and the Japanese soldier's notebook where I had written the names of the kind Japanese girls who had risked their lives and given us food on the dock at Moji. I had also written down the names and addresses of some of the men in camp.

"Do you have ammo for that rifle, soldier?" asked a navy shore patrol guard in a white helmet and armband.

"No ammo, it's a souvenir," I replied. "That Jap rifle's coming home with me where it will never threaten another American."

My thoughts turned toward the promotion which Captain Perrenot had given me in the Philippine battlefield. I wondered if headquarters received it. I never could locate Captain Perrenot or any of the others in G-Battery after the fall of Bataan. I heard a rumor that he didn't make it out of the Philippines, but I learned not to believe anything unless I saw it myself. He was the best artillery officer a soldier could serve under, he had even shown us how to hit a moving target from 300 yards with our 75-mm cannons. Those Japanese troops on the beach at Lingayen would never forget our four half-tracks either.

God, it was good to feel American clothes against my skin and real socks and thick American leather boots on my feet. I was in a daze. I was standing on an American ship among American sailors, with the smell of American food wafting up from the galley.

"Come this way, Buddy. It's time for you to see the doctor," said the sailor escorting me through the lines.

"Get this chow hound some of that food I smell, and I'll never have to see a doctor again," I joked with the sailor.

I stepped into the examination room and could hardly believe my eyes. Standing there was one of the most beautiful women I have ever seen, with gold oak leaves on her lapels.

She said, "Hello, Frank. I'm Major Rose Cafio and I'm going to check you out."

I didn't know what to say. I was stunned to see not only an American woman, but also a Spanish-American one at that. I was even more astounded, because she was also a high ranking officer, and a doctor. The world had changed since I'd been captured.

"Frank. You can call me Rosie," she said with a gorgeous smile and chuckle.

"Okay, Doctor Rosie," I said and I began trembling. As she examined my shaking body with her soft hands and gentle touch, I became increasingly weak-kneed. Here I was with a beautiful Spanish-American, Major Doctor who was checking me out from stem to stern. I thought I must have been in heaven.

"Frank, you look in remarkably good shape for all you've been through," she said. "Is there anything you would like? Anything?"

I didn't dare reveal all the thoughts that were spinning through my mind while I looked into her big brown eyes. I replied sheepishly, "Could I please have some ice cream?"

"What flavor?" asked Major Rosie.

"Vanilla," I quivered.

She called a corpsman and gave him my request.

"Is there anything else?" she asked, with her hands open and head tilted quizzically.

"Could I wire my parents in Albuquerque and tell them I'm okay?" I asked, coming back to reality.

The corpsman delivered a heaping bowl of vanilla ice cream. That first bite was sweet, cold heaven. Major Rosie summoned the corpsman to take my message and wire it immediately. This was the first communication that my parents received from me in three and a half years:

Dear Mother and Dad,

I have been liberated by our great American troops and I am in the good hands of Major, Doctor Rosie on a US Naval hospital ship at Nagasaki, Japan. I'll be seeing you soon.

God bless you all. Frank

I hopped off the examination table and dressed. Then I was led to the mess hall for a dinner fit for a king. Dr. Rosie had to attend the other sick POWs, so she dashed off. I never had a chance to see her again to say goodbye. I'll never forget her smile and how she made me feel human again.

For the first time in years I lay in a bunk, protected from anything that could hurt me or take my life. I couldn't remember the last time I felt this way. I slept like a baby in the arms of the US hospital ship, layered with sheets, blankets, and pillows. Even the paint on the wall was the color of my homeland. I dreamt of home. I could smell the roses blooming. I heard the whistle, as a Santa Fe locomotive pulled into the downtown depot. I tasted Mother's enchiladas and bacon-flavored refried beans. I saw the faces of my beloved parents. I thanked God with all my heart that I was going home. So many times during this war I could have died. *God bless you, Mr. Garcia.*

Generals MacArthur, Wainright , and Percival on deck of USS Missouri
*U.S. Archives*

*September 2, 1945*
*On board the USS Missouri*

The formal signing of the end of hostilities between the US, and all of the nations at war with Japan appropriately took place on the narrow quarterdeck of the battleship named after President Truman's home state. General MacArthur delivered a short speech, brief but true to his eloquent form, stated, " It is my earnest hope, and indeed the hope of all mankind, that from this solemn occasion a better world will emerge out of the blood and carnage of the past-a world dedicated to the dignity of man and the fulfillment of his most cherished wish for freedom, tolerance, and justice."

Following the formal signing in the leather bound document on the simple wooden table by each of the nations delegates one of the Japanese delegates remarked, "This narrow quarterdeck was now transformed into an alter of peace."

Early the next morning, a corpsman informed me, "You checked out okay for departure on the next available LST," the corpsman said. This meant I didn't have to stay on the hospital ship for further examinations.

*All right! I'm leaving today to go back home.* Everything was perfect so far. At times I thought it was a fantastic dream; it was too good to be true. Over and over again, the faces of my family flashed through my mind. These were my treasures. They were worth more than all the gold in Fort Knox.

As we pulled out of Nagasaki Bay on the small LST, I looked back at Japan for the last time. It was time to put the nightmare behind me. If this ordeal taught me anything, it was that every single moment might be my last. From this point forward I would do my best to make each moment count. The amphibious landing craft transported us to the small aircraft carrier USS Chenango, moored outside Nagasaki Harbor. Julian Trevino, a Spanish-American sailor from Texas told me that the carriers had been designed as escorts to protect convoys of supplies and troops. Everything I saw was completely new to me: the carrier, the B-29s, even the rifles, handguns and uniforms were new designs. No wonder the Japanese had been defeated. I wished we had these modern weapons and backup supplies when the Japanese landed at Lingayen Gulf. President Theodore Roosevelt said it well, "Walk softly and carry a big stick." Our stick was not big enough to repel the Japanese invasion force.

I checked the troops on the carrier, but I did not see any of my fellow Battling Bastards of Bataan, who had been part of the 200th or the 31st infantry. I would never forget the brave Filipino twins, who were horribly wounded by bursting shrapnel. They never gave up their side-by-side post on the rear machine gun. We were all soldiers, then prisoners without a home, fighting for our lives. I followed orders and did whatever was necessary to stay alive to fight another battle.

"We're headed for Okinawa, but it looks like the weather may prevent us from landing safely," announced a naval officer. We waited for two days onboard the carrier for a break in the weather. High winds screamed night and day across the choppy seas. The first part of my journey home had begun. Like everything else that had occurred since the war began, I knew this would not be a cakewalk. It didn't matter, because I was finally going home.

So here I was, ready and able to pursue the next phase of my dream, with all my body parts intact — though I was still skin and bones. I was one of the lucky ones because this horror story hadn't driven me stark raving mad. I was heading home to start a life that I hoped would include a loving wife and a family. I prayed that I would be blessed with a family, to love and nurture in my hometown for the rest of my life. I prayed that peace would reign over our lives. Hopefully the atomic bomb would ensure peace for a long, long time.

After a couple of days on Okinawa, I was informed that I could get a ride to Clark Field in the Philippines on a B-24 bomber. The old war-horse looked as if it had seen a lot of action. Its four engines sounded rough as it taxied down the runway.

"Are you sure this thing can fly?" I asked the pilots half-joking.

The pilots stationed me in the machine gun bubble directly behind and above them, and said, "Lovato, your job is to keep an eye on the engines in case of fire. Watch for smoke."

"What? Watch for smoke? Man, isn't any part of my trip home going to be easy?" I asked.

I gave the pilots the A-OK sign, and we took off, rumbling and shaking. I sat with my eyes glued to the fire belching engines. Once we were in the air, the shaking was reduced significantly. I thought this airplane sounded happier in the air than on the ground. It's when they are running at cruise speeds that they feel and sound their best.

Two propellers began to slow down and dark smoke belched out of both the side exhaust pipes. I pressed the seat release button and slid the track the seat down into the cockpit to tell the pilots. "Hey! Two of the engines conked out and I saw smoke!"

They looked at each other and grinned, as if they knew what was happening. "Don't worry, Lovato. This airplane flies on two engines if it has to," laughed one of the pilots.

"I'm glad to hear that," I said surprised. I think they were having fun at my expense.

"You get back up there and let us know if the other two quit," laughed the co-pilot.

"Right!" I answered.

Dad had said that airplanes would have a big impact on our lives in the future, and they had definitely impacted mine. If the airplane were the way of the future, I might consider transferring from the Army to the new Army/Air Force, when I re-enlist. I liked working on mechanical transports and they would probably need good vehicle maintenance support for all of their aircraft.

By now it was dark, and Manila Bay was lit up like a big city by battleships, cruisers, destroyers and aircraft carriers. One of the pilots said that the entire Third Fleet was anchored in the bay. It sent chills down my spine to see Manila back in US protective hands again. The last time I saw Manila was when I left for Japan on the Hell Ship in July 1943.

As we landed at Clark Field and I stepped down onto Philippine soil again, I felt a surge of strength and power rush through me like. My country and I had returned as General MacArthur had promised. Probably less than half of the Battling Bastards of Bataan were still alive. For a brief moment I closed my eyes and thanked God to be one of the lucky. I was grateful to be alive and in one piece even thought I still weighed less than one hundred pounds, had shrapnel fragments in my leg and a head full of horrible memories I hoped I could forget.

Fortunately, the time in Manila was brief. My only regret was that I was not able to see the "Miracle of the Roses" garden where the Virgin Mary appeared on the petals of a rose. I had to either board the available transport home, or stay and take my chances on the next ship going stateside. Needless to say, I didn't take any chances or push my good fortune.

Aboard the crowded ship I saw no one I knew from the 200th or from any of the prison camps. All the soldiers I met had arrived in the Philippines during or following General MacArthur's return. Occasionally, I would see another former POW in the mess hall or while wandering around the ship. We didn't look like the rest of the healthy, rosy-cheeked young soldiers. Our bodies were so emaciated that no uniform could fit them. My brief conversations with former POWs rarely went beyond asking what camp they were in or if they knew the whereabouts of Captain Perrenot, Brewster, Herman or some of the guys from the 200th. They, in turn, would ask me about their missing buddies. When we met again a brief nod and a "good luck" or "God bless you" was all we said to each other. Our eyes revealed the agony, but no one wanted to talk about the horrors buried deep in our souls. Like me, I'm sure they wanted to shove those painful days and nights of out of their thoughts. I kept busy doing little things to occupy my mind and to keep the past from destroying all the good and beautiful that now surrounded me. There was so much to look forward to when I got home.

The days passed slowly onboard the ship as it sailed east to Pearl Harbor. I passed the time by taking long, hot, soapy showers in the morning and sometimes at night. The other soldiers must have thought I was absolutely crazy as I sang and chuckled under the streaming showerhead. Getting accustomed to three hot American-style meals a day was more difficult than I expected. My digestive system was not capable of consuming a western-style diet of dairy foods and meats cooked in grease. At first, the smell of fried foods made my stomach turn. The medics warned me that this might happen, so I ate sparingly of the blander offerings like mashed potatoes, cooked vegetables, or scrambled eggs. My body did accept cakes, fruit pies and cobblers so I ate generous portions of those delectable treats. The thought of tasting my mother's fruit pies again made my eyes well up with tears of joy.

I was awake before sunrise and out of my bunk before most of the other soldiers. I watched the sun's golden rays stream skyward and I filled my lungs with the warm, salty tropical ocean air. I stood where I could see Old Glory and closed my eyes. I took out my harmonica and played "God Bless America" for the thousands of my fellow soldiers and POWs buried in shallow graves in the Philippines and for those who died in Japan and whose ashes were riding home with me. Little Victory's notes must have sounded like a solitary songbird in the wafting ocean breeze to the sailors on watch, but to me it sounded like the voices of the nine thousand men at Camp O'Donnell. Like my father before me, who played "Taps" each morning before the sun rose on the high plains of the Rio Puerco, I promised to forever dedicate this song to my buddies.

The soldiers on board had no idea of the horror that we soldiers experienced at Bataan and Corregidor. When they asked, I only said, "It was hell." I wanted to push the nightmares out of my mind. Maybe I doubted anyone would believe how badly I was treated as a prisoner. I wanted to enjoy all the wonderful things that I had now. Each day I kept to myself, took long showers, ate sparingly, and explored the big iron ship carrying me home.

After a brief stop for fuel and supplies at Pearl Harbor, we continued on to San Francisco, where four years ago I sailed out as an eager, wet-behind-the-ears National Guardsmen. Most of the soldiers crowded against the railing, sat on gun turrets, and craned their necks to catch the first sight of land. Exuberant cheers echoed out from men on the highest positions that signaled land had been sighted. I leaned over the deck railing and spotted a small dark mountain peak jutting above a wispy layer of mist clinging to the coast. *My God, I'm home!*

Everyone began to celebrate. Men whistled, cheered, jumped and danced while slapping backs, shaking hands, hugging, laughing, and crying. My heart felt like it was about to burst from my chest when I first saw the orange-red towers of the Golden Gate Bridge. Hundreds of people lined the bridge, waving flags as they cheered us home through the majestic gateway to San Francisco Bay. As the tugboats came out to bring the ship into port, tears spilled out of my eyes when I saw the red, white and blue of the thousands of American flags flapping on San Francisco rooftops and hanging from windows. Scores of other Americans waved flags on the docks to welcome us home at last.

Just as the ship was preparing to dock, a brass band struck up the "Star Spangled Banner." I peered over the edge of the boat one last time before getting in line to disembark. I heard a familiar voice cut through the cheers and music, "Frank! Frank!" I was shocked to hear someone calling my name. With the exception of the Chillicothe Kid and my friend Herman, I had been called everything but "Frank" for four years. I'd heard "Private," "Lovato," *"San beya ku ju hachi,"* or "American dog" to name just a few. My heart leaped. It was the strong voice of my youngest sister, Annie. She was jumping and waving above the crowds of cheering people on the wooden pier. My knees almost buckled when I saw my father and mother standing next to her with tears streaming down their cheeks, while they held each other close. I returned their waves, clutched my duffel bag and got in line to disembark into the arms of my loving family, the ones that had given me the strength and the courage to survive.

*My God I'm home, I'm really home! God Bless America!*

---

*April 1, 1945*

U.S. troops land on Okinawa only 400 miles from the Japanese mainland. Although the invasion was met with very little resistance, the inland battle to remove the Japanese from their dug-in emplacements and network of tunnels proved to be a bloodbath of attrition for troops and Okinawan civilians alike. Stepped up "Kamikaze" raids on Allied ships and even a suicide plan to run aground the massive Japanese battleship Yamato to be used as a fortress, unequivocally demonstrated the Imperial Japanese commands' intention to sacrifice every Japanese citizen's life for the sake of the Emperor and Japan. Admiral Mitscher's carrier-based aircraft sank the Yamato before it could carry out its final mission. By war's end "Kamikaze" pilots sunk 30 Allied ships and damaged over 300.

*April 29, 1945*

German commanders surrender in Italy

*April 29-30 1945*

U.S. 7th Army enters Munich as Hitler and Eva Bruan commit suicide in an underground bunker in Berlin.

*May 2, 1945*

The Berlin Nazi commandant surrenders the city to the Russians.

*May 7, 1945*

Unconditional surrender of all German forces to the allies is signed at Eisenhower headquarters at Riems. Fighting continues in several locations.

By the end of the war in Europe, the all African-American fighter pilots of the 332nd Fighter Group known as the "Tuskeegee Airmen" had downed over 450 German fighter planes in the air including the first ever Me 262 jet. Prior to their arrival, up to one third of the bombers had been shot down by enemy fighter plane interceptors and antiaircraft fire. The Tusked Airmen did not lose a single U.S. bomber to enemy aircraft.

*May 8, 1945*

Allies declare VE Day "Victory in Europe."

*May 25, 1945*
*Okinawa*

It appeared to the Allied command that the Japanese forces were on the verge of complete collapse because they had already suffered over 60,000 deaths and their remaining troops were pushed to the extreme tip of the island. American losses of over 6,000 killed were far above the original estimates. By now U.S. forces controlled all the airfields on Okinawa. Although the Japanese were completely cut-off from any support and had no chance of winning, much less surviving in their barren, dugout coral caves and emplacements, the final battle for Okinawa was still almost another bloody month away.

*June 22, 1945*
*Okinawa*

The final battle for Okinawa was fought with U.S. flame-thrower tanks and a month long mopping up operation to root out defiant, starved, and injured Japanese troops. In the bloodiest battle of the Pacific, almost all of the 110,000 enemy troops had been killed along with over 75,000 Okinawan civilians. Over 13,000 Americans died securing the last bastion of Japan's inner circle of defense. The next military objective was the Empire of Japan.

*Strategic Outcomes*

Once again, as witnessed on Saipan, Iwo Jima, and Okinawa, even after realizing it was hopelessly overpowered by allied troops and war materials, the Japanese military command opted not to surrender and chose to die fighting. Ancient teachings of the way of the warrior (Code of Bushido) prevailed over reason and all intelligence information. Their Navy had been annihilated, their air corps reduced to young suicide bombers, and the army clearly lacked the strength of manpower and materials to defeat the Allied powers on any front. The final battle and possible fight to the death by every Japanese citizen would now be fought on the mainland of Japan by what remained of their decimated army and civilians.

*July 16, 1945*
*Alamogordo, New Mexico*

The first atomic bomb was tested successfully in the remote, south central desert near Alamogordo, New Mexico.

*July 16, 1945 - Aug 15 in the U.S. 2, 1945*
*Potsdam, Netherlands*

The Allies develop and finalize terms of the Potsdam plan and sent it to Emperor Hirohito and the military dominated government cabinet ministers.

"We call upon the Government of Japan to proclaim now the unconditional surrender of Japan's armed forces and to provide proper and adequate assurances of their good faith in such actions."

"The consequences for Japan is prompt and utter destruction." Winston Churchill

*Tokyo, Japan*

Prime Minister Suzuki's answer to the Allies request to end the war was met with a one word response of "Mokusatsu" which literally means in Japanese to "kill with silence." This no action, no comment response was interpreted by the Allies as a complete rejection of the Potsdam plan to end the war.

"JAPAN OFFICIALLY TURNS DOWN ALLIED SURRENDER TERMS ULTIMATUM" New York Times headlines July 30, 1945

*July 31, 1945 (July 30 in the U.S.)*

The U.S. cruiser Indianapolis was torpedoed and sunk by a Japanese submarine I-58 after delivering its top-secret cargo to Tinian Island. Due a failure in communication, only 315 of the 1,196 men were rescued from the shark-infested water five days later.

The component parts for the "Little Boy" atomic bomb would eventually be dropped by the B-29 "Enola Gay" on its principal target, the port city of Hiroshima.

*August 7, 1945 (August 6 in U.S.)*
*Hiroshima, Japan*

At 8:15am the B-29 "Enola Gay" drops the first atomic bomb on the port city and populace of Hiroshima.

Colonel Tibbets, his crew, photographers and film crew witnessed the nuclear fireball blast that instantly killed over 100,000 inhabitants, including several American Prisoners of War held captive in the Hiroshima castle. The ensuing mushroom shaped cloud rose over 30,000 foot above the completely destroyed city.

President Harry Truman's press release announced to the Japanese Government and the world that "It is an atomic bomb...If they do not accept our terms, they may expect a rain of ruin from the air, the likes of which has never been seen on this earth."

*Tokyo, Japan*

Both the Emperor and the army dominated ruling cabinet continued to remain silent offering no response to either the presidents warning or the previously delivered terms of the Potsdam Declaration.

*The Kremlin, Russia*

Russia finally declares war on Japan and begins a military offensive against the Japanese army positioned on their northernmost borders.

*August 10, 1945 (Aug. 9 in the U.S.)*
*Tinian*

Early in the morning Major Charles Sweeny and his crew lifted off the airfield on Tinian Island loaded with another atomic bomb, code named "Fat Man" and headed to its primary target of Kokura, Japan. Kokura was the site of a large military arsenal. It was decided en route to change course to the port city of Nagasaki because high clouds rendered poor visibility over Kokura. Shortly after 11:00 am, Sweeny's bombardier released the plutonium-based nuclear bomb on Nagasaki. The city was completely flattened by the blast killing over 35,000 of its inhabitants.

*Tokyo, Japan*

News of the destruction of Nagasaki by another atomic bomb and the Soviet Unions entry into the war prompted Emperor Hirohito and the Foreign Minister to petition the Supreme War Council to immediately accept the terms of the Potsdam Declaration. After several hours of heated debate, War Minister Anami stated that Japan must never surrender and that all Japanese must fight to the bitter end in order to "find life in death." Understanding that there could be no agreement among his cabinet ministers, Emperor Hirohito broke prior precedence by announcing the need to accept the terms of the Potsdam plan and "bear the unbearable."

The next morning the full Imperial Conference approved the Potsdam plan. Following their approval, the Emperor prepared a recorded speech and had it secretly locked away overnight. During the night a group of military conspirators attempted to find the recordings and destroy them. Fortunately, the attempted coup was foiled, prompting War Minister Anami to commit Hara Kiri.

*August 15, 1945 –11:00 am (Aug. 14 in the U.S.)*

Radio message broadcast throughout Japan

For the first time ever, civilians and military personnel actually heard the high-pitched voice of their revered Emperor Hirohito. His recorded message stated that the United States has employed the use of a weapon of "incalculable" power which could "result in the ultimate collapse and obliteration of the Japanese nation." He stated that Japan must accept the terms of the Potsdam Declaration. It is interesting to note that the word 'surrender' was never mentioned in the Emperor's message.

Allied news media announce VJ Day 'Victory in Japan' and VP Day 'Victory in the Pacific' throughout the world.

September 2- was declared the official VJ Day commemorating the signing of Potsdam plan)

*August 23, 1945*

U.S. occupational troops land in Japan

*September 2, 1945*
*On board the U.S.S. Missouri*

The formal signing of the end of hostilities between the U.S., and all of the nations at war with Japan appropriately took place on the narrow quarterdeck of the battleship named after President Truman's home state. General MacArthur delivered a short speech, brief but true to his eloquent form, stating, "It is my earnest hope, and indeed the hope of all mankind, that from this solemn occasion a better world will emerge out of the blood and carnage of the past...a world dedicated to the dignity of man and the fulfilment of his most cherished wish for freedom, tolerance, and justice."

Following the formal signing by each of the nations in the leather bound document, one of the Japanese delegates remarked, "This narrow quarterdeck was now transformed into an alter of peace."

# Epilogue

The war was over. The former prisoners of war who had survived came home to create a new world for themselves, and even for their former enemy nations. Medals were handed out along with a few dollars in back pay, and of the original twelve thousand who had capitulated in Bataan, Corregidor, Wake Island, and in other Pacific Theatre locations, those of the approximately four thousand American survivors who could stuff their horrific memories into a place in their mind soldiered on to the next phase of their lives. The Philippines achieved their independence, and their soldiers and countrymen embarked on healing and rebuilding a new, free nation.

A few wrote their accounts of their POW experience in self-published books, which I have included in the appendices. Most preferred to put it all behind them like a bad dream. Others could not live with their daily nightmares and quickly succumbed to alcoholism, mental illness, or suicide. Those who could adapt, although never fully able to forget, returned to their home states and attempted to put the memories behind them, and to live out the dreams that they had so dearly prayed for in the prison camps.

After a short period of peace, a new enemy in the ideology of communism emerged, and young men as well as some of the same men who had fought the Nazis, Fascists, and Imperialists were called back into action to fight on foreign land in Korea. In the twentieth century, peace had become a fragile state of homeostasis, easily upended by charismatic leaders of nations and ideologies bent on achieving power, in a world that had created weapons capable of destroying whole cities with a single bomb. All the individual stories of the war in the Pacific, albeit the headline battles of Pearl Harbor, Midway, Guadacanal, Iwo Jima, and Okinawa, were largely forgotten to all but those who had lived the heroic battles and the surviving four thousand POW's who did not much want to dredge up the repressed horrors.

Staff Sergeant Frank Lovato stepped down off the ship in San Francisco and was greeted by his beloved mother, father, and two sisters. He spent a few weeks in a Santa Fe military hospital undergoing tests and inoculations, and quickly returned to active duty. Two parts of his plan that had sustained him through the Death March and forty two months in the prisoner of war camps had been achieved. "I need to get home, gain the rank I was promised, meet and marry the most wonderful woman in the world, raise two boys and two girls, then retire and live the rest of my life in my beautiful New Mexico. My dream would keep me alive, God willing."

He had returned home and also received his rank of Staff Sergeant.

Captain Perrenot had put in for his promotion during the battle for the defense of the Philippines, but no official word had been received. Fortunately for him, an officer in Captain Perrenot's command attested to his claim while he was in Santa Fe.

While on leave in Albuquerque, Dad went to a local department store to purchase a baby shower gift. There in the baby clothes section, he met the love of his life and my dear mother, Evangeline Celina Herrera. It was love at first sight. After a brief dating period and engagement, they were married and the third part of his dream was fulfilled. Soon after Dad transferred into the United States Air Force, I was born in 1947. He soon achieved Master Sergeant, the highest rank for an enlisted man by 1950. By 1961, three children followed just like in his "dream plan": Patrick in 1951, Marie in 1957, and Deborah in 1960.

Dad led a distinguished career in the United States Air Force, serving to help rebuild the infrastructure in war-ravished England, in Nevada during every above-ground nuclear bomb test, and in Pakistan during the Francis Powers incident. When the opportunity finally came in 1961 to end his career in the military service, Dad listened to the wishes of our beloved mother and retired, to live out the last part of his "dream plan" in their home town of Albuquerque, New Mexico. The military retirement pay for a Master Sergeant, four hundred dollars per month, was not enough to support a family of six. Believing his almost twenty years of management and leadership experience as a non-commissioned officer, several Good Conduct medals, four Presidential Citations (one from the President of the Philippines), Distinguished Service medals, two Purple Hearts, the Bronze Star, and a history of dependability and loyalty to his country would be at the least a better-than-average job history, he applied for a position in the United States Civil Service. Unfortunately, virtually none of his celebrated military history contributed to acquiring a comparable management position. Because he and his fellow buddies of the National Guard were whisked out of school and off to the Philippines as tensions arose in the Pacific prior to the commencement of the Pacific War, he had not received a high school diploma. Dad had to start over again from the bottom of the Civil Service government service scale. He swallowed his pride and put the welfare of his family first, and accepted a position as a mail room clerk. Although he eventually earned his G.Ed, he remained in clerk positions for the next fifteen years. No one of his fellow employees, bosses, or even his family knew of the remarkable history of his service to his country that is written in this book. Dad finally retired again in 1976 from government service to devote full-time personal support to our family. It was then, at a University of New Mexico football game, that I heard him quietly murmur the words that inspired me to later research and write this incredible story of his dedication, service, and survival.

During the course of interviewing and writing Dad's account, I attempted to discover what happened to his American buddies of G Battery. Because he was unable to locate Captain Perrenot and Burl Brewster in the prisoner of war camps, and there was no contact at any of the post-war gatherings of former POW's, he assumed they "didn't make it" like almost two-thirds of the POW's who were surrendered in Bataan.

I researched the National Archives and discovered that Captain Travis E. Perrenot had died shortly after arriving in Japan on the infamous "Hell Ship," the Oryko Maru. Through the internet, I was able to learn more of his pre-war life and locate his heirs, and related to them his heroic wartime command that they knew nothing of. A highway was named after him in his hometown in Texas. Prior to the war, he had worked for the Texas Highway Department, planting trees along the main highway that now bears his name. True to form, as Dad described, he was respected and loved by his family. Ironically, one of his nephews became a field artillery officer in the Army. It was an honor and a privilege for Dad and I to give him the gift of his legacy: the story of how his uncle was perhaps the first United States Army field artillery officer to lead an attack on the invading troops of General Homma's Imperial Japanese Expeditionary forces.

On Easter morning of 1999, almost fifty-seven years to the day that they were separated during the massive Japanese offensive, I began calling numbers of persons that I had located on the internet with the name of Burl Brewster, hoping to find an heir who might have background information as did the Perrenots. My second call was answered by a soft-spoken woman who, after I asked if they knew of a Burl A. Brewster who had served in the Army in the Philippines during WW2, politely said "just a minute," then called her husband to the phone. The gentleman responded slowly in a slight Texas drawl, "Yes, I am Burl Brewster, and I was in the Philippines during the war." Shocked, I could hardly speak. It was Brewster, the only other person alive (other than the Filipinos) that had experienced the heroic battles of G Battery, Second Provisional Group, Self Propelled Artillery (Mechanized), and that I unfortunately had no information on.

Mr. Brewster had also believed my father had been killed in the POW camps. He thought he had actually seen him lying in a pile of dead bodies waiting to be buried in a shallow mass burial trench. He asked questions about Dad and our family, then proceeded to invite me to visit him, his wife and daughter at their home in Southern California. The Brewsters welcomed me with open arms and hospitality befitting a family member. Dad and Burl had spoken on the phone, but because both had hearing difficulties, it was difficult for them to understand each other very well. They agreed to get together as soon as their respective wives' challenging health problems would permit. Mrs. Brewster was in the hospital frequently, and my mother was losing her ability to walk due to a spinal injury. I videotaped my interview with Mr. Brewster, and like my father, he related his respect for Captain Perrenot. When I related to him my findings of his demise, it broke his heart to hear, once and for all, that he had died that horrible way. It was as though he had held the hope that Captain "Perry" had "made it," and like he and my Dad, was living in peace with his loving family somewhere in Texas, pushing the past his days in that living hell, leaving them farther behind with each passing day. Mr. Brewster had returned after his liberation from the prisoner of war camps, chose to accept an honorable discharge from the military service, and became a watchmaker and jeweler. It was a business where he could go into his shop, a private world detached from the masses of people who didn't care what he had done or went through during the war, support his family, and try to forget the indelible pain. Each day in his retirement, he looked out from high atop his hilltop home to see the beautiful Pacific ocean, which he had been able to cross over, away from the horrific memories he had tried to leave on the other side.

Burl A. Brewster died in a Veterans Administration hospital in the winter of 2002.

The Chillicothe Kid proved to be the most illusive buddy of my father's saga. Not knowing his real name made it impossible to research in any of the existing records. Dad said he remembered he was from Chillicothe, Texas, and had related that he was in the import/export business. Dad knew little about his history prior to their brief time together. I began my research by contacting the editor of the Quanah Tribune-Chief, Vernon Daily Record, and Chillicothe Valley News newspapers, who was kind enough to publish a special supplement to the local newspaper, entitled "Who Was The Chillicothe Kid?" It was the entire chapter of their last day together; a day filled with an artillery barrage, an emergency baptism, finding the home brew, and finally reuniting with G-Battery inside the old mission church. The editor prefaced the story by informing the readers to contact me if they had any information leading to the discovery of the mystery sharpshooter. Although the residents of Chillicothe and the surrounding area were most supportive, only one eighty year-old gentleman had a theory of a specific person that fit the physical description that Dad had described. He related that prior to the war, the Stevenson brothers owned a family farm in the Chillicothe area. They were identical twins, but each had different life goals. One of the brothers wanted to farm, but the other left the farm to his brother and went to the Philippines in the thirties for business opportunities. According to this gentleman, the young man, known only as "Tag," perhaps short for Theodore, never returned and nothing more was known of his fate. The brother left no heirs, and the farm was inherited and later sold by a relative who lived in Los Angeles. Another local called to tell me that although he didn't know who the "Chillicothe Kid" was, he was certain he knew what early profession "The Kid" might have had prior to departing to the Philippines. Because my Dad had remarked that "The Kid" shot his western-style Colt pistols with deadly accuracy, so quickly appearing not to take aim in the traditional manner, the caller suggested that he might have been a true "gunslinger". A legitimate, professional sharpshooting guard that was hired by oil companies to guard the cash payroll taken out to the oil fields on pay day. He related that all boys growing up on farms and ranches in rural Texas learned at an early age to shoot a pistol, rifle, and shotgun. Most cattlemen and ranchers carried weapons for protection from rattlesnakes, sheep killing coyotes, and any other threats to the well-being of their property. According to the caller, when a young boy demonstrated a natural propensity to shoot accurately, he was given special privileges and further gun handling training by a local mentor. Known also as "Pistoleros", the gun handling coach would eventually develop the young boy into a fellow "Pistolero". Hired guns were highly valued at a time when bank robbers terrorized the rural towns. Depression era hardships turned desperate men and women into criminals. Oil field, underground mine, and ranch payroll wagons were easy targets for highly mobile crooks, thus necessitating hiring a trained guard. I, too, speculate that this might explain his lack of interest in farming as a career, his uncanny ability to shoot so well, and why he felt a need to guard my Dad when they went out on reconnaissance patrols. Perhaps we will never know in this lifetime who "The Chillicothe Kid" was, or how he lived and died, but he will live on as a life-saving angel and a true friend in my Dad's memory and this book for generations to come.

My research to see firsthand for myself the Philippines, Bataan, Lingayen Gulf, and the locations of the now demolished prisoner of war camps took me on an exodus of my own self-discovery. I discovered a country of wonderful people who remember the war on their homeland. Patriots who respect the freedom they enjoy, and honor the sacrifice of hundreds of thousands of their own countrymen as well as the thousands of Americans who died to preserve it. Every April 9th, they celebrate the heroes who fought, died, and liberated their country from the grip of foreign powers with celebrations, memorials, stories in newspapers, radio shows, and speeches. I salute our brothers and sisters in the Philippines, and welcome them to our country with open arms.

During the time of the initial writing of Dad's experiences, I was robbed of my livelihood as a jewelery designer and sales representative when a thief stole all of my inventory of precious gems and custom-made gold jewelery. The total loss was almost three hundred thousand dollars. For a brief moment, following the announcement by the police detectives that they had no clues, I felt like jumping off a bridge. Shaking like a leaf, I opened my laptop and thought I had better do something to take my mind off killing myself. When I scrolled to the last thing I had written on Dad's story, I stared in almost disbelief at the prophetical words before me: "Never, never give up!"

They were words spoken by my grandfather to my father, before he had departed to the Philippines prior to the onset of the war. I thought, how could I even consider taking my own life, when my father and his father before him committed themselves to the greater purpose of striving to live through any adversity because it was the right thing to do? So I gathered my wits and legacy of survival, and went about my own investigation, and it turned out that I delivered the thief to the police myself. Less than half of the jewelery was recovered, the thief was sent to jail for three years, and I was still in debt almost two hundred thousand dollars, but I had done something about saving my own life and finishing this book.

As of this May 2007 Memorial Day, my father is still alive and making a positive difference in the lives of his family and his country. He is a true American hero to me and everyone who has ever met him. He smiles with pride when he tells his VA doctors, who love him like a father, that he "bleeds red, white, and blue." Dad embodies and promotes the pure values of patriotism in his every day actions, from the time he awakes to the time he falls asleep. The horrors of the 42 months he and his fellow New Mexican and allied compatriots suffered torment him every night in his nightmares, and 3 or 4 times a day in 40 to 60 second seizure-like PTSD episodes. He never complains or talks about them; rather, he continues to soldier on doing his daily work of caring for other people who, in his eyes, are less fortunate. His home in Albuquerque is a sanctuary for relatives struggling to survive childhood cancer, homelessness, loss of jobs, or anyone needing positive and compassionate support.

When I asked him what he wanted more than anything for you, the reader, to receive from reading this book, he replied, "I pray we learn from our past and don't make the same mistakes again. We must forgive, but never forget."

"God Bless America"

# Suggested Viewing on Video

## Documentaries

*"Murder in the Sun"* Japanese War Crimes and Trial by Lou Reda Productions Inc.

*"NBC Presents "Bataan: The Forgotten WAR"* NBC television

*"A NEW MEXICO STORY"*
*"The Bataan Death March to the Atomic Bomb"*
A documentary by Aaron Wilson, McCaffey Films LLC

## Full-Length Historically-Based Motion Pictures

*Bataan* (1943) Director-Tay Garnett
Robert Taylor, Gary Murphy, Loyd Nolan, Desi Arnez, Thomas Mitchell, Barry Nelson,

*Bridge on the River Kwai* (1957) Director-David Lean,
William Holden, Alec Guiness, Sessue Hayakawa, Jack Hawkins, James Donald

*Empire of the Sun* (1987) Director-Steven Spielberg
Christian Bale, John Malcovich, Miranda Richardson, Nigel Havers, Joe Pantoliano, Leslie Phillips, Ben Stiller

*King Rat* (1965) Director-Brian Forbes
George Segal, Tom Courtenay, Patrick O'Neal, James Fox, William Fawcett, Denholm Elliot

*Merry Christmas Mr. Lawrence* (1983) Director-Nagisa Oshima
David Bowie, Tom Conti, Jack Thompson

*Paradise Road* (1997) Director-Bruce Beressfford
Glenn Close, Julianna Margulies, Francis McDormand, Cate Blanchett, Pauline Collins

*The Great Raid* (2005) Director-John Dahl
Benjamin Bratt, James Franco, Connie Nielson, Joseph Fiennes

# Acknowledgements

First and foremost, I thank my father, Master Sergeant Frank N. Lovato, for reliving his time in Hell and relating it to me to share with the world. His brave and noble spirit, a shining example to everyone who meets him, is his legacy to us all to create a better world. I salute him and the principles of forgiveness, compassion, and love for our great country, for which he has taken a stand to uphold until his last breath. I have become the man I am by witnessing his example.

I am grateful and humbled by the dedication of the men and women who gave everything to defend their families and countries from oppression. Their stories must never be forgotten.

I extend my heartfelt gratitude to the memory of Burl A. Brewster, for being a buddy to my father during the defense of the Philippines. Mr. Brewster's and Dad's taped dialogues of the battles they fought together are the only known accounts of the actual landing of the Japanese invading forces on Lingayen Beach, Luzon. Also to Captain Travis Perrenault, for being their intrepid leader, and to the Chillicothe Kid for saving Dad's life and being a true friend to him.

Thanks to my Filipino buddies: Reynaldo Cervania, who guided me through the back roads of Northern Luzon, and the military guidance of former Philippine Army sergeant Felix Ledda, as we explored records, maps, and trekked Bataan together in search of sites and proud veterans.

My eternal gratitude to my copy editors, Loretta Swit, Lori Ross, Gloria Meyers, Lori Gubera-Stengal, and Cassandra Clark. No computer program could ever replace the human factor essential in composition.

Hats off to the graphic designers; Lorraine Gervais's cover design and Katy Hight's crisp layout are much appreciated.

I thank Professor Emeritus Ben Steele, the artist, Bataan Veteran, and former POW, for allowing us to include his poignant drawings. Truth is revealed through the artist's eyes.

Thank you, Peter Collier, for believing in this project, and for reading and making recommendations to improve the overall quality and readability.

My head is bowed in honor and gratitude to you, the reader, who has read my father's story and who, I am sure, will gain another insight into creating peace between all humankind, as Dad would want for us all to do.

Francisco L. Lovato

# Order Form

To Order Books by Mail

NAME: ______________________________

MAILING ADDRESS: ______________________________

STATE ______________ COUNTRY ______________ ZIP __________

TELEPHONE: ______________________________

E-MAIL: ______________________________

QUANTITY __________ X $19.95 SUB TOTAL $ __________

SHIPPING PER BOOK: $1.50 $ __________

TOTAL $ __________

SALES TAX INCLUDED

Gift Delivery Orders

SEND TO:

NAME: ______________________________

MAILING ADDRESS: ______________________________

STATE ______________ COUNTRY ______________ ZIP __________

Del Oro Press
POB 2103
Nevada City, California 95959
530-477-1519
francisco@theunion.net
www.FranciscoLovato.com

# Glossary

**ammunition** (OAD) *n.* projectiles (bullets, shells, grenades, etc.) and their propellants.

**ammo** *n.* an abbreviation for ammunition.

**antiaircraft** (OAD) *adj.* used against enemy aircraft.

**antiaircraft weapon** a weapon capable of operating from ground or vehicle, used to defeat enemy aircraft.

**antitank weapon** (DOD) a weapon capable of operating from ground or vehicle used to defeat armor and other material targets.

**artillery** (OAD) **1.** large guns used for fighting on land. **2.** the branch of the Army that uses these.

**B.A.R.** an abbreviation for the Browning Automatic Rifle.

**Barelas** predominantly Spanish-American, residential and small business area adjacent to downtown Albuquerque, New Mexico.

**barracks** structures made for housing military personnel and supplies storage.

**barrel liners** highly polished, and spiral grooved artillery barrel inserts that seal against the fired projectile thereby spinning it as it leaves the barrel. The spinning motion improves the projectile's accuracy much like the action of a tightly thrown football.

**battery** (DOD, NATO) 1.tactical and administrative artillery unit or sub-unit corresponding to a company or similar unit in other branches of the Army.

**battalion** (OAD) *n.* an Army unit made up of several companies (artillery batteries)and forming part of a regiment.

**bayonet** (OAD) *n.* a dagger-like blade that can be fixed to the muzzle of a rifle and used in hand to hand combat.

**BB gun** a small caliber air powered pistol or rifle that shoots a BB size, round, piece of lead shot. Not considered a dangerous weapon.

**bivouac** a temporary camp set up by a moving military unit.

**boot camp** a training base for new military recruits that teaches military protocol, stresses physical conditioning, and prepares the recruits to fight in hand to hand combat and with a variety of weapons.

**bracketing** (DOD, NATO) a method of adjusting fire in which a bracket is established by obtaining an over and a short along the spotting line, and then successively splitting the bracket in half until target is hit or desired bracket is obtained.

**breech** the back part of a gun barrel where the ammunition is loaded.

**bombard** (OAD) v. to attack with shells from a big gun.

**bombardment** *n.*

**bullet** (OAD) *n.* a small round or conical projectile used in a rifle or revolver.

**bunkers** (OAD) *n.* a reinforced underground shelter.

**B-17** *"Flying Fortress"* Boeing manufactured heavy bomber.

**B-25** *"Mitchell"* North American manufactured medium bomber.

**B-29** *"Superfortress"* Boeing manufactured heavy bomber that delivered the atomic bombs on Hiroshima and Nagasaki.

**camouflage** (DOD, NATO) the use of natural or artificial material on personnel, objects, or tactical positions with the aim of confusing, misleading, or evading the enemy. (FLL) From the French word *"camoufle"* meaning to blind or veil.

**cannon** *n.* an artillery type gun that fires a large projectile.

**canteen** *n.* soldiers water carrying container that attaches to their belt.

**capitulate** *v.* to surrender.

**capitulation** *n.*

**casualty** (DOD) any person who is lost to the organization by having been declared dead, duty status-whereabouts unknown missing, ill, or injured.

**cavalry** (OAD) *n.* troops who fight on horseback.

**civilian** (OAD) *n.* a person not serving in the military.

**command post** (command center) (DOD) a facility from which a commander and his or her representatives direct operations and control forces. It is organized to gather, process, analyze, display, and disseminate planning and operational data and perform other related tasks.

**dengue** (OAD) *n.* infectious tropical fever causing acute pain in the joints.

**depot** strategically located supply station.

**deuce and a half** slang term used to describe the two and half ton rated GMC, troop and materials carrying dual rear axle truck.

**dog tags** slang term used to describe the individual soldiers stamped metal, identification tags worn around his or her neck.

**dummy emplacements** similarly appearing, but unoccupied emplacements set up for the purpose of deception.

**emplacement** (DOD, NATO) **1.** A prepared position for one or more weapons or pieces of equipment, for protection against hostile fire or bombardment, and from which they can execute their tasks. **2.** the act of fixing a gun in a prepared position from which it may be fired.

**fatigues** military issued work clothing, typically suited for the working environment.

**field artillery** (DOD) equipment, supplies and ammunition, and field personnel involved in the use of cannon, rocket, or surface-to-surface missile launchers. Also called FA.

**fighter plane** *n.* a highly maneuverable, typically single pilot operated, attack aircraft.

**foxhole** *n.* a soldiers individual, dugout emplacement used for protection.

**gun** (DOD) **1.** a cannon with a relatively long barrel, operating with relatively low angle of fire, and having a high muzzle velocity. **2.** a cannon with a tube length of 30 caliber or more.

**gunboat** (OAD) *n.* a small armed boat with heavy guns.

**gun carriage** (DOD, NATO) a mobile or fixed support for a gun. it sometimes includes the elevating and traversing mechanisms. also called carriage.

**GI** slang, Government Issue.

**half track** M-2 Half Track 75-mm Motor Carriage T12. main gun: mm mm French Quick-Firing M1897A with a rear mounted 30 caliber machine gun.

**hara kiri** (OAD) *n.* suicide involving disembowelment, formerly practiced by Japanese officers when in disgrace or under sentence of death.

**headquarters** *n.* the main place where military operations are controlled.

**helmet** *n.* a soldiers protective headgear.

**HQ** slang for headquarters.

**infantry** *n.* military troops who fight on the ground.

**incendiary bombs** bombs that spread fire through the use of materials such as napalm.

**internees** civilian prisoners held in confinement during wartime.

**kamikaze** Japanese term meaning "divine wind." (OAD) *n.* **1.** a World War II Japanese aircraft laden with explosives and deliberately crashed by its pilot on its target. **2.** its pilot.

**landing craft** *n.* boats designed to carry troops from the transport ship to the shore.

**lugao** *n.* a rice based gruel made by boiling a small amount of rice in a large quantity of water.

**machine gun** *n.* a hand held or mounted rapid firing gun that can deliver a large quantity of bullets in a continuous, automatic manner.

**M.A.S.H.** acronym for Mobile Army Surgical Hospital.

**mess kit** a military issued, portable, individual food preparation and eating kit.

**mine** (DOD, NATO) **1.** in land mine warfare, an explosive or material, normally encased, designed to destroy or damage ground vehicles, boats, or aircraft, or designed to wound, kill, or otherwise incapacitate personnel. **2.** in naval mine warfare, an explosive device laid in the water with the intention of damaging or sinking ships or of deterring shipping from entering an area.

**mortar** a short, mobile, cannon used by the infantry that fires a projectile at a high angle.

**napalm** (DOD) powdered aluminum soap or similar compound used to gelatinize oil or gasoline for use in napalm bombs or flamethrowers.

**nipa hut** a small, usually single room, dwelling made of locally grown materials, such as grass and bamboo.

**operation** (DOD) **1.** a military action or the carrying out of a strategic, operational, tactical, service, training, or administrative military mission. **2.** the process of carrying on combat, including movement, supply, attack, defense, and maneuvers needed to gain the objectives of any battle or campaign.

**order** (DOD, NATO) a communication, written or oral, or by signal, which conveys instructions from a superior to a subordinate. (DOD only) in a broad sense. the term's "order" and "command" are synonymous however, an order implies discretion's to the details of execution whereas a command does not.

**ordnance** (DOD) explosive, chemical, pyrotechnics, and similar stores, e.g. bombs, guns and ammunition, flares, smoke, or napalm.

**POW** abbreviation of Prisoner of War.

**P-40** *"Warhawk"* single-seat, Curtis manufactured fighter aircraft used by American forces prior to and at the beginning of WWII. It was made famous in China by General Chennault's American volunteer pilots known as the *"Flying Tigers"*.

**quartermaster** military officer in charge of stores and assigning quarters (lodging).

**ration** (OAD) *n.* a fixed quantity (especially of food) allowed to one person.

**regiment** (OAD) *n.* a military unit of ground forces organized into two or more battalions.

**rounds** individual units of ammunition.

**sabotage** (DOD) an act or acts with an intent to injure, interfere with, or obstruct the national defense of a country by willfully injuring or destroying, or attempting to injure or destroy, any national defense or war material, premises, or utilities, to include human and natural resources.

**saber** *n.* a long curved sword.

**shrapnel** *n.* originally named after it's inventor, Englishman Henry Shrapnel, who designed metal balls inside of an artillery shell, it generically refers to any metal shell fragments of an exploding shell.

**scuttlebutt** slang for informal news passed from mouth to mouth.

**shell** *n.* a piece of ammunition. v. to fire upon enemy targets.

**shell-shocked** a transient stress reaction to battle induced trauma characterized by dis-association from reality, confused thinking and a dazed appearance.

**slit trench** a small shovel width (approx. 6-9 inch) shallow (approx. 9-12 inch) continuous hole used by military personnel for defecation while in the battlefield or near bivouac area.

**small arms** (DOD) man portable, individual, and crew -served weapons systems used mainly against personnel and lightly armored equipment.

**SNAFU** slang acronym — Same News All F----ed Up.

**sniper** *n.* a soldier that fires upon another usually from a concealed and long distance.

**Springfield** rifle, model 1917- 30 caliber, bolt action, military rifle issued to infantry troops. Used during World War I and at the beginning of WWII.

**supporting fire** (DOD, NATO) fire delivered by supporting units to assist or protect a unit in combat.

**strategic advantage** (DOD) the overall relative power relationship of opponents at enables one nation or group of nations effectively to control the course of a military or political situation.

**strategy** (DOD) the art and science of developing and employing instruments of national power in a synchronized and integrated fashion to achieve theater, national, and/or multinational objectives.

**tank** a thickly armored, battle vehicle driven by continuous metal treads armed with a large gun and machine gun(s).

**target** (DOD) 1.an area, complex, installation, force, equipment, capability, function, or behavior identified for possible action to support the commander's objective, guidance, and intent. Targets fall into two categories: planned and immediate.

**trench interment** (DOD) a method of interment in which remains are placed head to toe.

**troops** (DOD) a collective term for uniformed military personnel (usually not applicable to naval personnel afloat).

**withdrawal operation** (DOD) a planned retrograde operation in which a force in contact disengages from an enemy force and moves in a direction away from the enemy.

# Japanese/English Definitions

**atama** – head

**atsu mare** – line up

**bango** – count off

**batai** – dead

**benjo** – toilet

**byoki** – sick

**domi domi** – no good

**hyacco** – hurry

**go han** – rice

**ki o tsuke** – attention

**mae susume** – quick march

**meizo ni** – no water

**mushi mushi** – telephone greeting

**ni** – no

**okie** – big

**segoto** – work

**shimpo** – penis

**tenko** – roll call

**to-mare** – halt

**wa do i** – bad boy

**wakuru** – do you understand?

**yasume** – rest/stand at ease

**yorosho ni** – no good

**domo arigato gomen mashita** – thank you very much

# Sources

## Books

Astor, Gerald. *Crisis in the Pacific.* NY: Random House.1966

Blevins, Bruce. *Pearl Harbor to Okinawa.* NY: Random House

Boisclaire, Yvonne. *In the Shadow of the Rising Sun.:* Clearwood Publishers

Browne, Courtney. *Tojo: The Last Banzai.* NY: Holt Rinehart and Winston 1967

Bywater, Hector. *War in the Pacific.* 1927

Costello, John. *The Pacific War.* NY: Rawson, Wade Publishers, Inc 1981

Daws, Gavan. *Prisoners of The Japanese.* NY: William Morrow and Co. Inc. 1994

Department of State, *Foreign relations of the United States, Conference at Berlin and Potsdam, 1945. Washington, D.C.:* Government Printing Office, 1947

Hearn, Lafcadio. *Japan: An Attempt at Interpretation.* Rutland, VT. Tokyo: Charles E. Tuttle Co. 1959

Ienega, Saburo. *The Pacific War 1931-1945.* NY: Pantheon Books.(Random House) 1978

Jansen, Marius B. *Japan and China: From War to Peace, 1894-1972.* Chicago: Rand McNally College Publishers

Kerr, E. Bartlett. *Surrender and Survival.* NY William Morrow and Co. Inc. 1985

Knox, Donald. *Death March.* San Diego. NY, London: Harcourt Brace Jonavich, Publishers. 1981

Levering, Robert W. *Horror Trek.* NY: Carlton Press. 1948,1979

Macaranas, Natividad. *Bravely They Fought.* Chapel Hill, NC: Professional Press.1990

Marek, Stephen. *Laughter in Hell.* Caldwell, Idaho: The Caxton Printers, Ltd. 1954

McCracken, Alan. *Very Soon Now, Joe.* NY: The Hobson Book Press. 1947

Pearson,Judith L. *Belly of the Beast.* NY: New American Library, a division of Penguin Putnam Inc. 2001

Sams, Margaret. *Forbidden Family A Wartime Memoir of The Philippines 1941-1945.* Madison Wisconsin:

Sides, Hampton. *Ghost Soldiers.* NY: Doubleday. 2001

Sneddon, Murray M. *Zero Ward.* San Jose, NY, Lincoln, Shanghai: Writers Club Press. 2000

Steele, Ben. *Prisoner of War.* Billings, Montana: Dept of Art. 1986

Toland, John. *But Not in Shame.* NY: Random House. 1961

Toland, John. *The Rising Sun.* NY: Random House. 1970

## Articles and Personal Histories

Loback, Bobby Ann Provencher. *Frenchy's War.* Unpublished memoirs of Raymond Joseph Provencher

Varias, Antonio. *Major Battle Lines in the Defense of Bataan and Corregidor 1941-1942.*

Ramos, Maximo. Agoo village resident who related story of Japanese landing and defense by artillery in hidden emplacements. 193 San Isidro Macabebe, Papanga, Phil.

*History National Guard of NM 1606-1963* by John Pershing Jolly Maj.Gen. AGC, NMARNG The Adjutant General. Santa Fe NM

Bataan Memorial Military Museum & Library, 1050 Old Pecos trail, Santa Fe, New Mexico 87505

Defenders of Bataan and Corregidor, Headquarters – Fort Bonafacio, MCC Makati, Metro Manila, Philippines

U.S. Latino & Latina WWII Oral History Project
School of Journalism
University of Texas at Austin
1 University Station A1000
Austin, TX 78712
Telephone: 512.471.1924